Children's Learning in Primary Schools

What does learning look like? What are different subjects really about? Why are transferable skills so important? How can we overcome the difficulties that children encounter in their learning? And what questions and prompts are likely to prove useful in helping children to get the most out of their lessons?

The over-arching role of Teaching Assistants is to support teaching and learning in schools. To do this effectively, they need to understand the curriculum content of all the subjects in which they provide support and know what learning outcomes are sought. This accessible book provides an overview of the knowledge, skills, understanding and attitudes that children learn in each subject in their primary years.

Written with the non-subject specialist in mind, and drawing on research and best practice in the classroom, this extremely practical book aims to provide the reader with the information they need to:

- deliver focused lessons to individual pupils, groups, or the whole class;

- concentrate on the most important elements when making classroom resources;

- make valuable assessments of the children's learning, and keep useful records of their achievements, progress and difficulties;

- take a full part in discussions with colleagues – selecting objectives, devising interesting activities and delivering exciting lessons in each of the subjects.

Including a wide range of examples and activities, this book will prove an invaluable companion for all students working on STLS and Foundation Degree courses, and Teaching Assistants currently working in primary schools.

Mike Cowdray is a former Assistant Headteacher. He has over 30 years' teaching experience in nine primary schools across the north of England and has led a wide variety of subjects including English, Mathematics, Science, ICT, and Design and Technology.

Children's Learning in Primary Schools

A guide for Teaching Assistants

Mike Cowdray

Routledge
Taylor & Francis Group

LONDON AND NEW YORK

First published 2013
by Routledge
2 Park Square, Milton Park, Abingdon, Oxon OX14 4RN

Simultaneously published in the USA and Canada
by Routledge
711 Third Avenue, New York, NY 10017

Routledge is an imprint of the Taylor & Francis Group, an informa business

British Library Cataloguing in Publication Data
A catalogue record for this book is available from the British Library

Library of Congress Cataloging in Publication Data
Cowdray, Mike.
    Children's learning in primary schools: a guide for teaching assistants/
    Mike Cowdray.
    p. cm.
    1. Teachers' assistants – Great Britain. 2. Education, Elementary – Great
    Britain. I. Title.
    LB2844.1.A8C64 2012
    371.14'1240941–dc23
    2012010325

ISBN: 978-0-415-53600-4 (hbk)
ISBN: 978-0-415-53601-1 (pbk)
ISBN: 978-0-203-11193-2 (ebk)

Typeset in Bembo and Helvetica Neue
by Florence Production Ltd, Stoodleigh, Devon

Printed and bound in Great Britain by the MPG Books Group

Contents

18 Science

Acknowledgements

It would be impossible to mention, by name, all the friends and colleagues who have unwittingly contributed ideas for this book – after all, you stretch literally from A to Z! My sincere thanks go to all of you:

- the teachers and subject coordinators, who spent many long hours telling me about *your* subject(s);
- the teaching assistants, who patiently devised ever more interesting ways to help the children to learn;
- Merrilyn, who pointed the way, and Alan and Colin, who kept me on track.

And of course, to Liz, who has given constant encouragement, support, and practical assistance throughout the book's gestation period.

1

An Introduction

Primary education – a starter kit

Primary schools are incredibly important places. Their job is to provide the children with a reliable *starter kit* – that is, a toolbox full of the essential knowledge, skills, understanding, qualities and attitudes that will give them a flying start in life, and at the same time act as a firm foundation for future learning. And it should be fun, satisfying and rewarding in its own right, too!

Life expectancy for people living in the UK is now more than 80 years and rising. This means that children starting school now can expect to see 75 years or more of change. If we look back 75 years from the present day, we find the 1930s – and it would be impossible to list all the changes that have taken place in the world since then. So, in order to be confident and successful through a lifetime of changes that are as yet unknown, the questions we need to ask ourselves are:

- What do children need to know?
- What skills do they need to learn?
- What do they need to understand?
- What qualities and attitudes do they need to develop?

In this book, we look at what children learn in their primary schools. Crucially, it is about what they actually *learn*, not just what they *do*.

But let's talk about you . . .

You obviously take pride in your work and enjoy working with children. You are extremely conscientious and want to do your best, both for them and for your own satisfaction. I expect you are fairly comfortable with the *pastoral support* part of the job, but would like to know more about *teaching and learning support* – perhaps, in some lessons, you are not always convinced that you are helping the children as much as you could.

Clearly, different schools have slightly different expectations of their Classroom Assistants/Teaching Assistants (from hereon in, called TAs) – some are employed to give general help around the classroom, others provide support for a particular child or group of children, while others might cover absent colleagues, provide assistance in particular subjects, or lead lessons. However, a common feature is that the role of the TA is to support the children's learning, as well as their personal and social development and welfare.

Ofsted suggested that the contribution of TAs towards a good maths lesson is one where they 'know the pupils well, are well briefed on the concepts and expected misconceptions, and provide support throughout the lesson that enhances thinking and independence' (Ofsted 2009: 5). I see no reason why this should not also be true in all the other subjects.

Being a conscientious TA, you want to contribute to every lesson in such a way all the children in your care are able to join in and benefit from the activities as much as they can, and therefore make progress in their learning. You will be asking yourself:

- What is this subject really about?
- What knowledge/skills/understanding/attitudes should the children be learning?
- Which of these are the most important in this particular lesson?
- How do these fit in with the child's whole programme?
- What should *I* be doing to make sure that the children get the most out of this lesson?
- How do I know when I am doing a good job?

And these are the very same questions that this book sets out to answer.

What does the book contain?

At the heart of the book is a desire that children should make as much progress as possible throughout their primary years – that is, every child, every day, in every area of the curriculum.

Clearly, we need to accept that children don't all start from the same place, and neither do they all progress at the same rate. Indeed, even an individual child is likely to learn at different rates in different subjects. But we do know that one of the greatest spurs to success is *success* itself. So – what should the children be learning in school, and how can we help them to step on to this upward spiral of success?

In the early part of the book, we explore the different types of learning that the children will meet (Chapter 2), and some of the difficulties that children might encounter in their learning (Chapter 3). In Chapter 4, we look at the children's first year or so in school, before their learning is divided into separate subjects. Later chapters focus on individual subjects. Each of these includes:

- a broad overview of what the subject is actually about;
- a description of some of the *experiences* offered through the subject;
- a description of what the children should be learning, in terms of *knowledge, skills and understanding;*
- opportunities offered by the subject for learning the so-called *transferable skills*;
- examples of questions and prompts that we can use, to help the children learn more effectively.

I believe this will help to clarify any areas you might have been a little unclear about, so that you can better:

- focus on the important elements of the subject when you make classroom resources, supervise activities and deliver lessons to individual pupils, groups, or the whole class;
- pinpoint particular objectives for individual children or groups;
- make helpful assessments of the children's learning, and keep useful records of their achievements, progress and difficulties;
- be confident that you are *making a difference* in the children's learning;
- take a full part in discussions with your colleagues, as you select objectives, devise interesting activities and deliver exciting lessons in each of the subjects.

And this will help the children directly to:

- learn new facts and remember them;
- gain new skills and develop them further;
- understand new ideas and clarify them in their mind;
- develop a positive attitude – to learning, to themselves and to other people;
- adapt and use their learning across a range of new and unfamiliar situations.

How is the book arranged?

I suspect that, when you were at school yourself, you were probably more interested in some subjects than others, and that, when you were about 14 years old, you were allowed to choose certain subjects at secondary school while dropping others. And I guess that the teaching was better in some subjects than in others. In short, your background across the whole range of subjects would probably best be described as *mixed*, with many strong areas and some less strong.

Therefore, this book is set out so that you can dip in anywhere and, in just a few minutes, get a good idea of what the children should be learning in each area of the curriculum.

Throughout the book I have used a lot of lists and bullet points. In this way, I hope to present the information in the most straightforward way possible, without your having to search through masses of text to find what you want.

I have also included lots of questions and prompts. These are intended only to be examples, but please do use them and adapt them in any way you see fit, to help the children make sense of the things they see, hear and do.

Finally, please accept that my intention is to give just a *flavour* of each subject, setting out the sorts of things the children should be learning – the lists cannot be exhaustive. In each area of learning there is a path along which the children will travel – younger children will just be starting out, while we hope that the older ones will be well along the way.

How do we know if we are doing a good job?

A simple model of good teaching is:

- Find out where the children are now in their learning (in terms of knowledge, skills, understanding and attitudes).
- Together with the children and their parents, decide where we want them to be.
- Then help them to move from one to the other.

Of course, the children don't need to have *mastered* something to have made progress – perhaps they have *become aware* of something new, or *joined in an activity* that requires the use of a new skill, or *gained partial understanding* of an idea. Each of these provides a foundation for further learning in the future and represents progress in its own right as well.

In order to judge how well we are doing our job, we need to ask ourselves:

- Do the children trust us and relate to us?
- Do we have a good idea of where they are now in their learning?
- Do we know what they are supposed to be learning next?
- Can we think of interesting and motivating ways to make ideas clear to them and take them to the next level?
- Can we tell when learning has taken place?
- Are the children learning?
- Do *they* know they are learning?
- Are they learning as well as they could be?

If you can answer *yes* to each of these questions, then it is likely that you are indeed doing a good job.

2

Different Types of Learning

What are primary schools trying to achieve?

The aims of each school are expressed slightly differently, but they usually include phrases such as:

> We week to provide an environment, where pupils:
>
> – are safe and healthy;
> – enjoy their learning and make good progress across the whole breadth of the curriculum;
> – develop personal, social and emotional maturity;
> – develop confidence and independence;
> – learn to contribute actively to society.
>
> (DES 2004: 9)

Our task, then, is to provide a rich diet of lessons, activities and experiences, through which the children can learn whatever is necessary to make progress in each of these areas (as well as any others mentioned in the school's aims, of course). Much of this learning will take place in formal lessons, but a significant amount will occur at other times of the day and through other events, such as assemblies, breaks, visits, and so on.

However, learning is not a straightforward process. For the most part, progress is made through a series of *steps and stairs* – with a few blind alleys thrown in for good measure! There is no guarantee that the children will make a smooth transition from one stage of learning to the next.

What are we trying to do in lessons?

This is a big question, but the answer is not so difficult: we want the children to *make progress* in their learning, that is, to move on from where they were before the lesson *in at least one area of learning.*

In terms of the subjects themselves, there are three distinct types of learning:

- acquiring facts and *knowledge*;
- learning and developing *skills*;
- *understanding* ideas and concepts.

(DfEE and QCA 1999: 17)

Then there are the so-called *transferable skills*, *attitudes* and *qualities*, which are not subject specific. These not only help the children to learn effectively across a whole range of subjects, but also help them to build and maintain sound relationships, develop independence and responsibility, maintain self-esteem and become rounded individuals, capable of becoming the sort of person they really want to be. Although they include a mixture of skills, attitudes and personal qualities, these are usually referred to, collectively, as *transferable skills*, and are described in more detail later in this chapter (QCDA 2010: 14–15).

In class, we balance these four types of learning by ensuring that the children learn the subject matter and develop these transferable skills at the same time. This is done by planning the lessons with four elements in mind:

- the subject matter;
- the way the lesson is to be delivered;
- the tasks the children will be asked to complete and the ways in which they are to be tackled;
- the kind of feedback we will give the children afterwards.

For example, when we teach the children their multiplication tables, we might ask them to work by themselves, copying the tables and trying to memorize them, or to look for patterns on a 10 × 10 multiplication square (such as 0/5 endings for all numbers in the 5-times table). Alternatively, we might ask them to work as part of a group reciting the tables, or making up multiplication stories. While the *subject* outcome will be the same, the *transferable skills* will vary considerably from one activity to another, with particular approaches selected according to the needs of the children at that time.

Of course, learning can't take place in a vacuum – the children need to be *doing* something – they need to be engaged in an activity, or an *experience*, which is both interesting and exciting.

The top part of Figure 2.1 shows the three different types of subject-based learning, floating in a sea of experiences, while the lower half highlights the importance of the transferable skills. Let's look at each of these areas individually.

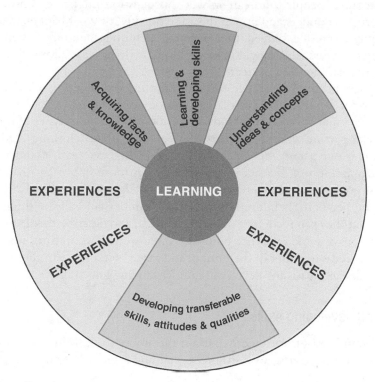

FIGURE 2.1 Types of Learning

Subject-based learning

Acquiring facts and knowledge

The first type of learning we want the children to be good at involves remembering facts and information, and being able to recall them. People who excel in this are frequently good at TV and pub quizzes.

Questions often beginning with:

- *What?* (What is the name of the highest mountain in Scotland?)
- *Where?* (Where is Buxton?)
- *When?* (When was Queen Victoria on the throne?)
- *Who?* (Who invented the electric light bulb?)

Questions and answers are often short:

- Q: When was the Great Fire of London?
- A: 1666.

Of course, people who can answer this question might not know where the fire started, or understand how it spread so quickly, or what happened to London's economy as a result. Indeed, they may not even understand the system we use for naming the years. But they do possess the knowledge that allows them to answer this particular question correctly.

We accumulate knowledge throughout our lives. There is no fixed order for this – what we learn depends largely on our experiences. If our parents own a horse, we build a reservoir of knowledge about horses (e.g. types of horses, events they take part in, their body parts, the equipment and clothing used by riders), whereas if our parents are interested in gardening, we learn about plants, tools, pruning, and so on. Neither of these subjects is more important than the other – we just grow up with different areas of knowledge.

In the beginning, children probably don't understand all the things they learn about, but they can recognize them, name them and describe them, and this means that they have some reference points for discussion. This, in turn, means that they can bring ideas together in their mind, and make better sense of them – using their knowledge as a basis for developing understanding and skills.

Learning and developing skills

This second sort of learning focuses on the ability to do things, to carry out tasks – for example, playing an instrument, painting a picture, tying a knot, skipping, and so on.

Once children have learned to carry out a skill at a basic level, they can build on this in various ways:

- increasing the ease with which they carry out that skill;
- improving their accuracy or subtlety;
- extending the difficulty of the task;
- expanding the range of situations where they can make use of it.

We are concerned with questions such as:

- How can I do this?
- How can I do this better?

Skills are vitally important in life, because they are what we do – they help us to convert our thoughts, dreams and desires into reality After all, we can learn the words of a song, but we won't get the thrill of performing it unless we also learn to sing, and sing in tune. We can read recipe books to our heart's content, but we won't be able to taste the food unless we cook it, and cook it just right.

Understanding ideas and concepts

Many people would say that this is the most important type of learning – the word *understanding* appears many times in national guidelines for teaching and learning in schools.

Whatever the topic under consideration, understanding enables us to answer questions such as:

- What is this about? Why is it like this?
- How does this work? Why does it happen the way it does?
- How does it link with other things I already know about?

Each question is likely to require an explanation, not just a one-word answer. For example, the children might explore scientific questions ('How does electricity work?'), religious ones ('Why do Christians use the symbol of the cross?'), or social questions ('Why shouldn't we run in the corridor?').

To extend our understanding, we:

- often have to deal with abstract ideas, concepts and beliefs;
- bring together facts, opinions and ideas, and interpret them;
- make hypotheses and check them out;
- extend what we already know and understand.

When we want the children to memorize facts, we might invent short rhymes or phrases, called mnemonics, to help them – for example, *Naughty Elephants Squirt Water* (NESW, the four main points of the compass). Understanding works differently. It allows us to link ideas together, so that the brain *walks through* a subject, giving itself a commentary along the way and triggering the recall of the words, names and facts we have heard before in this context.

The more links the children make between a new topic and all the other things they already know about, the better chance they have of seeing the full picture, and therefore understanding. An essential part of this process is modifying what they already know and understand, in order to accommodate their new insight.

Transferable skills, qualities and attitudes

Transferable skills – an overview

In addition to the subject-based knowledge, skills, understanding and experiences, there are a number of important skills, qualities and attitudes (the *transferable skills*) that the children make use of over and over again – in all lessons, in all subjects, on school visits, in concerts and performances, at break-times and at home. These general learning skills are called *transferable skills* because, no matter where they are learned, they can be transferred to many other areas of life, both within school and outside. They can be grouped into:

- personal and emotional skills;
- social skills;
- learning and thinking skills;
- working skills.

These really are *skills for life*. They are fundamental to success in school, at work and in life in general. They help children to be happy, healthy, confident and responsible, and contribute to successful learning across all areas of their lives. As such, they are at least as important as the subject-based learning – perhaps even more so.

Our aim is for these transferable skills to become part of the children's everyday *repertoire*, as they are gradually incorporated into their work and lives.

Unfortunately, these are not the sorts of skills that can be taught in a once-and-for-all fashion. It is rather like growing plants – they need to be cultivated and nurtured, so that they grow and mature. Long-term support and encouragement will be required. Let's take a look at each of these skills in turn.

Personal and emotional skills

Here we are talking about qualities and attitudes such as:

- self-confidence, self-esteem;
- healthy living;
- team-work, cooperation, respect;
- attentiveness, involvement;
- ambition, initiative, persistence;
- interest, enthusiasm, capacity for enjoyment;
- dealing positively with both praise and criticism;
- keeping emotions under control.

A more extensive list is included in Chapter 16.

When the children feel positive about themselves and in control, they can more easily take advantage of opportunities that come their way, overcoming any difficulties and making the most of life. Qualities such as these can bring satisfaction, pleasure and fulfilment.

Social skills

Social skills include:

- working well with others – taking turns, sharing equipment, resources and time;
- understanding other people's feelings;
- respecting others' rights and responsibilities, abiding by group rules, behaving well in a wide range of social situations.

Again, there is more about this in Chapter 16.

Skills like these not only promote and accelerate all types of learning, they also oil the wheels of relationships – within families, communities and society. For these reasons, they play an essential part in preparing the children for on-going success, both in childhood and as an adult.

Learning and thinking skills

Learning skills can boost learning in every part of the curriculum. Once the children have learned to carry them out and become convinced of their value, they can be transferred to any subject (or, indeed, to any interest out of school) to excellent effect. They include:

- *Research/enquiry* – this skill has several steps: asking questions clearly (after all, if we ask the right question, we have a better chance of getting the right answer); planning and carrying out research; collecting results carefully; discussing and analysing those results; judging the reliability of evidence; and reaching reasoned conclusions and explaining them clearly.
- *Thinking creatively and solving problems* – the children learn to be open-minded when exploring possibilities; to identify similarities and differences; to link ideas together; to make original suggestions and hypotheses (and check them out); and to experiment with new ways of doing things (accepting that they might not always work).
- *Weighing up the quality of ideas and results* – both their own ideas and those of other people, and suggesting how things might be improved next time.

While these skills might look rather complex, the children will have made a start on many of them even before they started at school and will continue to build on them over the years. There is a two-way relationship going on here:

- the children learn these skills in their lessons, by approaching tasks in particular ways;
- they make better progress overall by applying such skills in their lessons.

Working skills

Working skills include:

- being attentive and showing interest;
- being well organized and working accurately;
- using precise language to discuss their work;
- fine motor skills – drawing, cutting, etc.;
- seeking out help when necessary and thinking through advice;
- considering safety and ethical values.

Many of these skills are very closely related to the *personal and emotional skills* outlined above.

Bringing these types of learning together

Based on the previous sections, our Learning diagram might now look like this:

FIGURE 2.2 A more detailed model of Types of Learning

Of course, learning is much more disorganized than this diagram would suggest. In order to make progress in any one area, the children usually rely on one or more of the other areas to help them. For example, when they learn to recite a poem (a skill), they need to remember the words (knowledge), appreciate the mood of the piece and deliver it with feeling (understanding), and do enough practice to gain fluency and have the confidence to perform it (personal skills/attitudes).

It is perhaps worth reminding ourselves here that every child has *a unique profile of abilities*. We can all point to areas where we seem better than others – 'I'm quite good at sport, but hopeless at art', or 'I'm better at English than maths'. Some people seem to have quite an *even profile* and learn at a fairly consistent rate across all parts of the curriculum, while others have what has been called a *spiky profile*, being significantly better in some areas than others.

Our job, then, is to help the children to move from stage to stage, building on what they already know, understand and can do. During a lesson, or through a series of lessons, progress can be made in any one of these areas or, more likely, in two or three of them at the same time.

Where do national guidelines fit in?

A school's curriculum is perhaps best described as *everything the children experience in school, from the time they arrive in the morning to the time they go home again,*. On the other hand, national guidelines (the *National Curriculum* and various *strategies* in England, Wales and Northern Ireland, and Scotland's *Curriculum for Excellence*) include only some subjects (but not others), and limit themselves to a *core* of what children should experience and learn in each of those prescribed subjects, together with a short discussion on the personal values we would want the children to adopt.

Now nobody would deny that this central core is extremely important, but it is not as broad as a school's curriculum, where the children cover so much more. Moreover, national guidelines continue to evolve and change – there seems to be a major overhaul every few years, and the introduction of various strategies and changes of emphasis in between. But the fact remains that many of these developments do not significantly change what the children actually learn, because they were already learning it as part of their broader curriculum. For example, primary children were taught about the benefits of good hygiene long before PSHE education was formally introduced as a subject.

With so many different types of learning, how do we go about teaching?

Children absorb information and ideas all the time, from all kinds of places – from their friends and family, from the TV, the Internet, and so on. To them, school is just one more source – an important one, but nevertheless, just one more.

However, in school we have a responsibility to make sure that the children do indeed learn the *essentials*, that is:

■ essential knowledge, skills, concepts and ideas;
■ essential transferable skills.

We also need to make sure that these essentials are learned thoroughly, so that the children:

■ build a secure foundation for future learning;
■ are equipped to become active and confident participants in society.

It is generally agreed that the best way to teach a new idea is to relate it to something that the children already know something about and then extend the explanation from there, pointing out similarities and differences. For example, if the children are learning about the geysers in Iceland, we might describe them as being *a bit like a kettle in the kitchen*, and if they are learning about e-mail addresses, we might describe them as being *rather like the postcode on an envelope*.

There is seldom a single best way to teach a particular fact, skill or idea. This is because each of the children has a different set of experiences behind them and learns in a slightly different way from their friends. On the other hand, we do know that some areas of learning are best approached through hands-on, practical activities, where the children will be moving about, building things, experimenting and creating things, while in others the children generally benefit from sitting at their tables reading, writing, drawing or working at their computers. Discussion also plays an important part in the children's learning, both as an activity in itself and in conjunction with other activities.

But whatever the activity – whether it is a written exercise, a practical task, piece of research, discussion or game – the children will be *thinking* about what they are doing. Our job is to intervene in the best possible way and at the best possible moment, to help them along the way, so that they gain knowledge, learn and develop skills, and make sense of the situation. This means that, at different times, we can be a teacher, instructor, coach, facilitator, mentor or guide, depending on how we approach the task. To do this, we need to be able to use all of the following strategies:

■ **Demonstrating** (also called *modelling*): we show the children how to do something and then they have the opportunity to try it for themselves (e.g. drawing a circle with a pair of compasses).

■ **Directing**: we set the children a task that has a single correct solution, drawing their attention to particular points that they should take note of and include in their work (e.g. take three photos with different degrees of zoom).

■ **Explaining**: we give reasons why things are as they are or how things happen (e.g. how roots bring water from the ground into a plant).

- **Questioning**: we ask questions to discover the children's current knowledge and understanding, so that we can build on this and lead them to the next step. Questioning is particularly useful when the children appear to have misunderstood something; we need to know where they are coming from and what needs further explanation (e.g. can you tell me what this graph is showing us?).

- **Exploring**: we work with the children to explore a group of objects or words or numbers, and try to find connections between them. This might involve a certain amount of guesswork, so their suggestions need to be discussed with an adult to avoid making false connections and jumping to mistaken conclusions (e.g. I want to sort these things out, so that all those made from the same material are grouped together. Can you help me?).

- **Investigating ideas**: we help the children to discuss factual ideas in an attempt to help them understand why things are as they are. In order to bring fresh information to the investigation, they might carry out a brainstorming exercise, or look at evidence in the form of books, practical experiments, models, videos, and so on (e.g. is there always snow on the top of high mountains?).

- **Discussing**: we lead a discussion about a moral issue or a preference, where differences of opinion need to be teased out and weighed up. The discussion may end without agreement, but views will have been aired and justified (e.g. we've been thinking about sectioning off the playground, so that the younger and older children have their own areas. What do you think?).

- **Playing**: we join in games with the children, demonstrating behaviour and encouraging them to talk things through, introducing new words and ideas, and perhaps refining the rules or setting new problems, leading them towards a variety of solutions. (Hmm, I wonder what would happen if I . . .).

- **Listening, watching and responding**: we listen to the children's ideas and contributions and watch them working, so that we can gauge how we can help them further (this technique will be used in conjunction with all the other teaching methods).

It is worth noting that many of these strategies rely on talking. When children talk about their work, they generally get a clearer picture of the topic. After all, this might be the first time they have needed to be clear about an idea that has thus far been rather vague: What do I actually know and think about this? Does it make sense? How can I best explain it? Is this what I really mean? Of course, by talking they also expose any misunderstandings they might have, which we can help them to correct.

Unfortunately, deciding which of these teaching methods we should use in a particular lesson is not clear cut. Rather, it is a matter of judgement. We need to take into account, for example:

- whether the children have come across this topic (or idea) before, and what they might already know;
- the extent of their enthusiasm for the subject;

- whether they are learning alone, as part of a group, or as one of the class;
- their preferred style of learning – watching, listening or doing (visual, auditory or kinaesthetic);
- what facilities and equipment are available in the classroom;
- our own level of knowledge, skill, understanding and confidence when dealing with this topic.

Having taken all this into account, we need to be as imaginative, inventive and creative as we can be, so that the children find the lessons stimulating and intriguing.

Which is the most important type of learning?

We have been looking at seven types of learning:

- knowledge
- skills
- understanding
- personal and emotional skills
- social skills
- learning and thinking skills
- working skills.

And it will come as no surprise to learn that we need them all – the children need them all – to be successful in life. It's rather like our health – to stay fit and well, we need a good, balanced diet and plenty of exercise. And if we want our pupils to become confident, successful young people, then we need to provide plenty of exciting experiences and a good, balanced diet of learning, with just the right mix of challenge and support.

Enjoying experiences

But enough about learning. Sometimes it is sufficient for the children just to take pleasure from a fulfilling and inspirational experience. Perhaps something like holding a snake, or standing on top of a hill looking at the *toy* houses and cars below, or watching a marching band striding along the street, or tasting honey.

An everyday activity, such as finger-painting, may have been planned so that the children learn about the texture and qualities of the paint on different surfaces, and to reinforce the importance of good hand-washing techniques afterwards, but we should not underestimate the value of just enjoying the experience. Of course, we can't be sure just what will inspire each individual child, but we do know that when we hit the button, that moment will stay with them as a positive memory for years.

3

Barriers to Learning

What barriers are we talking about?

In every classroom there are some children who seem to learn effortlessly – picking up new ideas, asking and answering interesting questions, developing and refining quite intricate skills, and so on – and then there are others who don't seem to learn so easily. While the Government might set standards for how quickly they think children *should* be learning, we know that many of the children in our classes are facing barriers that make this very difficult indeed.

Three barriers that affect a significant number of children are:

- having a difficult start to school life;
- having little or no experience of the English language;
- having an *additional* or *special need*.

If we are to help the children, we need to:

- be aware of the barriers that each child faces;
- think ahead and make a judgement about how those barriers might affect their performance in a particular lesson;
- vary the lessons, so that the children can either make progress towards overcoming their barriers, or complete tasks in spite of them;
- ensure that the children gain some measure of success in every task we ask them to do. For example, if we ask them to read a page, it is our responsibility to make sure they can read it – or at least most of it; if we want them to listen to a story, we need to make sure they are sitting in a suitable place in the room; and if we want them to catch a ball, we need to make sure that the ball is the right size and is thrown in the right way.

Of course, the children need to be challenged, but their *next step* must always be attainable.

Equally important is the children's own recognition of their successes, so that they can be proud of themselves for bringing them about. It is also helpful if the children can be persuaded to judge their progress against their own previous performance, rather than against the best that is happening in the class. In this way, they will build confidence in their ability to attempt future tasks with an expectation of further success.

Children who might have a difficult start to school life

Some children are at a disadvantage before they even begin school. For example, they might have:

- a general developmental delay;
- spent time in hospital during the early part of their life, and therefore have missed out on essential experiences and learning;
- been born in the summer, so they are among the youngest in their class – when they are 5 years old, this can amount to 20% of life experience thus far;
- faced emotional trauma of some kind early in their life;
- received only limited support and encouragement from their parents.

These children tend to lack some of the knowledge, skills, understanding and transferable skills that are normally learned during the first four or five years of life and which provide a springboard for learning in school.

Clearly, they might need to continue working towards some of the early learning goals (see Chapter 4) at the same time as embarking on the normal primary school curriculum. With support, some will catch up with their peers quite quickly, but others will continue to perform less well, even up to the age of 16 and beyond.

Children whose first language is not English

The second group of children are those who have gained their early experience of speaking and listening (and perhaps reading and writing) in a language other than English, either in this country or abroad. They might join the school at any age.

We need to remember that their language level (in English) in all probability does not reflect their knowledge, skills and understanding in other areas. These are just ordinary children who might be quick to pick up new ideas, or not; they might have well-developed language skills in their first language, or not; and they might be good at art, music, maths or physical education (PE), or not. However, they find themselves in an environment where the main language used around them is different from the one they have grown up with. This represents a barrier to learning because English is the main medium for teaching, learning, discussion and explanation in the classroom.

Of course, these children don't attend school just to learn English – they are at school to receive a full, all-round education, just like all the other children. So our job is to help them:

- to feel relaxed and confident;
- to learn to speak, listen, read and write in English;
- to access all the other areas of the curriculum and make good progress in each of them.

(DfEE and QCA 1999: 37, paragraph 8)

It is understandable if they do not speak much at first, as they will be adjusting to their new circumstances, listening intently and trying to make sense of their surroundings. We should actively encourage them to use both languages – English and their own first language – as this helps them to do their thinking in whichever language suits them best. It will also help them to keep in touch with their extended family – it would be very upsetting to gain one language and lose another.

The extent to which the children's limited language interferes with learning in the classroom depends largely on whether activities are purely practical or whether they entail discussion of abstract ideas. For example, in Music and physical education lessons, the children can often follow the lead of their classmates in the practical activities, as they can when *making and doing* in Art and Design and Technology lessons. Similarly, some areas of maths can be accessed through numbers, symbols, charts, graphs, and so on, rather than through words, and many information and communications technology (ICT) tasks can be adapted to reduce the amount of language involved. However, history, geography, citizenship, religious education (RE), and personal, social, health and economic (PSHE) education are often more problematic, because the topics tend to focus on abstract issues and ideas. This is also true of English lessons when stories and poems are being discussed, and of the more practical subjects at those times when projects are being planned and finished pieces are being evaluated.

To help these children learn effectively, we can borrow a variety of techniques from the ways in which we:

- teach language and literacy skills to younger children who do have English as their first language;
- work with children who have a language delay;
- work with children who have a specific difficulty such as dyslexia;
- teach a modern foreign language.

The children are not normally withdrawn from lessons to learn English. Rather, they learn English *through the lessons*, meeting words and phrases in a meaningful context at the same time as learning the subject content. However, there might be circumstances when it is appropriate to withdraw a child, or a group of children, from the class:

■ where a certain amount of *catching up* or *filling gaps* is required, perhaps using the essential *core language structures* and *vocabulary* that we use every day (see Chapter 13, p. 158);

■ where it would be beneficial for the children to prepare for a lesson beforehand, by discussing the activities they will be asked to undertake, the key vocabulary that will be used and the questions they are likely to be asked;

■ after a lesson, where it can be useful to revisit the content, to clarify any points that might have been only half understood or missed altogether.

Children with a special need

The third group of children to encounter significant barriers to their learning are those with additional difficulties or disabilities. These difficulties might be short-lived or might affect them throughout their school career, and may even extend well into their adult lives. For the most part, teachers and teaching assistants (TAs), working closely with the children, can ensure that they don't miss out on any of the experiences offered in school and so continue to make progress. However, for a small number of children, their barrier disrupts their life and their learning to such an extent that they are judged to have a *special need*.

For a *need* to become a *special need*, it must be a specific and identifiable barrier, which interferes with a child's life and impedes learning to such a degree that additional help is required to access the curriculum and make progress (DCSF 2010: 59).

Special needs are usually described as:

■ **Academic** – to do with the child's intellectual ability, particularly where this affects the tasks required of them in school; this includes *general learning difficulties*, which are usually classified as mild, moderate, severe or profound, and *specific learning difficulties*, such as reading and writing (dyslexia).

■ **Sensory** – to do with impairment of vision or hearing, and sometimes the sense of touch.

■ **Physical** – problems with mobility, motor skills, strength, balance, coordination, speed or flexibility; includes dyspraxia and problems with self-organisation.

■ **Medical** – long-term illnesses, such as diabetes, anaemia, cancer, cystic fibrosis, epilepsy, heart conditions, and so on, which interfere with both independence and learning; includes many syndromes; also includes the side-effects of treatment, for example, lack of concentration from anti-epilepsy drugs, or the need for frequent repositioning when confined to a wheelchair for prolonged periods.

■ **Communication difficulties** – the mechanics, e.g. vocabulary, clarity of speech, pronunciation, fluency; and the social aspects, such as autism and Asperger's syndrome.

■ **Behaviour, emotional responses or social interaction difficulties** – to do with the child's relationship with oneself and others; self-esteem, empathy, self-control, concentration, relationships with adults or other children, obsessions, dealing with change, etc.; includes conditions such as Attention Deficit Hyperactivity Disorder (ADHD), responses to trauma and mental health issues.

(DCSF 2009: 6)

Clearly, each of these difficulties can interfere with learning in school, particularly in terms of the children's:

■ ability to retain facts and knowledge;

■ understanding;

■ development and mastery of skills;

■ rate of learning;

■ speed of working and the amount of practice that can be fitted in within the time available;

■ ability to complete tasks and respond to challenges in the same way as other children;

■ ability (or willingness) to take a full part in lessons and activities;

■ concentration, confidence, and so on.

Our task is to help the children either to *overcome* or to *manage* their barriers as far as possible, noting that these two are quite different.

Overcoming a barrier involves helping the child to improve their skills, or change their behaviour or attitude in a way that reduces the height of their barrier, or even makes it disappear altogether – for example, we can teach a child with Asperger's syndrome how to read people's facial expressions, and we can give children with a stutter strategies to speak more fluently.

When *managing a barrier*, on the other hand, we accept that we cannot change the disability (blindness or cerebral palsy, for example) and need to find ways for the children to work around it, so that they can lead as normal a life as possible and make as much progress in their learning as possible. We need to teach *coping strategies* that help the children both to access the curriculum and meet the challenges posed by everyday life.

Whatever the children's needs, they will be working very hard to make progress in spite of their difficulties, so we need to help them to:

■ maintain their interest, motivation and enthusiasm;

■ experience regular successes, which they themselves recognize;

■ maximize their attainments and achievements;

■ develop the *transferable* skills that will enable them to tackle unfamiliar tasks with confidence;

■ achieve to a level that provides a sound platform for future learning at secondary school and beyond;

■ prepare for independent, confident activity in the worlds of home, family life, community and leisure;

■ remain confident and feel good about themselves.

Of course, having a special need does not mean that the children are destined for a life of failure. In recent years we have had many successful entrepreneurs, MPs and government ministers who have variously been dyslexic, blind, deaf or diagnosed with ADHD. On the other hand, there is no avoiding the fact that these types of disabilities can have a negative effect on a child's learning.

A common thread running through these difficulties is a *lack of time* – children with special needs often take longer to get through their work and therefore learn more slowly. With this in mind, not only can we not afford to waste any time, but decisions need to be made about prioritising certain activities and areas of learning. These priorities are usually set out in a *personal plan* or an *individual programme* (such plans come with a variety of different names).

Personalized learning and individual programmes

Set against the backdrop of a supportive classroom environment, our starting point for helping children with special needs to learn more effectively is to gather together information about their performance by:

■ identifying their levels of attainment in the different areas of the curriculum;

■ noting the rate of progress being made in each area;

■ recognizing any other achievements, both inside and outside of the classroom;

■ pinpointing their needs, disabilities and difficulties;

■ identifying the child's interests and strengths – not just strengths when compared with other children, but also areas of *relative strength* within the child's own performance;

■ inviting advice from specialists, as necessary, starting with the school's Special Educational Needs Co-ordinator (SENCO) and the child's parents.

As an essential part of this information-gathering process we need to find out not only what difficulties the child is having, but also how one *need* might be having a knock-on effect in other areas.

Let's take the example of a boy with a significant hearing loss. *If he is having difficulty adjusting his hearing aids,* does he know how to adjust them? Or does he just forget? Or does he need support in terms of his personal organisation? Or is he turning the aids off in order to avoid the lessons? Or to attract help from the TA, who is always patient and whom he considers to be his friend? *If he is making slow academic progress,* is the hearing loss causing him to miss the teacher's explanations and therefore perform below his potential? Or has he got an academic difficulty? *If he has a quick temper,* is he frustrated because his hearing loss makes him feel isolated from the other children? Or because of his lack of progress in lessons? Or because of his lack of confidence when speaking out in class? Or is there some other cause of his anger? And *if he is reluctant to join in group play,* does he feel as though it requires just too much effort to join in, competing against the background noise, constant chatter and lack of opportunities for lip reading?

To sum up, we need to keep our diagnostic assessments up-to-date, logging each child's difficulties, attainments, achievements and progress. Then, we can draw up a programme to guide our actions. This comprises:

- a series of realistic but challenging targets for the child;
- a personalized plan of action, which sets out what the child should be doing to achieve the targets, and what we should be doing to help.

And then we need to carry out that plan and continue to track the child's progress towards the targets, so that we know whether it is being effective (not forgetting to record other incidental achievements along the way).

Targets can be set in one of two ways:

- We might seek to accelerate the child's progress in a particular subject area. We might ask the question *What is the next thing for the child to learn?* And the answer might be, for example, *To read a particular set of words,* or *To learn the number bonds to 20.*

- We might focus on dealing with an aspect of their disability or barrier to their learning. We might ask the question *What is the main thing that would help the child perform better in many different areas?* And the answer might be, for example, *To complete five minutes of written work before asking for help,* or *To check that spectacles are smudge-free and adjusted at the beginning of each lesson,* or *To control a computer mouse around a screen.*

There might be one target or several, depending on which barriers we are concentrating on and how severe they are. But whatever targets are set, they need to become a priority in the child's learning, so that they are taught, revisited and practised often, usually several times each day.

Of course, we don't want to compromise the breadth of the curriculum these children receive, but at the same time, we do need to keep the whole package both manageable and relevant to their personal abilities and aspirations. So we need to strike a balance between the normal classwork undertaken by the class on the one hand, and the individualized activities on the other. Depending on their needs, some children will require only minor modifications to the daily routines of the classroom. Others might need additional support in a few specific tasks, or for most of the week, or they might even need some separate, individual activities. Children with the most severe needs might require a completely individualized curriculum that concentrates on self-maintenance and basic life skills.

In many good schools, it is normal for children of all abilities to work to a personalized programme – this makes individual programmes far less intrusive in the classroom.

How can we best support children with special needs?

Like all the other children in school, children with special needs should be helped to develop knowledge, skills, understanding and transferable skills to the very best of their ability, across the whole curriculum. While they need rather more help to overcome or manage particular barriers to their learning, they will often surprise us with what they *can* do, when given the right sort of help.

However, we do need to be vigilant, as the difficulties of children with special needs are not always obvious and may show up in all sorts of unexpected areas. For example, children with dyspraxia (a *specific difficulty*, which interferes with physical coordination and movement) might encounter difficulties across a broad range of activities:

■ *gross motor skills* – balance, coordination, changing direction, left/right, stairs;
■ *fine motor skills* – doing up shoe laces, using a knife and fork, guiding a computer mouse, turning the pages of a book one at a time;
■ *handwriting* – holding a pen in a relaxed way, speed and neatness, keeping to the line;
■ *speaking* – organizing the sequence of words;
■ *personal organization* – losing things, being on time for lessons, dealing with longer pieces of work;
■ *concentration* – attention span.

Between them, our children might have a whole range of needs, so the support we offer needs to be equally varied. For example, we might need to focus on:

■ *keeping them physically safe and well:*
   – managing medication, life-saving equipment, and health and exercise routines;

- accompanying them as they move around the building, to avoid falling or sustaining injury;
■ *helping them to access the lessons and maintain their concentration:*
  - accompanying children, so that they arrive at the lesson on time;
  - organizing seating arrangements;
  - ensuring additional equipment is to hand and working properly;
  - helping them to organize their own equipment and belongings;
  - sitting alongside, or near, particular children – maintaining a physical presence close by;
  - reminding them of what they did in the previous lesson;
  - repeating or describing in more detail what the teacher is showing the class or is saying;
  - clarifying what they are actually supposed to do;
  - keeping notes;
■ *re-presenting lessons in a way they find more manageable:*
  - breaking up activities into smaller chunks;
  - helping them to plan a piece of work;
  - using simpler vocabulary;
  - enlarging worksheets;
  - reading to them;
  - scribing for them;
  - discussing an object or a picture, rather than a piece of text;
  - discussing the main points of the lesson again;
■ *presenting tasks that have been designed specifically to make progress towards their personal targets:*
  - reading and maths programmes;
  - communication programmes, perhaps set up by a speech and language therapist;
  - social skills programmes, through discussion or counselling;
  - self-organization programmes – to help manage equipment such as hearing aids, spectacles, inhalers, etc.;
■ *keeping an eye on the balance between classwork and tasks prescribed through the individual programme;*
■ *keeping assessments and records up-to-date:*
  - making observations and keeping notes;
  - carrying out more formal assessments;
■ *liaising with parents, teachers and other professionals (where these are included in the individual programme):*
  - reporting on how the children respond to tasks that have been set – for example, any significant changes in their mood, attitude or achievements;
  - keeping parents informed;
  - ensuring that the children keep appointments with speech and language therapists, physiotherapists and other professionals.

In each case, the aim is to enable the children to make good progress in their learning.

However, before we do any of this, we first need to read the children's records, find out about their targets and programmes and, crucially, get to know the children and gain their confidence. The bond between a child with special needs and their TA is not to be underestimated – the TA becomes their friend, their confidant and their first port of call when they feel excited, worried or frustrated.

By meeting the children's special needs – that is, by helping them to over-come or manage the barriers to their learning – we see so many other benefits in terms of the children's personal qualities, social skills and attitudes as they become happy, content and confident in school, while making progress in their learning. Of course, progress in some areas will be slow (but it will be real pro-gress), and yes, some children will require long-term support, but the effects can be so very rewarding both for the children themselves and for the adults supporting them.

4

Before the Subjects Begin: The Early Years

The world isn't made of subjects

In the world of the under-fives, there are no subjects – there is just *life*. Subjects are artificial – just a convenient way for adults to package knowledge, ideas and skills that have a common theme.

When young children *play shop*, they find out about so much more than maths. At the very least they learn English (speaking, listening, reading and writing), maths, PSHE education, geography, citizenship, and design and technology. For example:

■ the names of the items for sale in the shop, where they came from, what materials they are made from, what they are used for, their colour, texture, shape, and so on;

■ socializing with the other children, speaking politely and taking turns;

■ asking and answering questions;

■ writing and reading labels, which might contain words or numbers;

■ counting objects and counting money;

■ using money to pay for things;

■ handling small coins without dropping them;

■ listening to a follow-up story about a fictional family who go shopping together.

So we adults need to be clear about what the children are learning through each of their *play* activities, and how this learning leads on to the various subjects, as we help them to:

■ explore the world around them – to play with it, feel it, taste it, get involved with it, absorb it – and try to make sense of it;

■ make a start in English, maths and some of the other subjects;

■ learn some of the more *generic* (general) and transferable skills, which will stand them in good stead throughout the primary years.

(Department for Children, Education, Lifelong Learning and Skills, Welsh Assembly Government 2008: 14)

Where do we begin?

Every child is individual and starts school with a particular mix of knowledge, understanding, skills and attitudes. There could be any number of reasons for this. For sure, they will have encountered differing family circumstances – parental background, the size and closeness of their extended family, whether they have older brothers and sisters, the family culture, and the personality, interests and achievements of family members. And they will have enjoyed differing social experiences – opportunities to play with older or same-age children, more formal opportunities through playgroup and nursery, toys, games, visits and holiday experiences. Importantly, they will also each have a personal *profile of abilities* across the various areas of learning. Information like this can be very useful to us, as we build on the children's previous experiences and successes, and help them to make further progress in the best way they can.

What important things do the children learn in this early stage of their school career?

If the primary school really is a *starter kit* for life, then clearly, the first few terms at school are crucial. It is here that we begin to create that foundation for success, as we:

■ set the tone – perhaps *purposeful fun* describes it best;
■ establish positive attitudes to learning – curiosity, concentration, and so on;
■ teach and encourage social skills;
■ help them to organize the things they need for their work and play;
■ ensure that each child experiences early success, so that self-confidence flourishes;
■ begin to cultivate those *transferable* skills that are essential for future success;
■ prepare the children for more formal ways of working.

The children begin to develop *personal qualities and attitudes*, such as:

■ increasing self-confidence when speaking with adults and other children about themselves and their work;
■ taking an interest in what is going on around them;

- being willing to ask questions and ask for help when they need it;
- feeling excitement when trying new activities and finding out new things;
- understanding the difference between *right* and *wrong* in familiar situations;
- controlling negative emotions, such as jealousy and impatience.

Children also learn to cope with the *social and emotional demands* of spending several hours a day with other children in the classroom, for example:

- behaving well – being polite and getting on with, and respecting, the other children and the adults;
- working cooperatively, taking turns and being productive when sharing a task with a friend;
- beginning to understand and accept that the things we say and the things we do have consequences, both for ourselves and for other people;
- being alert to the feelings of other people;
- sitting at tables and sharing space and equipment agreeably;
- accepting changes to classroom routines.

They develop *physical skills*:

- the *gross* motor skills of running, hopping, skipping, jumping, throwing and catching, and so on, and avoiding collisions with other children;
- the *fine* motor skills of using pencils, crayons, paint, scissors and simple tools, achieving some measure of control with their preferred hand;

and learn the basics about *keeping themselves safe, healthy and tidy*:

- the foods that contribute to a healthy diet;
- that exercise is good for you;
- personal hygiene – face and hand washing, nose wiping, toileting, etc.;
- dressing themselves, including buttons and perhaps laces.

They extend their skills in *listening and speaking*:

- understanding and responding to instructions involving one or more steps, and asking for more information if it is not quite clear or they can't remember what to do;
- listening attentively in a larger group, such as a school assembly or the dining hall, where there might be more distractions;
- reporting past events in a straightforward, logical way, using appropriate vocabulary;

- giving a clear explanation when asked a question such as 'How did XX happen?' or 'Why did XX happen?';
- making up their own stories, expressing their ideas clearly and coherently, and adding to the mood and atmosphere by using gesture and tone of voice.

They take their *first steps in reading*:

- listening to stories, enjoying them, understanding them, joining in with key phrases, and perhaps commenting on the plot and characters;
- taking an interest in books – holding them the right way up, following the story through the pictures, and appreciating that the print on the page carries meaning;
- referring to letters according to their name and sound;
- reading some words *by sight* and others through straightforward *phonics*;
- retelling the sentences or the story they have read;

and *writing*:

- making marks to represent letters and words;
- writing recognizable letters, perhaps along a line;
- copying individual words and then writing them from memory, for example, their name;
- using phonic knowledge to build short words;
- starting to compose longer pieces of writing for different audiences and for different purposes.

Maths is all around us and helps us to make sense of the world in so many different ways, so the children learn about:

- what numbers are and how they are used;
- addition and subtraction;
- the language of measurement in everyday situations – size, distance (including length, height, width, etc.), weight, time;
- comparing objects according to their size – bigger/smaller, longer/shorter, heavier/lighter, etc.;
- positions – on, under, next to, etc.;
- the names and some of the properties of two-dimensional and three-dimensional shapes.

And the children extend their *skills* and expand their *knowledge and understanding of the world* by making a start on some of the *subjects*:

- *Art and design* – making pictures, patterns and models, using a variety of materials and media, cutting and sticking, taking note of colours, textures and shapes.

- *Citizenship* – learning about similarities and differences between their own life and that of children from other cultures.

- *Design and technology* – using construction materials, investigating how machines and equipment help us at home and in the classroom, including the various ways we use ICT.

- *Geography* – describing local places and places further afield, exploring the ways in which people interact with and influence their environment, for good or ill.

- *History* – recalling and relating past events in their own lives and the lives of people in their family, learning about the way different people lived in the past.

- *Music* – rhythm, clapping, dancing, singing, playing instruments.

- *PSHE education* – the realization that other children might have different likes and dislikes from them, and that this is acceptable.

- *Science* – observing and describing plants and animals, investigating floating and sinking, noting shadows, carrying out simple experiments.

(QCA 2008: 24–82)

Then there are the skills the children learn, which are not linked to any particular subject, but will help them to understand more about the world around them, and at the same time give them a huge advantage when they begin to learn more formally through subjects. Skills such as:

- considering their own likes, dislikes and strengths, and being able to discuss the quality of their work;

- developing their imagination – what it would be like to be somebody else, or in a different place or time – *let's pretend . . . how could we? . . . what could this be used for?*;

- exploring, describing and comparing unfamiliar objects – what's the same and what's different;

- making a record of what they have seen, heard or experienced, through talking, drawing, model-making, role-play, story-making, ICT, and so on;

- finding out how things work;

- appreciating the idea of *cause and effect* (this is also called *cause and consequence*);

- using ICT.

(Tickell 2011: 78)

All of these basic learning outcomes – knowledge, understanding, skills and attitudes – have also been included in the appropriate subject chapters in this book, where they are developed further to show just how the children build on these early steps through the remaining years of their primary education.

In the classroom

It is essential that children are motivated and excited by the things they do in school. This is particularly true of the youngest children, as we try to establish a life-long love of learning. We also need to ensure that the children feel secure, respected and cared for, have confidence in the adults working with them, and know that they will be given time to work things out for themselves when they can, but will receive help when it is needed.

Naturally, no two classrooms are the same – there is no reason why they should be, as each class has a different mix of children. As each child develops and matures from day to day, and from month to month, so the classroom needs to be constantly evolving too, by introducing new activities and equipment, rearranging spaces, altering the children's groupings, varying the way adults lead and support activities, extending the length and complexity of tasks and challenges, and gradually increasing the formality of delivery.

These variations introduce the children to the ways of the primary classroom, where they will be required to:

- sit on the floor, at desks or on stools, or stand, as appropriate to the lesson;
- receive help individually, or in a small group, or as part of the whole class;
- work alone, or alongside other children, or contribute to group tasks;
- maintain their concentration on an adult-led activity for an extended period;
- make judgements about how successful they have been in a task and how they could do better next time;
- learn what sorts of activities and topics might be included in a particular subject.

And so on . . . *as the subjects begin.*

5

Art, Craft and Design

What are art, craft and design really about?

The purpose of art, craft and design education in primary schools is twofold:

- to get children interested in the art, craft and design around them;
- to involve them in art, craft and design in a practical way.

The three elements that make up this subject – *art, craft* and *design* – have much in common with each other and overlap to a great extent, but they are not quite the same thing. The main difference between them is the motivation of the person carrying them out (Dutton 1990).

To take them in reverse order, we can say that:

- A designer arranges and presents ready-made components – materials, pictures, words and media – to create a visual piece of work that contains a message for the viewer. The piece is planned and designed with a particular purpose in mind.

- The craft-worker focuses on the practical skills – the processes and techniques – trying to complete them as carefully and as accurately as possible, to create a usable object of the highest quality.

- The incentive for the artist, on the other hand, is to explore the world and make an emotional response to it through the process of creating something imaginative and unique. Artists express themselves through their art, carrying the viewers with them on their journey of discovery.

Other art forms – dance, drama, literature, music, etc. – make a similar distinction. For example, in music, the *designers* might write advertising jingles, the *craft-workers* endeavour to play their instruments as beautifully as possible, while the *artists* seek to use the sounds and harmonies of instruments and voices to convey emotions and ideas in an original way.

Overall, we can say that artists have the greatest amount of freedom – they might even begin a piece of work without knowing how it will look, sound or feel at the end of the process. Perhaps they also show most *creativity* by:

- looking at the world with a fresh eye, using their imagination to come up with something new;
- then, crucially, converting that idea into reality (an *idea* is not, of itself, *creative* – it needs to *become* something).

Clearly, these three roles are very similar, as they all make use of materials, media, technical skills and aesthetic judgement to create a finished piece. To cover all bases, therefore, in school we help the children to become designers, craft-workers and artists (from here on, for convenience, I shall refer to them all as *artists*), by helping them to:

- explore the world around them;
- imagine what might be possible when using visual media – *what if . . .? how can I . . .?*
- make connections between things that seem quite different, linking ideas together in an interesting way;
- experiment, and become proficient, with a wide range of materials, tools and techniques;
- combine the different elements of a piece to create a *whole,* which makes a visual impact;
- use unexpected results as a way of gaining new insights and creating something fresh and new;
- ensure that the *message* or the *idea* or the *emotion* shows through;
- importantly, *make it happen* – in their own unique way.

With this in mind, the children might create pieces that:

- describe people or objects or scenes;
- celebrate an event;
- tell a story;
- explore an idea;
- give an opinion;
- express a feeling or an emotion – wonder, love, fear, excitement;
- try to persuade somebody to a particular point of view;
- praise or congratulate somebody;
- have a particular tactile quality.

After all, each of these might be used as a starting point by *real* artists. For example, if a group of artists were discussing *waves*, they might portray the thrills and spills at the national surfing championships in Cornwall, or express an opinion on the way wave power is being developed to generate electricity off the Scottish coast, or they might prefer to explore the shapes and textures that are made when waves curl on to a shingle beach.

At this point, it is probably worth reminding ourselves that art, craft and design are all about *illusion*. If we sculpt a squirrel out of plaster, there is no real squirrel. If we draw a room, there isn't really a room – there is no carpet or furniture, and no sun shining through the non-existent windows. The job of the artist is to make the viewer *see* something that isn't really there.

So, while the subject called *art, craft and design* is evidently a practical subject, it is also a *thinking* subject, which requires knowledge, understanding, skill and imagination. The children learn:

- to observe things carefully and to extend their *visual vocabulary*;
- to interpret formal works of art, making informed judgements;
- to make decisions about *composition* in their own work and that of other artists;
- about a wide range of materials and media, the effects they can produce, and how to work with them in a controlled way.

And they produce their own pieces of art, which are an honest response to a subject, as seen through their eyes.

Observational skills and describing what we see

An overview

Our aim, with regard to observational skills, is to help the children to really notice, and then to describe, what they see when they interact with the natural environment, with man-made objects or with pieces of art, so that they:

- become more sensitive to the visual and tactile qualities of objects;
- develop an *art vocabulary* to describe what they see and feel;
- use their observation skills to learn about the world in which they live;
- develop an eye for beauty, and take pleasure and delight in what they see.

Artists believe that any object or scene can be explored and described by referring to five main *elements* – **colours, lines, textures, tones and shapes** – and that this applies equally to man-made objects, works of art, and the natural world (DES 1992a: 4 and 6).

The children learn to take particular notice of these elements, as they explore the world around them. The aim here is to *say what they see* as precisely as possible, and to avoid being distracted by preconceived ideas about what they think they might have seen – how high up a person's face are the eyes? what colour is grass in winter? Let's look at each of these elements in turn.

Colours

The children learn to recognize and describe:

- hues, tints and shades, tonal values;
- primary colours (red, yellow, blue) and secondary colours (orange, green, purple);
- other colours e.g. brown, lilac, turquoise, crimson, ochre;
- black, white and grey;
- skin tones;
- variations within a colour, for example, *red* might be *scarlet, crimson, pillar-box, blood, maroon*.

They learn to describe colours as:

- bold, vibrant, brilliant, dark, light;
- pale, watery, opaque;
- warm, cool, earthy;
- monochrome (not just black and white, but shades and tints of any single colour).

In the classroom, we need to be aware of any children who have a degree of colour-blindness.

Lines

When we make a line-drawing of an object, we often have to invent lines that don't exist in reality. For example, there are no actual lines on a chair, but when the children draw one – that is, when they create the illusion of a chair on a piece of paper – they usually draw the *edges* of each component (the seat, legs and back-rest). And just where are the lines on a human body?

Another imaginary line is the one where two areas of colour meet – for example, the top of a wall where the wallpaper meets the ceiling. In the world of cartoons, this edge might be shown with a black line – in more sophisticated pictures, the two colours just butt up to each other.

The children also learn to use lines to represent texture in their pictures (for example hair, fur, creases, wrinkles). This is a useful way of representing three dimensions in a two-dimensional format. Lines can also suggest speed and movement.

Despite the fact that these lines are imaginary, the children are taught to identify them in the real world as they learn the language of art, craft and design.

The children learn to describe lines as:

- thick, thin, dark, light, hard, soft, heavy, bold, faint, delicate;
- straight, curved, wavy, swirly, spiral;
- flowing, fast, jerky;
- vertical, horizontal, diagonal, zigzag, parallel;
- long, short, broken, dashed, dotted.

Textures

Texture describes the quality of a *surface* and how it feels to the *touch*. Surfaces can be:

- hard, soft, spongy;
- wet, moist, damp, dry;
- flat, high relief, low relief;
- smooth, slippery, coarse, rough, knobbly, spiky, sharp, abrasive, uneven, grained, corrugated, furry, hairy, prickly, velvety, leathery.

In our world of make-believe, it can also mean an *implied* texture − a skilful artist can make us believe in the texture of a rabbit's fur or a fishmonger's hands.

Tones

Tone refers to variations in light, brightness, shade and shadow. For example, the light from a window falling on one side of a vase makes that surface appear lighter and brighter than the other side, which is in the shade, and we might also see a shadow behind it. Some people prefer black-and-white photography just because of this effect, but really, we can talk about *tonal scales* in any colour, grading from light to dark, in the same way as we talk about the white−grey−black spectrum.

When drawing and painting, the children learn to use tone:

- realistically − to show where light would actually fall on a subject, and where we would see shade and shadows;
- or creatively − perhaps to draw attention to a particular part of a scene, or to create a sense of menace in the shadows.

Artists often use variations in colour to create lightness and brightness, and use colour, lines, shading and hatching to create shade and shadow.

Words associated with tones include:

- light, dark, bright, contrasting, shadow, shade, clear, dim, gloomy;
- shiny, dull, reflective, flashing, matt, glossy;
- subtle, muted, dramatic, misty.

An underwater photograph of a shoal of fish creates great variations in tone, as the sun reflects off the darting silver bodies, set against the darkness of the deep.

Shapes

We can use the word *shape* to describe both:

- two-dimensional (2-D) objects – flat ones, such as pictures, and
- three-dimensional (3-D) ones – solid objects, with height, width and depth.

However, artists sometimes also use the word *form* to mean *shape* when talking about 3-D objects.

Artists say that a shape *occupies a space*. The children learn that shapes and spaces can be:

- *positive* – the shapes we actually make when we draw, or the objects we are actually looking at, or
- *negative* – the areas around and between objects – the bits that are left when we look at the main shapes.

So, for example, a tree (or a picture of a tree) has a positive shape and fills its own positive space, but the space around and underneath the tree is a negative space.

We can also make a distinction between *geometric shapes* (square, circular, etc.) and *organic* shapes (which are also called *natural shapes*).

Of course, shapes are not always simple. They might be quite elaborate, or they might be a *composite* shape, made up of a number of smaller ones (for example, a single book has a shape, but a row of books on a library shelf creates an interesting composite shape).

The children learn to describe shapes as:

- long, short, wide, thin, narrow, curly, angular, stretched, squat;
- round, circular, oval (or any other geometric shape), symmetrical, regular, irregular;
- curved, flat, concave, convex;
- rugged, tapering, pointed, smooth;
- erect, vertical, rigid, stiff, dangly, floppy, bulbous, suspended, globular;
- above, below, next to (or any other positional words).

And they learn to talk about:

- composition, arrangement, the shape of a group of objects;
- foreground, background, focal point;
- viewpoint, perspective;
- scale, proportion.

Understanding and appreciating other people's art, craft and design

Designers, craft-workers and artists have different reasons for making their pieces, so the children are encouraged to discuss, appreciate and understand them in the context of the makers' intention, perhaps focusing on:

- For **designers** – did the piece deliver its message clearly and elegantly?
- For **craft-workers** – was the piece beautifully made? Did it *work*?
- For the **artist** – did the piece reveal the artist's emotions? Did it draw us in and take us on the artist's own journey?

Designers have a hand in all manner of objects that we see around us. Even a cardboard cup from a coffee shop will have a particular shape and colour, and might have a logo on it, as well as other pictures, a bar code, and several pieces of text – all of this has been planned, designed and made, and the people responsible will want us to notice their work and find it interesting.

An appreciation of the work of a *craft-worker* is a little harder to achieve, because it relies to an extent on the children's appreciation of the skills involved in making the object. However, they can still say whether they like it, what aspects really appeal to them, and so on – probably referring to those same five *elements*. As they work with a broader range of materials, tools and techniques in their practical lessons, the children learn more about the processes involved in making artefacts, and begin to develop an appreciation of what a *quality* object might look like.

In each unit of work in their art, craft and design course, the children explore the work of a particular artist or genre. For example, when a unit focuses on *colour*, the children might take a close look at the work of Paul Klee or Henri Matisse, and when working with clay, the children might examine some Greek pots, with an eye on *shape*, *texture* and *pattern* (QCA 2000).

When the children discuss pieces of art like this, how can they know what an artist intended? Well, first, it can be helpful to know something about the context within which the piece was created, so they discuss when it was made, and where, what materials and techniques were available at the time, what social conditions were like, what historical events had just taken place, why the piece would have been made, who was funding the project, evidence of any particular artistic or cultural tradition at the time, and so on.

Next, the children look at the piece itself, and ask questions such as:

- What can I see?
  - What is the subject of the piece?
  - Which part seems to be the most important?
  - Is it treated in a realistic way, or are some parts exaggerated or distorted?
  - Is it really about the subject, or is it designed to make a social, religious, moral or political comment?

- How has it been put together?
  - How has the work been arranged? What is in the foreground, middle-ground and background? How is the eye drawn to particular points?
  - Is the piece made up of just one object, or does it bring together several ideas or objects around a central theme?
  - How balanced is the piece? Does one area overpower another? Is it significant that there are objects of different shapes, sizes or colours?
  - Do any parts overlap? Why?
  - Which of the five elements is most important – colours, lines, textures, tones or shapes? What effect does this have?
  - Which colour or colours dominate?
  - Are the lines straight or curved or . . . ?
  - Does the work have one texture or more?
  - Are any elements (lines, colours, shapes, etc.) repeated within the piece? What effect does this give?
  - What contrasts are offered, in terms of colours, sizes, shapes, content, etc.? Are these contrasts dominant, or is the piece mostly harmonious?
  - Is any movement suggested – either actual movement, or something that indicates movement (such as a pointing finger, or the direction of a person's gaze)?
  - Does it hold together as an overall entity, or are some parts more striking, or pleasing, than others?

- What techniques were used?
  - What is it made from?
  - What tools, processes and techniques did the artist use?
  - What skills were needed to produce a work like this?
  - Would the artist have used sketches, or anything else, in preparation? What stages did the work pass through?
  - Was it completed quickly, or did it evolve over a long period?

- What is the mood of the piece?
  - How do the people in the piece feel?
  - Is the work quiet or noisy, happy or sad, relaxing or edgy?
  - How does it make me feel? Is this feeling a temporary reaction or does it continue to affect me afterwards?

Discussing questions like these can lead the children to make links between what they *see* and what they *feel* (in an emotional sense), and moves them closer to appreciating what the artist has done, and understanding what was intended. And, of course, the children can use these same questions to reflect on their own work and that of their friends. Can we tell from a child's picture whether he enjoys bonfire night, or is frightened by it? Is he happy or bored on the beach?

Luckily, there are some useful conventions the children can use, and they learn a little about these, in order to help them interpret works of art. For example, colours can suggest moods – red might suggest anger, blue hints at sadness, muted colours are calm and peaceful, while strong and contrasting colours can indicate drama and conflict.

The children learn that, while these are not exactly *rules*, they might give an indication of what an artist intended. One of our jobs is to help the children crack that code, so that they notice particular features and recognize their significance – for instance, if the whole picture is full of reds, purples and sharp points, the children might suggest that it looks like an angry picture.

In addition, of course, examining artworks at this level of detail will help the children to improve their own art, craft and design, as they make connections between their own work and that of professionals, in terms of colours, patterns, the use of motifs, practical techniques, and so on.

Doing art, craft and design

We want the children to become confident artists, craft-workers and designers in their own right:

- using their imagination;
- creating their art through a variety of materials, media, tools, techniques and processes;
- communicating messages, thoughts, ideas and feelings in a visual format;
- experiencing the excitement of expressing their ideas in this way.

Our task is to offer opportunities that will lead them to develop knowledge, understanding and skills in each of these areas.

For the most part, younger children simply portray the world around them. Their artwork is often immature because their understanding of the world is limited. At first they might miss out some body parts, but gradually include them as they realize that they exist – for example, one day they will notice that people have nostrils, and they will then include nostrils on every face they draw. They give their dog *some* legs, only later refining this to *four*. Most young children use a single line at the bottom of the page to indicate ground-level and a single blue line at the top of the page to represent the sky, until they discover distance and perspective.

But we need to remember that the children's pictures and other works of art are their representation of the world as they understand it – their art is real art and should be recognized as such.

Doing art has two distinct stages, both of which require the children to make some major decisions:

- *Imagining the subject (in the mind's eye)* – Should the piece represent an object, an event, a scene, an emotion or a feeling? Should it be something the child has noticed, remembered, dreamt or imagined? Should it be taken from their own lives, or from their family and friends, from the news, or from topic work in school, or . . . ? Should it be two-dimensional or three-dimensional? Should they work alone or collaboratively? Should they use paint, collage, textiles, construction, clay, print, photography, digital media, or some other material? Should the piece focus on lines, colours, textures, tones or shapes? What about composition?

- *Next, converting that image into a picture or an object* – What techniques should I use? What is the process? What tools will I need? How long will it take?

Once these decisions are made – even if they change later in the process – work can begin.

At the earliest stages, the children work intuitively, doing what they think and feel is right. As they mature, we can guide them towards a more methodical way of working, so that they:

- Explore a subject or an idea – whatever the starting point or stimulus, it is important that the subject should be open-ended, and leave room for imagination, fantasy, expression and invention.

- Carry out research on how other artists have treated the subject, collecting up ideas from photos, galleries, magazines, artefacts, and using these ideas as inspiration to develop their own ideas further.

- Select a particular part of their preparatory work for their final piece.

- Consider the materials and media available to them and choose a suitable medium or combination of media.

- Select appropriate tools, equipment and processes, and make a plan to create the piece, through all its stages of construction.

- Use the media skilfully, to complete the piece, being mindful of how the various elements can be used to best effect.

This is by no means straightforward. The children need to:

- Experiment with ideas – drafting different versions and imagining how the piece might look from different angles and from different distances, how different colours might affect the look of the piece and, in the case of a 3-D piece, deciding whether it is stable, and so on. The children might use ICT tools (for example, cameras, drawing and painting programmes, and cropping tools) to try out their ideas.

■ Experiment with the materials, media, tools and techniques – working through problems that arise during the creative process, such as producing a particular effect that they have visualized in their head.

■ Evaluate, modify and improve their work-in-progress – it can be helpful to discuss their work with an adult, using specialist vocabulary so that comments are clear and decisions are supported by reasons:
  – Is the piece as I imagined it in my head?
  – Which parts of the piece are fit for purpose and which parts need to be amended?
  – What do I need to do to improve the piece?
  – Have I got the colours / lines / textures / tones / shapes just right? What about the composition? Do I need to brush up on my practical skills?

Because of its exploratory nature, a guiding principle of artwork should be *trial and improvement* – but not *trial and error,* which we hear so often and sounds so defeatist!

After all the thinking, imagining, planning, decision making and judgements, this stage – the *making* stage – is the one that enables artists to bring their ideas and thoughts to a successful conclusion, so it should never be neglected.

Sketchbooks are among the most valuable tools in the art-room, having a hundred and one uses at each stage of the process. They should be seen as the property of the children, so that they can use them whenever they think it would be useful to do so. A well-used sketchbook might contain:

■ a collection of photos, magazine cuttings, stimulating poems – rather like a scrapbook;

■ background information about different subjects;

■ notes on artists and how they have treated subjects;

■ examples of a particular style;

■ reminders of all sorts – notes and diagrams on particular techniques, colour mixing, etc.;

■ jottings, sketches and notes, which explore and trial ideas;

■ practice pieces to perfect a technique – a shape, a close-up, shading, perspective, views from different angles – before adding these to the final piece.

Another useful device is the *viewing frame.* This is used in the same way as we use a camera's viewfinder to select the best view for a snapshot. It helps the children to identify the boundaries of a scene, homing in on particular parts of the composition and filtering out irrelevant information, so that they can clarify their thoughts on what combination of shapes, colours, textures, tones and lines they wish to use as a basis for their work.

Children are encouraged to act as real artists, and this includes labelling their work for class displays, giving the title of the piece, the artist's name, the materials used, and the methods or techniques employed. It goes without saying that, as these are real pieces of art, they should be well mounted, so that they both celebrate the children's achievements and enhance the appearance of the room.

So far, it sounds as though doing art might be a solitary activity, but this is not necessarily the case. The children can learn a huge amount by working on collaborative projects – planning together, sharing each others' experience of using materials and methods, working in a larger scale (which can pose all sorts of perceptual and technical problems), negotiating and making joint decisions, and so on. Mixed-media friezes are very popular for this purpose, perhaps based on a theme such as *A Tropical Rainforest* or *Under the Sea*.

Clearly, a balance between thinking and practical work needs to be achieved in lessons, but equally clearly, at primary school level, the *process* of making art is far more important than the finished *product*. Once a stimulus has been given, the children should be allowed to develop their work in their own way – with help and advice as necessary, of course, but we should not be over-prescriptive. Unexpected ideas and accidental effects should be welcomed – after all, in art there are no right or wrong answers, just individual responses to a subject, springing from the artist's previous experiences, understanding of life, imagination and skills.

Materials, media, tools, techniques and processes

In their primary years, the children sample a wide range of materials, media, tools, techniques and processes that need to be combined if they are to make their own pieces with imagination and skill. For each of these, the children learn about:

- The properties of the materials and media – what they are capable of, what they are particularly good for, and their limitations.

- The tools that can be used with each material, and the skills and techniques required to get the best results.

- How processes work and the skills needed to create particular effects – for example, how batik works.

Realistically, of course, we cannot expect every child to enjoy every part of the subject, nor to demonstrate equal levels of skill and technique, but they should be encouraged to *have a go* in every area - in line with the primary ethos of providing a starter kit, or a taster – before they begin to specialize later in life.

Common activities include:

- *Drawing and painting* – drawing, shading, hatching, painting, pattern making, calligraphy, colour mixing – using pencils, crayons, pastels, paints, charcoal, inks, felt tips, brushes, pens, rollers, body parts, computer programs, different surfaces.

- *Printing* – repeat patterns, marbling, rubbings – using relief blocks, stencils, potatoes, tiles, cutting tools, inks, ICT.
- *Modelling and sculpture* – carving, sculpting, modelling, origami, collage, assembly, construction kits, jewellery making – using plasticene, paper, dough, papier-mâché, soap, plaster, wire, moulds, wood, building blocks, recycled materials, found objects, natural materials, collage materials, leaves, shells.
- *Clay* – decorating with pattern and texture, tiles, pots and free-form pieces, slabs, coils, pinching and throwing, slip-trailing – using rolling pins, wheels, engraving pens, sieves, cutting wires, clay guns, glazes, slips, stains and oxides.
- *Textiles* – sewing, embroidery, appliqué, batik, weaving, knotting, cutting, printing, fashion, interior design – using fabrics, dyes, fabric paints, wool, threads, needles, pins, sewing machines, bodkins, scissors, shears.
- *Digital media* – drawing, painting, image manipulation, cropping, photo-montage, animation, video – using cameras, video cameras, computer programs.

The children will meet each of these materials, media, tools, techniques and processes many times in the course of their primary school career, learning a little more on each successive occasion. Sometimes lessons will take the form of *short focused tasks*, where the children concentrate on developing particular craft-based knowledge, skills and understanding. At other times, they will complete *open-ended creative assignments*, where they combine their imaginative ideas with their practical skills to create an original piece.

As the children work to convert their ideas into a product, they will inevitably encounter all sorts of problems, for example:

- How do I show depth and distance on a flat piece of paper?
- How do I make that particular shade of lilac that I have seen?
- How do I paint my Mum's hair, when it seems to have several different colours in it?
- How do I make sure the design on my potato will be the right way round when I print it?
- How do I stop my fabric from fraying at the edges?
- How can I make sure my papier-mâché man does not fall over?
- How do I tint a black-and-white photograph using a computer program?

The list is endless. There is, perhaps, some comfort in knowing that experienced artists face problems like these every day as they struggle to bring their ideas to fruition. Clearly, the best way for the children to learn about a material is to work with that material – as well as looking at the ways in which other people have worked with it, of course.

As the children come across problems like these, they become more sensitive to the skills employed by other artists, craft-workers and designers – when they see a painting of a cat and a dog, they might notice that different brushstrokes have been used to represent the fur and the hair, and when they look at a religious painting, they might notice the way the illusion of light has been created, to bring meaning to the picture.

Art lessons (or, more usually, series of lessons) are planned around themes that allow the children to focus on:

- just two or three of the main elements – *colours, lines, textures, tones* or *shapes*;
- perhaps an aspect of *pattern* or *composition*;
- two or three different *materials* or *media*;
- just one or two *techniques* for each material.

So, for example, in a unit linked to a *Rainforest* topic in geography, the children might use pastel crayons for their individual work and textiles for a whole-class collage, and focus on mixing new colours (specifically variants of green), depicting the way light filters through leaves and how best to portray their foreground against an interesting background.

The final pieces will reveal to what extent the children have used the visual elements (colours, tones, etc.) in a considered way, shown technical control over the materials and techniques, and made a personal response to the subject matter.

When the work is completed, the children are given the opportunity to discuss their own artwork and that of their classmates in the same way that they would discuss professional art. Older children will be able to comment on whether their piece was influenced by the work of professional artists and, if so, in what ways (subject, materials, colours, shapes, techniques, etc.) – this is a very mature step.

Transferable skills and personal qualities

Children in primary schools acquire information and ideas in many different ways – by listening, discussion, practical activities, problem solving, investigations, etc., and it is likely that each of these strategies is used in every subject at one time or another. However, there is one other powerful strategy we should include in this list – a lot of our teaching and a great deal of the children's learning relies on *visual images*. These images include:

- pictures and photos – of people, places and events close to home and further afield;
- illustrations in books;
- diagrams to explain processes;
- charts and graphs;
- three-dimensional models;
- TV and video – drama, documentaries, news, films;
- displays of their work.

Visual images such as these help the children to make sense of their lessons in all subjects. There is no doubt that the activities they undertake in art, craft and design lessons can help to sharpen their skills in observation and description, so that they might make even better sense of the images they see, and therefore learn more in every subject.

In addition, art, craft and design activities offer opportunities for the children to develop knowledge, skills and understanding of a more general nature:

- research skills;
- the ability to make connections between things that have no obvious link – this is, after all, the basis of understanding new ideas in every area of the curriculum;
- imagination, inventiveness, thinking *outside the box*;
- aesthetic awareness, making judgements about the *quality* of their own work and that of others;
- understanding other cultures, both historical and contemporary ones;
- creativity – that is, transforming imagination into reality;
- understanding and carrying out technical skills, routines and processes;
- drawing – which can be a great help when drafting ideas (in any subject or context), and when trying to make sense of other people's ideas and suggestions;
- manual dexterity, hand–eye coordination;
- problem-solving and decision-making skills;
- self-organization – taking care of tools, equipment, materials, the room and themselves, including basics such as wearing an overall, covering surfaces, setting up, clearing up spills and packing away;
- communication and discussion.

Beyond this, the subject also provides fantastic motivation for the children to develop positive personal qualities, such as:

- self-control, self-discipline, care;
- concentration, persistence;
- a willingness to experiment;
- a willingness to deal with problems flexibly, and to start again if the first approach is not working;
- an appreciation of the value of *trial and improvement*;
- an appreciation that problems do not always have a single correct solution, and so we don't always have to be *right*;
- overcoming insecurity when making decisions and taking risks;

- an appreciation of the benefits of cooperation, sharing and collaboration;
- a willingness both to accept and to give criticism in a positive way;
- valuing individuality;
- a willingness to take responsibility for their own actions;
- playfulness and curiosity, interest and excitement;
- pride in one's achievements.

And of course, it is always possible that the lessons might lead the children to an absorbing hobby, which provides fun, interest and satisfaction into adult life.

However, in the end, we return to the idea that art is a means of expressing oneself, of communicating. If the children know in their heart what they want to say, but can't think of the words (or they don't speak English very well), they can always draw it, paint it or create a model of it – perhaps that is why their home-made cards and presents are so touching.

6

Citizenship

What is Citizenship really about?

In the subject called Citizenship, we are helping the children to:

- understand how society *works*;
- grow up happy, healthy, safe and confident, feeling that they *belong* to their communities, and are able to participate fully and positively in them.

(DES 2004: 9)

The starting point is for the children to appreciate that *society* is made up of many *communities*, that is, groups of people with something in common. At the simplest level, the children are in the same class at school, which is a community in its own right. Other communities to which they might belong include:

- their family, friends, local neighbourhood, village or town;
- clubs or groups they belong to, based on sports or hobbies;
- fans of particular kinds of music or football teams;
- people who speak the same language, or have similar religious beliefs.

The children learn something about the ties that bind these communities together, what makes them distinct and different, how they operate and how they interact with the other communities around them. Two large communities that the children might not realize they belong to are the UK and the global community – which, of course, includes everybody in the world.

Recognizing that we are a part of these communities helps us to *belong* in society. And this helps us to play an active and positive role, contributing to each of our communities in a morally and ethically sound way.

The children develop their knowledge and understanding of *society* by considering four broad themes:

- the rich variety of cultures to be found across the communities that make up our society;

- how the actions of one person (or group) are likely to affect others;

- how decisions are made in society;

- the importance of having good laws, and abiding by them.

(QCDA 2010: 35–40)

The rich variety of cultures that make up our society

There are more than sixty million people living in the UK, from a wide variety of backgrounds. In this part of the Citizenship curriculum, we help the children to find out how other people live, and to recognize where and how we all combine to create a thriving society.

The children learn about these other cultures – their beliefs, social traditions, language, food, dress, art, literature, games, celebrations, history, and so on. They do this by carrying out research, viewing television programmes, watching films and video clips from the Internet, talking with people from different cultural backgrounds, and perhaps speaking with representatives from voluntary groups.

Throughout, they are encouraged to note what is different and, crucially, what is the same as in their own culture. For instance, we might speak in different languages, but the messages we give and receive will largely be about the same things. In many schools, this can lead to the children exchanging information about their own lives – not just immigrants to the UK, but also long-standing cultures such as those found in fishing, farming and mining communities, steel towns, market towns, cities, villages, etc.

This can lead to one of two outcomes:

- excitement, delight and joy at discovering new things; or
- suspicion, fear and a feeling of being excluded.

Our task is to help the children build the knowledge, understanding, skills and attitudes that will allow them to adopt the first of these responses.

By learning about other groups, understanding their needs and aspirations, and rejecting any myths, prejudices and stereotypical views about them, the children can go some way to building and maintaining trust, respect and harmony in society, and enriching their own lives as a result.

In schools, we aim to help the children to adapt to change in a positive way, seeking out new experiences, welcoming new ideas from other sections of society and, at the same time, doing what they can to ensure that everybody else gets as much as possible from their lives. Society does not stand still: people have always moved house from one place to another; scientific, technological and industrial changes have always brought us new opportunities; and cultural and economic changes have always taken place.

How the actions of one person are likely to affect others

As citizens, we all have rights. These include human rights, of course, but also social, political, legal, and moral ones. And with rights comes a responsibility to ensure that other people can also access their rights. Here, we are talking about what is right and wrong, fair and unfair, just and unjust (DfE 2011).

As a first step, the children need to understand the difference between *wants* and *needs*, and to appreciate that, in most cases, *needs* should take priority over *wants*. And if we are to reach a balanced and satisfactory solution to a situation in which people have differing wants or needs, then it is essential that, before reaching a conclusion, we:

■ research and investigate the situation thoroughly, learning all the facts;

■ listen carefully to views and opinions that are expressed fully and honestly from all perspectives;

■ identify all the ways in which this issue is related to other issues – the *knock-on effects*;

■ identify who the potential *winners* and *losers* might be, and the level of benefits for some people compared with the negative consequences for others.

When trying to balance the positives and negatives, we must not forget that any negative effects will be happening to real people. The children are helped to *empathize*, that is, to imagine how other people will be feeling, when a decision is not made in their favour.

In the classroom, the children discuss questions such as 'Should the boys be allowed to play football on the playground, when the ball might hurt a younger child?' This question goes right to the heart of Citizenship:

■ Where is the balance of rights and responsibilities on the playground?

■ Should it be a case of *might is right*?

■ Should staff take a unilateral decision, or should the children themselves be included in a negotiated settlement?

There are many situations within the children's experience that can prompt discussions like this, some based in the classroom and others with a worldwide perspective:

■ Turn taking/always wanting to go first/calling out in class.

■ What games should be included in sports day, and what is a fair scoring system?

■ Should a parade of family-run shops be pulled down in order to build a new supermarket?

■ Should we buy strawberries and green beans from Africa?

■ How should Lottery money be spent?

The children also learn that decisions can have long-term consequences – how do we balance the benefits for people who are alive today with possible implications for future generations? After all, we know that the way we live today is the product of centuries of change and development in society, so it makes sense that the decisions we make and the things we do now will affect the lives of people in the future. Older children are capable of discussing quite complex topics such as these, developing a strong sense of social justice and moral responsibility with regard to people in their own communities and those who are further away.

Of course, our aim is not just for the children to gain knowledge about all these issues, understand them and be able to discuss them – we also want them to play their part as citizens and *do something about it*. This might involve something like giving practical support to a charity, but it might also include changing the way they go about their everyday lives, such as giving others a little more respect and valuing what they do.

However, some children find this difficult, perhaps because some classroom discussions come to conclusions that are very different from the views they hear at home. Or maybe they themselves have *needs*, which may be quite serious or complex – for example, they might suffer from Asperger's syndrome, which hampers their ability to empathize with other people. So we may have to accept that they may not yet be at a stage where they can give as much to the community as we would like.

While we, and the children, might agree on what is required if we are to meet everybody's needs in our society, there are likely to be many different and valid ways of going about it, and we simply do not know beforehand which method will be the most successful in the end. So there are often disagreements about the best way to bring about change for the better. Just how far can we influence the decision-makers?

How decisions are made in society

This part of Citizenship looks at *government*:

- who makes decisions;
- how those decisions are made;
- how we can take part in, and influence, the decision-making process.

In an ideal world, everybody would contribute directly to every decision that we, as a society, need to make. However, that is just not practical – we all lead busy lives and, realistically, we are not always interested enough to explore all the issues and make the best possible decisions. So we select other people to make decisions for us. This is the democratic process.

The children learn that there are various levels of government, and each has its own roles and responsibilities:

- central government, that is, the UK Parliament (with its two Houses, the Commons and Lords), the Scottish Parliament, and the Welsh and Northern Irish Assemblies;
- local government – parish councils, town councils, borough councils, county councils;
- the European Parliament.

And within school, there is a Governing Body and a School Council.

Although these *councils* go by many different names, they all operate in a similar way. The children learn that:

- councils are made up of councillors who have been elected (their title changes from one institution to another, of course);
- in this way, individuals' views are represented through their councillor, when decisions are made by the council;
- councils make decisions in the interests of the communities they represent and of society as a whole;
- with few exceptions, anybody can become a councillor, by volunteering to be one, and then winning enough votes in an election;
- each council is controlled by a set of rules, which lists the types of decisions it can make;
- decisions are made by counting the votes *for* and *against* a proposal;
- there is a principle of *one person, one vote* in all elections.

When exploring particular kinds of council, the children learn about the types of decisions that they make. Importantly, they are also helped to appreciate that these decisions can often be very difficult, as they relate to situations where, if one section of the community gains a benefit, it is likely that another group will be disadvantaged, and that there is rarely a single solution to any problem.

The children are also introduced to the idea of political parties, that is, groups of people who tend to be in agreement about the way society should be run and therefore tend to vote in the same way as each other. However, while parties may seem to have more power than individuals, each member still has only one vote.

These might be the facts and ideas we want the children to learn, but if they are to be filled with enthusiasm, they need to engage with real issues – either local ones (such as the suitability of the play equipment at the local park), global ones (reducing waste) or even historical ones (should Victorian children have been working when they were only nine years old?).

Responsible decision-making requires both serious thought and practice. So, if we want the children to make good decisions, both now and in the future, they need to take an active part in decision-making from an early age, preferably in a safe environment such as the classroom. That means creating opportunities for this to happen. At an everyday level, this might involve the children debating and voting on particular play activities or particular classroom displays, or how to carry out and present projects around school, or choosing their class member on the School Council.

In addition, the older children might study the decision-making process in their local community, perhaps following a planning application for a site close to the school, where various factors are considered by the councillors before permission to build is granted (or refused). A councillor might be invited into school to explain the issues and the children might visit the site themselves.

It is important that the children recognize that not every proposal they make will be adopted – this is because there might be implications that they have overlooked – or there may be implications that other voters believe are more important. But even if they are over-ruled (this time), they have at least been able to take part in the democratic process, where all sides of an argument are entitled to an airing.

The importance of having good laws and abiding by them

Every community has its rules, regulations and laws – families might have rules about behaviour, bedtimes, television viewing and computer use; clubs have rules about membership, meetings and subscriptions; and the country has rules (which we call *laws*) that cover many areas of our lives.

It is good practice (and now very common practice) for the children in a school to be involved in the discussion stages before rules that affect them are introduced – either in class or through the School Council. In this forum, the benefits of any proposed rule change are explained, together with an acknowledgement that certain people might be worse off and what this means in practice for everybody. Through this process, the children learn that rules are neither arbitrary, nor taken by an individual looking from a single perspective, but are an even-handed response to an unsatisfactory situation, where one group in society is in danger of being treated unfairly and a balance needs to be regained.

Children learn that the police (in the context of the wider community) and supervisors on the playground (in the context of the school) have a wide-ranging role when upholding the law, including:

■ protecting people and property;
■ preventing crime;
■ reminding people of what is expected of them;
■ apprehending people who break the rules.

They should do this in a way that:

- is respectful towards the people in the communities they serve;
- is even-handed.

All crime – that is, when a rule or a law is broken – involves behaviour that is *unfair* and has the potential to cause harm or upset both to the victim and to the wider community – for example, a child running in the school building (or a speeding motorist) might bump into somebody and hurt them physically; ethnic harassment is both upsetting for the individual involved and it also hinders society's drive to create harmonious and inclusive communities for everybody.

Perhaps, in an ideal world, we would not need laws – their function is really only to set boundaries and reinforce the ways in which we should lead our lives.

Knowledge, understanding, skills, personal qualities and attitudes

Knowledge

If the children are to make good judgements, it is essential that they have the relevant information on which to base their decisions, for example facts about:

- different cultures – the beliefs, languages, customs and values that members hold dear;
- rights that people are entitled to;
- responsibilities we have to make sure that others are able to exercise their rights and have their needs met;
- how central and local government work and how to take part in the democratic processes available to us in society;
- the process by which decisions are made;
- rules and laws.

Understanding

In order to be a good citizen, the children need to understand:

- that we are all individuals and, while we have differences, we also have many things in common with other people;
- that beliefs and values may differ from one culture and community to another, but that these are not necessarily right or wrong just because they are different;
- the key features of different cultures;
- the difference between a fact and an opinion;

- how peer pressure can change the way we think and behave, and appreciate that this can lead to better or worse choices, depending on the peers;
- how advertising and the media seek to influence what we think, what we do and the way we behave;
- that differences of opinion can be resolved amicably, through discussion and negotiation;
- that we might need to change the way we live in order to accommodate others;
- how to influence decision-making responsibly;
- why rules and laws are important in society, and why we should keep to them.

Finally, and importantly, we need to understand ourselves and our own emotions, and how to control negative feelings.

Skills

The facts and the understanding outlined above could be learned passively and in a detached way while sitting at a desk, but our aim is for the children to be actively involved in their communities. To this end, they need to learn some skills:

- enquiry – that is, knowing where to find information and views, asking the right questions in the right way, and weighing up the responses;
- debate:
  - preparing thoroughly beforehand, and clarifying their own opinions about an issue;
  - explaining their ideas and beliefs clearly – defending them logically, and restating them in a different way where necessary;
  - listening attentively to other people's views, and taking turns in the discussion;
  - weighing arguments and evidence, taking all information and alternatives into account, and being prepared to change their opinion;
  - keeping their emotions in check;
- speaking and writing persuasively, to get a point across;
- representing others who cannot speak for themselves, such as animals or people who cannot be present at the debate;
- negotiating and resolving disagreements peaceably and to everybody's satisfaction;
- taking part in community activities and decision-making.

Personal qualities and attitudes

Unfortunately, such knowledge, understanding and skills will come to nothing if the children fail to develop personal qualities and attitudes such as:

- care and respect for others – that is, all other people regardless of age, race, gender, ethnicity, religion, special need, social background and so on;
- belief in the principle of equal opportunity for all;
- respect for the environment and for other people's property;
- cooperation, helpfulness and consideration;
- willingness to listen and try to understand;
- willingness to take responsibility for oneself and one's community;
- empathy – appreciating how other people feel;
- willingness to stand up for what they believe to be right, including giving a voice to those who cannot speak up for themselves;
- willingness to consider what is right and what is wrong, and make the right choices, resisting peer pressure if necessary;
- willingness to follow rules for the greater good, even if personally disadvantaged by them;
- willingness to contribute to the life of the class and the school.

Many of these attributes grow out of the belief that we really can *make a difference* in our community.

How is Citizenship taught in schools?

Although citizenship is usually seen as a subject in its own right, with its own content and knowledge base, it often shares a timetable slot with PSHE education. However, this is only part of the story, because the children also learn about it through other subjects such as history and geography, through class-based activities such as decision-making, rule-making, caring, supporting and campaigning and, crucially, through being part of a school that demonstrates the principles of good citizenship through its everyday practices.

In timetabled Citizenship lessons the children might be introduced to new ideas through television news clips, video and so on. Or they might carry out their own research. Or explore issues through discussion, circle time and role-play. Or visitors (such as members of local community groups, charities, social clubs, public organisations and the council) might be invited into school to make presentations and discuss issues with them. At other times, the children might investigate real situations in school or in the local community where a decision needs to be taken and perhaps lobby decision-makers for a particular outcome, either to bring about a change or to resist a proposal.

Other subjects also offer opportunities to extend the children's learning about citizenship. For instance, in history lessons they might learn about the Roman Senate (as a type of council), in English lessons they might read the legend of Robin Hood (who allegedly robbed the rich to help the poor), and they engage with local and world cultures through art and music. Science and geography lessons offer opportunities for discussion about sustainability, and RE introduces the children to a range of values, beliefs and customs in the main religions in the UK. There are also strong links with PSHE education.

Activities that are not subject-based, but which can also provide rich learning experiences in the area of citizenship include:

- assemblies;
- the election of class councils and school councils, and the process of decision-making by these committees;
- taking responsibility for aspects of school life, such as serving lunch for younger children, buddying up with pupils who are new to the school, and preparing music for assemblies;
- looking after pets;
- recycling unwanted items;
- supporting deserving causes through fund-raising, campaigning or physical support, perhaps supporting children with special needs, or helping with local environmental projects;
- visits to community venues, such as a fire station, church, police station or council chamber, to find out about their contribution to the community;
- a day (or week) off regular timetable, when children throughout the school come together to explore a theme such as world clothes, children's health, old age, or how to make the school building more accessible to those with physical disabilities.

Every school has a statement of its aims and ethos, and the children should be able to see that the school lives up to these ideals by the way:

- the school shows a positive interest in the similarities and differences between the children's community and other communities, both within the UK and further afield;
- the school rules protect all members of the school community and are fair;
- class rules are drawn up through negotiation with the children;
- all the children are involved in democratic processes, such as elections;
- the children's views are listened to and they are helped to explain themselves clearly;
- local, national and international news items are discussed.

The approach here should be twofold – the school needs to ensure that these processes are the natural and accepted way of doing things, and it needs to make clear to the children that things are not done this way by accident, but rather because staff at the school really believe that they should be done this way.

Different schools will need to approach the subject of Citizenship in different ways, depending on the cultural resources available to them locally. For example, rural schools in which most of the children were born locally might have close links with local councillors, but will perhaps need to work harder to provide the children with experience of life in different cultures, such as those in multi-ethnic communities found in many cities in the UK.

7

Design and Technology

What is Design and Technology really about?

This subject is about making things – anything and everything. The whole of the *man-made* environment, at home, in the street and throughout the world. From paper clips to aeroplanes, from curtains to power stations, from pencils to pizzas – wherever we make something, that is an example of Design and Technology. It includes both *high-tech* things, such as medical equipment, cars, the latest communication devices, and *low-tech* things, such as clothes pegs, plastic bags, garden paths – they all need to be designed, before being made.

Technology in society

The pace of technological change is faster than at any time in history, and it shows no sign of slowing down. We read of scientific breakthroughs nearly every day in the newspapers. And wherever science increases our knowledge and understanding, technology uses that new knowledge and understanding to change the way we live and, hopefully, improve the quality of our lives.

Technologists are creative people who find ways to:

- meet people's needs;
- satisfy people's wants and aspirations;
- exploit opportunities, perhaps developing a new use for something already familiar to us.

They are practical problem-solvers who come up with ideas, inventions and innovations, either creating new products, or redesigning existing ones to improve efficiency or provide greater appeal to the user.

We know when objects have been designed and made well, because they have two particular qualities:

- they fulfil their intended purpose – that is, they *work*; and
- they are also aesthetically pleasing – that is, they satisfy people's preferences in terms of their look, sound, taste, touch and smell.

Some technologies move very quickly indeed (for example, electronic communication devices) – these tend to be the ones that appeal to consumers and promise profits for the innovator. Other products seem to stand still for decades because there is no perceived need to develop them further (pencils, for example). It is valuable for the children to trace the way individual products have changed over time in response to scientific and technological developments.

A key part of technology is examining objects critically, identifying both the good points and any possible design faults – sliced bread makes it possible for us to have regular-sized sandwiches, but a knitted swimsuit might stretch out of shape when it becomes wet. Issues such as energy use and sustainability are also considered.

Design and Technology lessons in school aim to prepare children to take part in this fast-moving technological revolution:

- both as knowledgeable consumers;
- and as technologists and innovators in their own right.

(QCA 2004: 15)

What is included in Design and Technology in the primary school?

In school, the children design and make things using three types of materials:

- **food**;
- **textiles**;
- **resistant materials** – paper, card, wood, metal, plastic, stone, clay, etc.

These are combined, as necessary, with:

- **components** – ready-made parts that can be assembled to make an object;
- **mechanisms** – that is, parts of objects whose function is to *do* something, for example, a table is inactive, but a tin opener has a mechanism.

Of course, many objects are manufactured using a combination of materials, components and mechanisms – for example, a go-cart might be made of wood (*a resistant material*), but incorporate wheels (*components*), and steering and brakes (*mechanisms*). And when an object is controlled by a microchip – either following a programmed instruction from a computer or reacting to a sensor, this is called *control technology*, and is also included in this subject.

How Design and Technology usually happens

Most real-life Design and Technology projects move through the four stages shown in this model. They usually begin with *identifying a problem* and move clockwise through the other three stages:

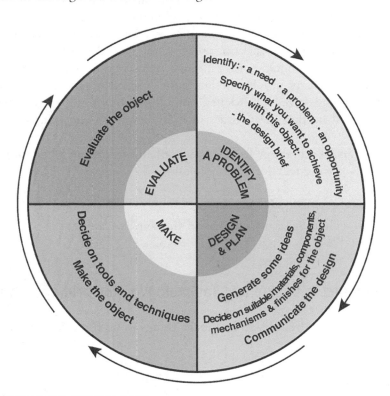

FIGURE 7.1 The Design Cycle (QCA 2004: 16–19)

If we consider putting up a shelf in the house, for example, we:

- *identify a problem* – which could be a need, a want or an opportunity (in this case, 'I've nowhere to store my DVDs');

- draw up a list of minimum requirements – a *specification* or *design brief* – how long, how wide and how strong it needs to be;

- discuss it with friends, generating ideas about how to solve the problem and dream up some appealing *solutions*, before making a final decision on the *design*;

- think about what *materials* it should be made from and how it should look in its finished form;
- write it down, perhaps with sketches, so that we don't forget anything;
- select some *tools* and decide on the construction *techniques*;
- *make* the shelf;
- offer it up to the wall, to see how it will look in practice – that is, we *evaluate* it – before making any final amendments and then fixing it – job done!

Of course, this is only a simplified model of the *design and make* process, because we might have looked at other people's shelves first and thought that we could do a better job (in which case we would have started at the *evaluation* stage); or we might have decided that we fancied doing some joinery (our starting point, then, would have been *deciding on suitable materials*, in the Design and Plan stage), and we would have moved around the other stages in a different way, before *making* and *evaluating* our new shelf.

Although the whole process has four main stages, school projects are often called *design and make* projects, reflecting the tendency to focus more on these two practical stages than on the two discussion-based stages.

The Design and Technology process in the primary classroom

The Client, the Designer and the Maker

It can be useful for the children to think of a project as a commercial undertaking, featuring a Client, a Designer and a Maker (the *maker* is essentially a craft-worker, who might be a cook, a dressmaker, a joiner, furniture-maker, stone-mason or even a computer programmer, depending on the project):

- the *client* identifies a problem, or expresses a need, a want or an opportunity;
- the *client* hires a *designer* and explains what the problem is, or what is needed or wanted, and draws up a list of criteria for the project (the design brief);
- the *designer* draws up a detailed plan, and discusses this with the *client*, which might lead to modifications and the design being fine-tuned;
- the *designer* then shares the design with the *maker*, who selects the best tools and techniques and carries out the practical work;
- while it is being made, the *designer* and *maker* evaluate the product and modify and improve the design as necessary;
- when it is finished, the *designer* and the *client* evaluate the product together;
- further modifications may be required, involving all three people, until the *client* is satisfied.

Of course, in class, the children take on all three roles – they are the Client, the Designer and the Maker. Let's start at the beginning.

Identifying a problem

Identifying a need, a want or an opportunity

Real problems are particularly motivating for children, especially when they produce a final object that they can use themselves. For example, they might need to keep track of pencil sharpeners in class (a *need*), or they might want to be able to change the water in the fish tank without spilling any on the carpet (a *want*), or they think they might be able to attach lights to the crossing patrol's lollipop, to help children cross the road more safely (an *opportunity*).

At this stage, the children might also undertake research into how other people have tried to solve the problem – using the Internet and perhaps interviewing people to find out how successful these other solutions have been.

Specifying what we want to achieve with this product – the design brief

A *design brief* is a list of features to be incorporated into the product, to make it *fit for purpose* and *for aesthetic reasons*. Features might be described as *possibilities* (positive features) or *constraints* (problems that need to be overcome). Possibilities might include:

- its function – what it is supposed to do, perhaps with specific *performance criteria*;
- who the intended user is;
- ease of use;
- quality of build – strength, durability, balance, stability;
- appearance and finish – shape, colour, pattern, sound quality, smell, taste, feel.

Constraints might include:

- size, weight, safety issues;
- cost, timescale for production;
- environmental, social or cultural considerations;
- a particular technology to be exploited during its construction.

Of course, not all these criteria apply to all projects, but children should be encouraged to consider these. It is likely that some features will be prioritized as *essential*, while others are merely *desirable*. Many of these features will be quite general at this stage, for instance, *it must be easy to see in the dark*. The detail will be added at the next stage, when it is designed with detailed characteristics. Older children will list their specification, so that they can refer back to it when they come to build and evaluate the object.

Designing and planning

The next job is to *design* the object, so that it is both *fit for purpose* and *aesthetically pleasing*. This involves a great deal of decision-making, which can be undertaken in three stages:

- generating and discussing ideas, and deciding how each of the features in the design brief are to be accomplished;
- deciding what materials, components and mechanisms should be used, and what finishes to apply;
- deciding how to communicate the detailed design to the person who will be constructing it (the maker).

Generating ideas

In the classroom, ideas are often collected together and explored through *brain-storming*. At this early stage the ideas can sometimes seem like little more than flights of fancy, but subsequent discussion will bring them back to earth, as the final solution will need to be rooted in what is possible in the real world. The final best option may draw elements from several of the suggestions made during the discussion.

When referring back to the design brief, useful prompts to help the children generate ideas are:

- what do you need in order to satisfy this particular requirement?
- how can you . . .?
- why do you think . . .?

It is not uncommon for some elements of the design brief to appear contradictory, for example, the product must be *strong* but *light in weight*. These issues need to be highlighted and resolved at this stage.

Deciding on suitable materials, components, mechanisms and finishes

Importantly, whether working with food, textiles or resistant materials, the children (as designers) need to know about the qualities and properties of those different materials, and of any components and mechanisms as well, and how they can be used. They also need to know what will happen when they are combined in different ways.

With this in mind, they learn about different materials by playing with them, exploring them and investigating their properties, finding out what they are good for and where they are not appropriate:

- materials that can be moulded and shaped – dough, marzipan, plasticine, clay, papier-mâché;
- materials that are good for making frameworks and structures – wood, art-straws, pipe-cleaners, tubes;

- sheet materials – pastry, lasagne, fabric, felt, paper, card, MDF, tiles;
- materials that can be used to join things together – icing, thread, string, sticky tape, adhesives, pins, screws, staples, elastic bands;
- materials that will provide a good finish to a product – icing, glaze, stitching, batik, appliqué, inks, dyes, paint, varnish, polish.

And different sorts of components and mechanisms:

- wheels and axles, nuts and bolts, hinges, levers, gears, pulleys, electric motors;
- pneumatics, hydraulics;
- electricity;
- electronics.

And by asking questions, such as:

- **Food** – Is it solid, liquid, sweet, savoury? What happens when it is heated, boiled, grilled, frozen? What are its nutritional qualities? How long will it keep without spoiling?
- **Textiles** – Is it strong, warm, waterproof? Can it be dyed? Will it scorch, melt, catch fire? What is the texture like to the touch – rough, smooth, soft, scratchy?
- **Resistant materials** – How heavy, strong is it? Is it waterproof? Is it flexible, bendy, rigid, stretchy? What tools are needed to work with it or cut it? How can it be joined? Can it be melted and moulded? Will it keep its shape?
- **Components** – What function does it fulfil? What material is it made from and therefore what qualities does it have? Does it look good?
- **Mechanisms** – What does it do? How does it do it? What do *we* have to do to make it work? What is it usually made from? What alternatives are there that do the same job? How much does it cost?

As well as exploring these in isolation, the children also look at manufactured objects, finding out how they work (such as staplers, scissors, pens) and using construction kits of different sorts.

Communicating the detailed design to the maker

Depending on the maturity and skills of the children, and the sort of object being created, this can be done in a number of ways. Younger children might simply discuss their ideas with an adult and add pictures as a more permanent record (these are not intended to be works of art, but rather to clarify thinking and communicate with the maker).

Older children will use a variety of drawings, sketches and diagrams, perhaps showing the intended appearance of the finished article, or a particular detail of the construction, or views from above, front or side, or the order of the stages of construction (rather like the instructions for self-assembly furniture). Or it might be an *exploded* drawing, showing all the components. These will usually be supplemented by written descriptions, including lists, notes and measurements. Or, indeed, the children might make a *mock-up* of the piece, using easy-to-work materials such as card, plasticine, a computer image or a paper pattern.

Making

This is the practical, hands-on part of the process. For many children, this is the part they enjoy most, and, if allowed to do so, they tend to rush into it without adequately completing the design stage. For others, it is the part they dread because the finished article can end up as a jumbled mess.

Like designers, makers need to have extensive knowledge of the properties of materials, components and mechanisms, and of which tools are appropriate for different tasks. Crucially, they also need the skills to use these materials, components and tools to make a *quality product*.

A re-evaluation of the object, when it is perhaps half-made, can often lead to improvements to the design. This is a fundamental part of completing a quality *design and make* project, and it should be actively encouraged.

Deciding on tools and techniques for making the object, and then using them with skill

The *making* part of the process has four main stages, whatever the material:

- measuring and marking out;
- cutting and shaping (in two- and three-dimensional materials);
- assembling the parts, by joining and combining;
- finishing and decoration.

While this is the usual order of play, the children won't always work through the stages in this order – for instance, when making scones, the *combining* stage comes before the *cutting and shaping* stage; and when making a fabric bag, the pieces might be *finished and decorated* before being sewn together.

Tools that the children learn to use, when using the various materials, include:

- for measuring and marking out:
  - food – templates, spoons, jugs, scales;
  - textiles – tape measures, chalk, paper templates, pins;
  - resistant materials – rulers, tape measures, compasses, pencils, pens, set squares;
- for cutting and shaping both flat and three-dimensional materials:
  - food – biscuit cutters, knives, graters, fingers;
  - textiles – scissors, shears;

- resistant materials – scissors, saws, knives, files, rasps, planes, drills, heat cutters, sand-paper;

■ for assembling the parts (that is, joining and combining materials, components and mechanisms):
  - food – forks, knives, spoons, whisks, mixers, blenders, fingers, cookers, grills, microwaves, kettles, pans, dishes, bowls;
  - textiles – pins, safety pins, needles, adhesives, sewing machines, staplers;
  - resistant materials – sticky tape, glue guns, spanners, hammers, screwdrivers, staplers, string, rope;

■ for finishing and decoration:
  - food – shaping tools, sieves, shakers, icing bags, syringes, nozzles;
  - textiles – needles, sewing machines, wax, dyes;
  - resistant materials – brushes, sandpaper, files, polishes, paints, dyes, varnishes.

If they are to make a quality product, the children need to know what techniques are suitable when working with any particular material, what each technique is used for and when it is appropriate to use it. They will also need to know what tools are needed to execute each technique and exactly how to hold and use those tools with precision so that the object they make is fit for purpose and looks good.

Safety is, of course, paramount. As children learn to use sharp, abrasive and heated tools, they need to understand the dangers and the possible consequences of an accident. They also learn how to reduce risks by holding tools and equipment safely, wearing protective clothing (overalls, gloves, goggles, etc.), behaving sensibly, moving about carefully and giving each other space to work.

A crucial part of this process is taking care of the tools, the equipment and the working environment, so tidying, washing and sweeping are all necessary, too.

Evaluating

The idea of a *quality product* has two elements – *function* (does it work?) and *form* (does it look good?). Evaluations need to take account of both of these elements. To do this for a particular item, we need to refer back to the design brief, remembering that this might include *constraints*, such as *cost* and *environmental impact*, as well as positive qualities that should be included in the design. Ideally, evaluation would take place at every stage in the *design and make* process.

At the beginning of a project, it is often helpful to look at ways in which other designers have solved the same problem (or met the same needs, or satisfied the same wants) – which elements would help towards meeting our own design brief and which elements are best avoided?

During the *designing* and the *making* stages, the children should be checking whether the current set of actions are likely to lead to a quality product that satisfies the design brief: Are these the most suitable materials? Is this the most suitable way of joining these two components? Is it stable?, and so on.

At the end of the project, all aspects should be re-evaluated: Have we satisfied every part of the design brief? Does the product do everything that was intended? Does it look, sound, taste, smell, feel good? What elements were particularly good? Could it be improved further? If so, how? What would we do differently in similar circumstances in the future? Is it a *quality product*?

It can be valuable for the children to carry out stand-alone evaluations of professionally made products, such as a flask for hot drinks or a pair of shoes. Or they could carry out *group tests*, where a number of similar objects are evaluated and compared – for instance, they could compare the merits of different rucksacks in preparation for a school visit.

The children might find it useful, as a group, to build a bank of questions that can be applied to any product they choose to evaluate. They might ask:

- What is its purpose? Who is it for? Is it fit for purpose?
- How does it work?
- Is it safe, easy to use, long-lasting?
- What materials, components, mechanisms have been used?
- How are the pieces joined together?
- Why is it that shape?
- How has it been finished? Is this functional, as well as decorative?
- What good qualities does it possess?
- How could we improve the design?
- Are there any environmental or sustainability issues?
- Is it good value for money?

Additional notes on particular aspects of Design and Technology

Food

The children study all sorts of different food and drink, including snacks and simple meals, savoury and sweet foods, world foods, healthy foods, etc. And they use all sorts of ingredients – fresh, dried, tinned, frozen.

A food-based design brief might include elements such as health/nutrition requirements, cultural requirements, number of servings, shape, size, appearance, taste, smell, texture, cost, and even qualities such as local availability and seasonality of ingredients, and how long it will stay fresh with and without refrigeration.

The traditional cookery lesson concentrates only on the *making* part of the process, and, as such, the children are not required to make decisions about ingredients (the *materials*), equipment or techniques as these are given in the recipe. In this respect, it is more of a *short focused task*, which allows the children to give particular attention to developing their practical skills, in the same way that the children might practise sawing wood by making a set of draughts from a large-diameter broom handle. This is a useful first step.

Later, the children might use their design skills to adapt recipes for particular clients' tastes, for example for young children, older folk, vegetarians or people with allergies or strong likes and dislikes, by substituting ingredients and devising original recipes.

An important part of learning about food is gaining an understanding of nutrition and how the principles of nutrition contribute to making a quality product, perhaps in contrast to what we see on television cookery programmes, where taste and texture seem to override health considerations. And we also encourage the children to try new tastes and textures to broaden their taste horizons.

Textiles

In the *textiles* part of Design and Technology, the children use a wide range of fabrics and threads to make clothes, furnishings, bags, accessories, etc., and learn about their qualities – strength, flexibility, absorbency, stretchiness, waterproofing qualities and colour possibilities. So children learn not just how to stitch and sew, but also how to choose particular fabrics for particular purposes – for example, a baby's bib and a kite would need fabrics with decidedly different qualities.

Resistant materials – stability in structures and products

Stability is an important feature in most products and deserves special mention here – after all, we would not want our products to fall over when they are in use. In some cases, this would be annoying (wobbly chairs, for instance), but in others it would be disastrous (unstable cups filled with hot tea).

Balance and stability depend on design features such as the intrinsic strength of the materials being used, how individual components are shaped, joined and reinforced, and the shape of the whole piece. Considerations like these should be included in any design brief.

Mechanisms, moving parts and control

In order to fulfil their intended function, many objects make use of features such as moving parts, electricity and switches, or electronics. So the children learn about:

- moving parts:
    - strings and rods – string puppets, weights on a grandfather clock;
    - winches and handles – fishing reels, tuning pegs on a guitar;
    - levers – door handles, scissors;
    - gears – bicycles, clocks;
    - pneumatics (pressed air) – pumps;
    - hydraulics (pressed liquid) – syringes;

- electricity and switches, to produce:
  - light – torches;
  - sound – buzzers, alarms;
  - movement – fans, toys;
- electronics, to control:
  - light – alarms, traffic lights;
  - sound – games, keyboards and other musical instruments;
  - movement – robots.

Of course, for electrical objects to *work*, they need a number of electrical components – wires, batteries, switches, motors, bulbs, buzzers, and so on – and the children often use construction kits to learn about how electrical circuits and electronic programming work.

The children also learn a little about *computer-aided design* (CAD), often using computer programs to try out ideas. At a simple level this might be trialling colours before finally painting a product, or checking out how some of the children would look in different styles of spectacles. Later, children might investigate how to arrange paving slabs of differing sizes to build a new patio; or they might use specialist programmes to draw three-dimensional diagrams.

As well as using it themselves, children are made aware of how manufacturing industries use CAD – there are many examples on the television that show models of cars under construction, crash simulations, etc.

They also learn a little about *computer-aided manufacture* (CAM), the process of cutting, assembling, joining, etc. automatically to a pre-programmed schedule. Again, there are some entertaining advertisements on television, showing cars being built by robots.

8

English

What are English lessons really about?

English in primary schools is usually described in terms of learning about *speaking, listening, reading* and *writing*. However, in truth, our language offers so much more than this:

- it is fundamental to the way we think and the way we learn; and
- it allows us to communicate with other people successfully and confidently – at school, in the home, socially and at work.

This makes it far and away the most important subject in school.

Language helps us to think clearly and learn faster

The first aim in English lessons is to help the children to use language to understand what is going on around them. When, as adults, we hear or read something, we try to make sense of it and understand the implications – for example, if we are in the kitchen and a voice from the hall calls out: 'Bye, see you later', we consider whose voice it is, where they might be going, what time it is now, when they might be back, whether they will need any tea tonight, how we feel about them going out at this time, and so on. Notice that we *received* just four words, but we immediately launch into a discussion with ourselves, using many more words. In fact, we use words to think much more than we use them to speak or write. However, our thoughts are rarely formed into proper sentences – they are more jumbled than that, with false starts, a good deal of repetition, and going back over old ground – but the words will all mean something to us.

Once in a while, the children's thoughts will drift away and they will find themselves daydreaming. But more often, when they are thinking, they are sorting out their ideas. Sometimes they will be trying to work things out logically and rationally, and at other times they will be focusing on their feelings and emotions, or they will be exercising their imagination. For example:

- mulling over new ideas and trying to make sense of them;
- memorizing information so they can recall it quickly later;
- revisiting how they did something and planning how they could do it better next time;
- dreaming up new links and connections between ideas, and new ways of doing things;
- examining their feelings about a person or a situation so they might feel more at peace with the world;
- rehearsing what they might say in a conversation, or how they might approach a task, to assess the effect before doing it for real;
- analysing problems and working out how to solve them;
- making judgements about things they see and hear;
- planning what they will be doing in the next few days or weeks.

Of course, they could cover the same ground by discussing it with somebody else, and it is our key role in the classroom to be that somebody. While we help children to find out about the world by offering experiences at first hand, it is only through discussion that they really come to understand and clarify their ideas. For example, when the children are experimenting with sand and learning about the concepts of *heaviness* and *lightness*, the discussion will necessarily involve new words, such as *heavy*, *heavier*, *light*, *lighter* and *weight*. The children's understanding of the world and their language skills grow hand in hand, each one supporting and stimulating the other.

In the same way, the children can use writing to explore new ideas, bringing elements together, clarifying them and refining them, until they understand them. This can often involve the use of lists.

To sum up, in schools, we use a great many techniques to help the children learn, in all subjects, but these are almost always used in conjunction with words and language, because these are among the most powerful tools we have at our disposal for making sense of the world and articulating our feelings.

Language helps us to communicate with other people

Why do we communicate – for what purpose?

The second aim of English lessons is to help the children to become skilled and confident when communicating with other people. **When we are speaking or writing**, this comes about when the listener or reader understands our message.

When we are listening or reading, it is when we understand the message that the speaker or writer intended.

When we communicate, we do so for a reason. The range of reasons – or purposes – is huge, but generally falls into three groups: *functional, social* and *creative*. The purposes listed below are phrased in terms of the intention of the person speaking or writing, but the listener or reader will also be joining in for their own purposes.

Functional purposes (that is, language to get a job done) include:

- recounting events, giving news;
- describing things – people, objects, scenes, emotions;
- giving instructions on how to do something, perhaps describing a series of steps;
- explaining a process, such as how something works or how plants grow;
- persuading somebody to do something or to adopt a particular point of view;
- advertising, negotiating, bargaining;
- discussing an issue, presenting and considering arguments from both sides;
- planning;
- collaborating with other people in order to get a job done;
- asking for (or giving) help, advice or information;
- discussing ideas, clarifying them and making sense of them.

Social purposes include:

- greeting, praising, congratulating, thanking;
- complaining, criticising, apologising;
- giving sympathy, comfort;
- chattering, entertaining, telling stories and jokes;
- agreeing, disagreeing;
- expressing feelings and opinions;
- being friendly – inviting, accepting, offering, flattering;
- being unfriendly – warning, refusing, insulting, deceiving.

Language is also used *creatively* in poems, songs, stories, drama, and so on.

While the idea of *communicating for a particular purpose* might sound rather manipulative, this is exactly what we do every day. It makes sense for the children to know beforehand what they are trying to achieve, so that they can present their message in the best possible way.

Paying attention to the audience and situation

The *purpose* is not the only thing the children need to think about when planning and delivering their message.

If they are to fine tune the way they compose and deliver their messages, they also need to take account of the person who will be receiving that message – the *audience* – and the circumstances in which they will receive it. So they need to ask themselves:

- Who is the audience – a friend, a brother or sister, a parent, a grandparent, an older child, a baby, a teacher/assistant, the headteacher, a visitor, a shopkeeper?
- Where might the audience be when they receive the message – in the living room, in the garden, on a football pitch, in a shop, in the classroom, in the street?
- When will they receive the message, and what might they be doing at the time – at a mealtime, at night, on their birthday, after a success or failure, while playing, while working together?
- And what might the listener or reader be feeling like – happy/sad/angry, relaxed/nervous, interested/bored/excited?

Children very quickly learn that they can vary the way they speak to their friends, depending on the location – chatting when parents are about, speaking quietly in the library, or shouting on a football pitch. Here, we extend this idea to include all communication.

What is the most suitable format for our message?

Keeping all these considerations in mind, the children also need to decide what form their message should take – speech or writing. They each have their advantages and disadvantages.

Speech is more immediate and personal, and is particularly well suited to discussing questions where details need to be clarified or where agreement needs to be reached. This might take the form of:

- a chat or a conversation;
- a transaction (in a shop);
- a discussion;
- a more formal meeting;
- a telephone conversation;
- video conferencing.

In most cases, both the speaker and the listener need to be available at the same time.

Because it is spontaneous and unrehearsed, everyday speech isn't *composed* in the same way as writing is, so it tends to be littered with phrases such as 'um', 'er' and 'you know', sentences are rarely finished, and we repeat ourselves, or we stop half-way through an idea and then start again – and the listener is fine with all this. However, if we wrote in this way, the reader might wonder what is going on.

Writing, on the other hand, is better suited to situations where the writer and the reader are separated in terms of place and time – indeed, writers often don't know their readers at all. It is also well suited to explaining complicated topics, where the writer can draft and redraft to achieve a polished piece, and the reader can keep referring back, which would not be possible in conversation without continually interrupting the flow by asking questions.

Writing might take the form of:

– notes (to self and others)	– advertisements, notices, announcements
– leaflets and posters	
– diary entries	– captions, menus, bullet points
– lists, tables, charts, graphs	– poems, songs
– signs, symbols	– play scripts, dialogue
– reviews, arguments, records	– stories (what genre to use?)
– invitations	– magazine and newspaper articles
– factual accounts, classroom projects	– instructions, recipes, manuals
	– notes, letters, formal letters
– greetings cards	– social networking comments
– e-mails, blogs	– text messages (SMS)

The children are also taught to use *multimedia communication* to deliver their message, combining words, images, video and sound.

What tone should we use?

Whether our message uses speech, writing or multimedia, and whatever its format, the tone of the message is the final judgement the children need to make. In order to achieve their purpose, the children can present their message as questioning or assertive, sympathetic or challenging, warm or threatening, amusing or serious, casual or formal, up-beat or pessimistic, etc.

Bringing it all together to create a message

How would Jack handle it? He is six years old and wants a toy dinosaur for his birthday. He needs to communicate this to the people most likely to make it happen for him:

■ What exactly is his purpose?

■ Who is the best person to approach?

- What is the best time and place for the contact?
- What is the best format and tone for the request?

Standard English – overcoming cultural differences

People from many different geographical and cultural backgrounds use English as a medium of communication, but they don't all sound alike, and they are not always easily understood by others – perhaps they have a strong accent, or they speak quickly, or they use dialect words and phrases. While these variations are all legitimate, they can present an obstacle to full communication.

While the children we teach will have their own *language culture*, which is shared with their family and friends and others in the locality, they will inevitably meet people with different language cultures, and they need to be able to communicate with these people as well. Our task is to help them to learn Standard English – the version of English that is understood across international and cultural boundaries. In this form of English, vocabulary, grammar, spelling and handwriting are all standardized (DES 1989a: 38, paragraph 20). Of course, the children don't need to use it all the time, but they do need to be able to use it as necessary.

Speaking and listening

Speaking and listening – an overview

Although a great deal of lesson time is given over to reading and writing in schools, we use speech much more in our daily lives, both for thinking and for communicating. Therefore, we need to do everything we can to help the children build skills and confidence in speaking and listening, and give them a head start in their personal, social and working lives.

Listening tends to take two forms:

- One-way communication – listening to stories, news, television programmes.
- Two-way communication – for example, conversation and discussion with other people in the classroom, at home, on the telephone, in shops, with friends, and so on.

Like most skills, listening does not develop by itself – the children need to be clear about what is required of them, and they need to practise in a wide range of controlled situations. After all, listening to a story on CD is very different from listening to an adult in the classroom, and a news bulletin on the radio is more demanding than a report on the television, because the listener does not receive any visual cues.

Speaking has the same two forms:

- One-way communication – making a speech, giving a report, etc.
- Two-way communication – conversations, chat, discussions, etc.

In everyday conversation we tend to alternate between the speaking role and the listening role. These are usually cooperative in nature, moving quickly as people shift their views and make new links in their understanding. In the classroom, speaking and listening is the usual way for staff and children to interact when learning about new ideas, but we do need to ensure that the children have sufficient time to think through their responses and ideas, so that they can express them as fully and clearly as possible, because it is *thinking and talking things through* that so often leads to fresh insight and a shift in understanding.

In order to make a contribution to a discussion, the children need a whole raft of skills, including:

- knowing when it is appropriate to make a contribution, and then gaining the other person's attention in an acceptable way;

- understanding and remembering what has been said by different people, while at the same time thinking about what they want to say themselves;

- keeping their comments relevant to the current discussion;

- choosing the most suitable words to get their point across;

- pronouncing words clearly and with appropriate volume;

- understanding how to compose questions, statements, commands and exclamations, as required;

- knowing how to fine tune the meaning and impact of their contribution, by the way they deliver particular phrases;

- asking questions in a constructive way to make sure they get the information they require;

- being able to summarize the important points that have been made;

- maintaining a friendly and cooperative tone, however much they might disagree with what is being said.

Body language and social considerations

However, words are only one aspect of communication. We also convey our message through *body language* (such as our stance, our distance from the other person, whether we decide to sit or stand, hand gestures, touch), *eye contact* (staring, looking away, looking down, etc.), *facial expression* (nodding, smiling, frowning, etc.), and our *tone of voice* (do we sound interested, sympathetic, angry or bored?).

It has been suggested that, in some face-to-face situations, a listener will take more meaning from the combined effect of the speaker's body language, facial expression and tone of voice than from the words actually spoken. The children need to learn about all these shades in communication. However, it is not always easy — many are confused by sarcasm, for instance, where friendly words are spoken with a disparaging voice. Children (and adults) with a degree of autism or

Asperger's syndrome find this particularly difficult, and may need specific help in reading facial expressions and understanding the words people say at anything other than a literal level.

No matter how well we think we have judged our message, it is by no means certain that every part of it will be fully received or accepted in the way we intended. Perhaps it was composed clumsily, or there was a misinterpretation of the sender's signals, or cultural differences got in the way, or the recipient's mood at the time got in the way, or perhaps the recipient just didn't want to hear that particular message. Whatever the reason for a communication failure, the children are taught that they might sometimes need to start over again.

Writing

Writing – an overview

In the classroom, children have the opportunity to practise each of the writing formats listed above, so that, in real life, they can choose the one that they believe to be the most effective for their particular message in their particular circumstances. For example, a persuasive eco-message might be presented as a story for publication in the local newspaper, or a poster, or perhaps a letter to a councillor. Whatever the decision, the piece is usually improved by being planned out beforehand, with a second draft if necessary, before the final version is produced.

In the classroom, we come across many children who are reluctant to write. This may be because they intrinsically do not enjoy the activity, but it could be that they lack confidence in their ability to do the job as well as they would like. The process of writing is certainly a complex one – there are so many skills to master and so many things to remember:

- composing and structuring the piece;
- the tone of the piece;
- grammar and punctuation;
- spelling;
- handwriting.

If children believe that their skill in any one of these areas lets them down badly (perhaps their spelling or handwriting is poor), then the easiest way to avoid exposing themselves is to say, 'I can't think of anything to write, Miss'. In many cases the problem lies in one of the last two areas – the so-called *secretarial skills*. Our task here is twofold – to help the children find a way around the immediate problem, perhaps dictating their work to a TA to sidestep the spelling problem, or word-processing to avoid a handwriting issue - and, in the longer term, to tackle the real difficulties.

Composition and structure

When very young children begin to make marks on paper, they can often tell us what their *writing* means. As they progress, we will be looking for the whole piece to be more coherent and more consistent, so that readers know where they are being led. Each format has its own pattern, and the children gradually learn these as they read them and then try them out for themselves – for example, a recipe usually sets out the ingredients in a list, before describing the method, while a poem and a song will be separated into verses and may have a repeated section (a chorus).

Stories are singled out for particular attention in the primary classroom and children learn to structure their own stories so that they have a beginning, a middle and an end. The beginning will tell us about the setting (that is, the time, the place and the general circumstances when the story starts) and introduce us to some characters, and, importantly, what they are trying to achieve. The middle section will explain how these characters run up against a problem and describe their efforts to solve it. This is usually the main part of the story – the plot. Further problems (and subplots) might also be introduced here. The end of the story will describe how the problems are resolved. It will bring us back to evaluate how well the characters achieved what they set out to do in the first place. As well as written stories, television programmes and films provide countless examples of this format.

When listening to stories, the children learn about various genres in fictional literature, such as adventure, folk tales, fables, science fiction, fantasy, mysteries, and so on. We help them to identify the particular characteristics that make each genre what it is. When they do their own writing, older children are encouraged to write in a range of genres, using their reading as a model.

While stories have a definite structure, factual writing is often more difficult to organize. The children need to decide what to include and what to leave out. Then the piece needs to be given a structure: How will the information be divided up into sections? What order should these sections be in? How should one section be linked to another, so that the reader can follow the development of the piece?

The key to all this is planning. In the early stages, we might help the children by dividing up their page and giving prompts as to what should appear in each section. Later, they learn to plan the structure of the piece for themselves before setting about the task of writing it, jotting down subheadings, with a few notes under each one, and moving these around until the order seems logical. This approach is effective in all types of writing – stories included – and will prove useful to the children for years to come as they progress through the education system, writing essays on all kinds of topics on all sorts of subjects.

Tone

The tone of a piece of writing is a really important consideration. It can draw readers in or it can alienate them. The children learn about a number of ways they can adjust the tone of their writing. They decide whether to use handwriting or print, depending on how personal or intimate they want the message to be.

They choose vocabulary carefully, deciding among near synonyms (such as *large, big, huge, enormous*), and vary the length of their sentences. They decide how much detail to include, and whether they should use pictures, drawings and diagrams to give additional information or to clarify points. They are also taught to reread their text, to check for potential misunderstandings, and to judge how it looks and sounds from the reader's viewpoint.

Grammar

To begin with, young children base their writing on everyday speech. As they gain more experience, they learn to write in a more considered way – sentences become longer and more complex, while remaining clear and coherent. And if they are to ensure that their message will be received as intended, they need to be aware of how grammar and punctuation can affect meaning. So they learn things like *what a sentence is* (it must mean something, it must be able to stand by itself and it must have at least one verb that matches the subject), *how to form statements, questions, commands and exclamations*, and *how to write in different tenses* (past, present, future).

They learn that some words provide the basic meaning of the sentence, while others add colour and interest for the reader. Considerable changes can be made by using one word rather than another – for example, he *ate* his dinner/he *gobbled* his dinner. In order to explore possible alternatives, the children learn to categorize words as:

- nouns – objects, emotions, abstract ideas (properly called *common nouns*), singular and plural;
- proper nouns (those that always have a capital letter) – people's names, days, months, places, nationalities;
- pronouns – words that stand in place of a noun, such as *he, she, it, they, them, these*;
- adjectives – words that tell us something about the noun, for instance, its size or colour; also, the variations on these words, such as *tall, taller, tallest*;
- verbs and all their variations – past, present and future; positive and negative; for example *go, goes, went, has gone, did not go, is going, will go, will not go*;
- adverbs – how the *verb* was carried out, such as *quickly, happily* – adverbs often have *ly* on the end;
- conjunctions – also called *connectives* – words such as *and, then, so, but, however, moreover*, which join phrases and clauses together to make longer, more interesting sentences;
- prepositions – telling us where and when something took place, such as *soon, after, behind, on top of*.

By knowing about these *parts of speech* and what they do, the children can construct their messages as precisely as possible.

Punctuation

Punctuation is used to help the reader make sense of the message. It includes marks such as:

$$. \quad , \quad ; \quad : \quad ' \; ' \quad `` \; '' \quad ? \quad ! \quad ' \quad - \quad (\,)$$

as well as capital letters and starting a new line or paragraph.

The children learn that punctuation is not limited to showing the reader when to take a breath; it also shows when a whole idea has been explained (*commas, semi-colons* and *full stops*), when somebody is speaking (*quotation marks*, also called *speech marks*), whether a particular tone of voice is to be used (*question* and *exclamation marks*), whether letters are missing from a word (*apostrophe*), whether something is owned by a person (a different use of the *apostrophe*), and so on.

Accurate punctuation is essential if writers are to help their readers to fully understand what they are trying to convey. Readers also need to remain alert. Sometimes they may need to read ahead to catch the full sense, particularly in the case of a question mark or an exclamation mark, which appears only at the end of a sentence.

Spelling

Spelling is not an end in itself. Rather, our aim is to help the children to spell words accurately without too much thought, so that they can concentrate on all the other aspects of writing, and make their compositions as effective as possible.

Children generally learn to spell in three ways:

- through *phonics* (using letter sounds);
- by *look and say* (often using letter names);
- by referring to other similar words.

The phonic approach is the most efficient way of learning to spell, as the sound patterns are repeated again and again in different words. Young children begin by listening – without writing anything down – first learning to identify individual *words* within a piece of speech and then to separate out the *syllables* in each word, and then individual *sounds* in each syllable.

Only then do children move on to learn about the relationships between the sounds they have identified (*phonemes)* and the letters that usually represent them on paper (*graphemes)*:

- single letters representing single sounds;
- two consonants representing a single sound (*ch, sh*);
- two consonants blended together (*cl-, dr-* at the beginning of a syllable, *-nd, -ft*, at the end of a syllable, and *-st* wherever they meet it);

- three consonants blended together (*str-*, *spl-*);
- two vowels making a single sound (*oa*, *oi*, *ea*);
- a vowel and a consonant making a single sound (*er*, *ar*, *ew*);
- a group of vowels and consonants making a single sound (*igh*, *eigh*, *ear*, *our*);
- a letter being changed by another that follows it (*ca*, *ce*, *ci*, *co*, *cu*);
- vowel sounds that are changed by the *magic e* (properly called a *split digraph a-e*, *e-e*, *i-e*, *o-e*, *u-e*);
- words with more than one syllable.

There is a well-defined progression through this series of steps, with plenty of word lists available to provide examples at each stage. In order to avoid confusion and a great deal of frustration, we need to be sure that a child's knowledge is secure at each stage, before they move on to the next.

A particular problem in English is that there are a number of sounds that can be spelt in several ways – for instance:

- the sound most commonly spelt as *er* can also be *ir* (girl), *ur* (nurse), *or* (tutor), *ear* (early);
- the sound most commonly spelt as *ee* in *see*, can also be *ea* (tea), *ie* (field), *e* (she), *ei* (conceit), *ey* (key).

The vowel sound we make at the end of the word *the* can also prove troublesome. It sounds like a very short *er*, perhaps more of a small grunt, and is also the way we pronounce the word *a* when we say 'I have just bought *a* dress.' When this sound is found in the second syllable of a word, it can be spelt with any one of the five vowels, for instance *salad*, *seven*, *basin*, *common*, *tantrum*.

So, while the phonic method of spelling can give us a good start, it needs to be checked by having another look at the word to see whether it *looks right* – and that can only come when the children have become used to the look of the word through their reading.

Many words are very old, originating from the English spoken tradition, and have been altered and distorted through centuries of use. These generally do not conform to phonic patterns – words such as *the*, *of*, *a*, *to*, *you*, *he*, *was*, which the children use more often than most other words. There is little chance of building these words phonically, so the children just have to remember them, so that they become part of their *look and say* spelling repertoire, and write them automatically every time.

Then there are words which, while not phonically regular, do share some features that can be used as an aid to remembering how to spell them. For example, words such as *here*, *there* and *where* (all denoting places), or those containing *ough*, or those (like daisy) that form their plural by replacing the *y* with an *i* before adding *es* (daisies).

Some children have a stronger feel for sound and others have a stronger feel for a visual approach to learning, so different children inevitably learn to spell in different ways, some relying on phonics while others prefer to use visual patterns. Both groups will need both approaches if they are to spell all the words they need to make their writing clear and easily understood by the reader.

Handwriting

For many people at work, writing by hand has largely been replaced by typing on a keyboard. However, if we are to send personal messages (such as love letters or letters of condolence), we really cannot achieve the most suitable tone if we word-process our letter or send a text message – handwriting is essential.

The quality of handwriting can be judged by:

- whether it is easy to read (legibility);
- whether it is formed quickly and easily (fluency);
- whether it is neat and even in size;
- its attractiveness as a style (the font).

The most important of these is legibility. If the reader struggles to understand the words, even if they are neat and regular and the page looks beautiful, then part of the message is likely to be lost. This skill needs to be maintained even when the children learn to write more quickly or join their letters.

Fluency in handwriting helps writers to write more quickly, so their hands can keep pace with the flow of their thoughts. When children find the act of writing laborious, they tend to stumble over the formation of sentences, and sometimes do not get around to writing everything that is in their head. This is a great pity, as the message (the important part) might have been of the highest quality, and been expressed in the most powerful and moving way, but no one will ever know. In effect, a lack of talent in this low-level skill may have prevented the production of a wonderful piece of writing.

Fluent handwriting, and joined writing in particular, can also aid spelling. The fluency helps the pencil to flow through groups of letters, so they do not need to be remembered individually – groups such as *ght* or *ment*, or whole words, such as *was*. Here, the children use *muscle memory* alongside their mental memory, giving them a double chance of using the correct spelling.

We do so much of our writing on a keyboard these days that it makes sense for the children to become skilled in this, as well as in handwriting. Maybe speech recognition software will take over in years to come, but, in the meantime, slow typing is not merely frustrating and time-wasting, it also impedes the flow of ideas. Spending a few hours learning to type efficiently would allow many children to type automatically, and therefore be able to concentrate fully on producing their best work.

Using ICT

ICT can be an extremely useful tool in all areas of learning about writing. Children can practise handwriting patterns, using whole-arm movements on a whiteboard, and smaller movements on a touch-screen monitor or tablet; and they can play spelling games to reinforce spelling patterns and highlight irregular words. They can rearrange sections of text, using *cut and paste*, and seek out the best word for a sentence using a thesaurus. They can also present their work to its best advantage, using features such as layout, borders, indents, fonts, colour, and so on. Probably the main benefit of using ICT is that the children can refine and improve their work quickly and easily, and just as easily revert to an earlier version if necessary.

Reading

Reading – an overview

Once we understand that the black squiggles on the page correspond to the words we say, reading is, in theory at least, fairly straightforward. All we need to do is:

- recognize the words, and say them fluently;
- then understand what the writer is trying to tell us (both in general terms, and in more detail).

However, we do need to become skilled in both of these aspects – capability in one area is just not enough.

In the early stages, when children are concentrating on increasing the number of words they recognize, it is easy to forget about the second strand. However, it is essential that they realize that their main task is to make sense of what they read, and when eventually they reach the stage when they recognize the words automatically, they can certainly put all their effort into understanding the text.

As in all areas of learning, the motivation of the learner is very important.

The key to motivation is success – that is, repeated successes that the children themselves recognize. When the children work hard in their reading lessons, doing as they are asked and gaining praise both for their effort and for their progress, they begin to believe that they have cracked the code. So it is not unreasonable that they should expect to be able to read other print that we, as trusted adults, put in front of them – reference books related to their various lessons, worksheets, writing on the whiteboard, helpful comments in their books, and so on. So let us make sure we do not undermine their confidence; rather, let us do all we can to reinforce their growing self-belief by making these texts as accessible as possible:

- The words used and the complexity of the language should match the skills and maturity of the reader (more than one version of a worksheet might be needed to accommodate different children in the class).

- Texts should be uncluttered and the lines well spaced, without too much on a page.
- Handwriting should be clear, legible and a good model for the children, otherwise print should be used.

The range of material that children read is huge – the forms of writing listed earlier in this chapter give an indication of its magnitude. However, that list only covers the kinds of writing the children are expected to tackle in lessons. Their reading will also include comics, food packets and labels, information books, signs and posters, advertisements, television screens, websites, games consoles, text messages, and so on.

Clearly, an increasing proportion of the children's reading experience now comes from screens of one sort or another. These frequently use a combination of words, signs, symbols, logos and abbreviated text-speak to create the message and therefore fulfil the writer's purpose.

However, we need to be aware that these on-screen presentations are generally more difficult for the children to read than paper-based text. There are a number of reasons for this: the children can see only a small amount of text at any one moment, which stops them from scanning up and down the page to make sense of the text as a whole; the layout is far more varied than a page in a book, and fonts and colours (particularly mismatches between foreground and background colours) can hinder clarity; and the text is often accompanied by distractions – the words are likely to be only a part of a busy page, which may also contain flashing lights, moving pictures and sounds.

Saying the words

A necessary part of reading is *saying the words*. Without this, we can make no progress towards understanding the message. As adults, we will come across several thousands of words in our reading that we have come to recognize. However, some of these words are written in two distinct ways, with capital letters and with lower case letters, and how different they can look. Who would have thought that *THE* is the same word as *the* – all of the letters look different!

As experienced readers, we use three main methods to help us say the words, and our aim is for the children to develop skills in all three areas, as they move towards combining fluency with accuracy:

- We use the *look and say* method of reading most of the time, remembering words from our previous reading.
- We often use *phonics* when we see a word we do not recognize. To use this strategy, the children need to know the ways in which letters and groups of letters can represent sounds and, crucially, recognize those letter groups when they appear in unfamiliar words (see p. 82, Spelling, for some of these). As an aside, reading through phonics is generally a less precise skill than spelling through phonics, and therefore is a little easier.

■ Perhaps surprisingly, we also *guess* at words. We can do this when we are in tune with the text and the flow of the sentence, and therefore have a good idea of what word we would expect to see next (*John really wanted this to be the best picture ever for his Mum, so he sharpened his _____ and got started*).

Of course, these three methods overlap and support each other. When reading words by the *look and say* or *phonic* methods, we still need to check that the sentence does indeed make sense. It is useful, when using the *look and say* and *guess* methods, to glance at the first letter or two to ensure that we haven't substituted a completely different word into the space. There is some evidence that we sometimes combine all three methods, in much the same way as we understand text messaging on a mobile phone – so long as we know what the message is likely to be about, take note of the significant first and last letters of a word, and judge roughly how long it is, we can often read it accurately even when it has been badly misspelled.

It is at this early stage in the reading process – recognizing the words – where people with dyslexia encounter their biggest obstacle. There may be disagreement over the causes of dyslexia, but what is clear is that some 4–8% of children have a particular difficulty in this area (Rose 2009: 11 and Snowling 2008: 3).

Our task is to help them recognize which of the three approaches they personally find most effective and then help them to develop their skills, emphasizing those areas where they have most success. In my experience, many dyslexic children find the *look and say* method most troublesome, so a combination of *phonics* and *making sense of the whole sentence* can be useful.

Understanding the message

Being able to *say the words* is all well and good, and is a necessary part of reading, but in itself it is no guarantee that the writer's message will actually be understood. In order to fully understand what the writer intended, the children need to appreciate that reading is an *active* pursuit. They need to relate to the text, using both their intellect and their imagination to weigh up the implications of what they are being told, mulling it over and internalizing it, and deciding whether they understand it and how they might react to it. They need to constantly compare any new information they read with their own previous experience. For example, if they are told that 'Monty is a very big mouse', they need to decide just how big Monty is likely to be, referring back in their mind's eye to how big mice usually are.

At a more sophisticated level, the children might concentrate on understanding the characters in a story – their feelings, their relationships, the dilemmas they face, their behaviour, how they are presented to the reader through description and dialogue. Or they might focus on how the plot develops – how incidents link together, subplots and red herrings, or how dialogue moves the plot along.

The language used in writing is often much more complex than that used in everyday speech, so the children need to be helped to continue to develop their language and comprehension skills to keep pace with the material they are likely to meet in their reading.

Judging how well children have understood a text is not always clear cut, and we may need to spend some time discussing texts with them. We ourselves need to be clear about what the piece holds so that we can lead a discussion through open-ended questions, helping the children to find meaning where they had not done before.

However, we don't usually read for its own sake. We read for a purpose:

- we read to find information; and
- we read because we enjoy reading.

Finding information

Sometimes, we read factual material for no better reason than idle curiosity and our response is 'Mm, that's interesting. I didn't know that.' However, it is equally likely that we will read it in order to make a decision or to plan an action. For instance, before we book a holiday, we search the Internet and read through brochures to get a flavour of the places we think we might like to visit, and then we base our plans on what we have found out. The children need opportunities to carry out practical projects like this. In school, projects might be subject based (*Can you find out how much it costs to visit Chester Zoo?*) or of personal interest (*What is the best way to look after my new guinea pig?*). In order to organize and remember the information they find out (and perhaps make a presentation afterwards) the children need to develop the skill of taking notes as they read.

Factual material comes in many different formats, from bus timetables to encyclopaedias. In order to become skilled in finding information, the children learn how to find information from directories, textbooks, reference books and the Internet, using alphabetical order, catalogues, indexes, classification systems, searches, and so on.

Through guidance and experience the children gradually learn to carry out research in a disciplined way:

- being clear about what they want to find out (simple prompts can be useful, based on *who? what? where? when? how? why?* questions);
- deciding on the best place to find that information;
- reading carefully and understanding what they find out;
- deciding whether it is relevant to their original question;
- deciding whether the information is reasonable and reliable, and whether it is fact or opinion.

Skills that are particularly useful for finding information are *skimming* and *scanning*.

The children use *skimming* to gain an overall impression of the main ideas to be taken from a book or an article, where it would take too long to read word-by-word. This might involve looking at the contents page, headings, subheadings, diagrams and pictures, as well as *skimming* through the text quickly.

Scanning, on the other hand, involves looking quickly through a text to find a specific piece of information. The children can also use this scanning technique to judge whether a particular article is worth further investigation – for example, if they are researching Mozart, they can scan pages looking for his name, while ignoring references to Beethoven, Dvorak and others, and then follow this up by marking the most promising sections and reading these in more detail.

A useful place to start skimming and scanning is on the cover of a book, or the headline in a newspaper – children can often learn a great deal about its contents before needing to read further.

Reading because we enjoy it

Different people enjoy reading in different ways. Many people read stories and poetry in order to gain enjoyment, inspiration and perhaps a new perspective on life. They invest time, mental effort, imagination and involvement in their stories, and see new worlds laid out before them and fresh ideas explored. They meet new characters and gain insight into what makes these people and their civilizations tick. If the book is a good one, readers may even need to take a breather after the final page and reflect on what they have read, for they have lived with the central characters through trials and tribulations for a hundred or more pages.

A second group sees fiction primarily as an escape, a quiet time that they can enjoy on their own, perhaps filling a bus or train journey, or whiling away a summer's afternoon on the beach.

Others tell us that they are either not very interested in reading stories and poetry, or that reading a book takes too long. They prefer to read shorter articles of interest to them in newspapers and magazines or on the Internet, and generally use reading as a tool to support other pleasures in their lives, such as keeping up-to-date with the news, learning more about their hobbies, or reading about the latest exploits of celebrities.

All of these viewpoints are perfectly legitimate. In fact, most people read in each of these ways at one time or another. So when children read for any of these reasons, they are making good use of the knowledge, skills and attitudes they have learned in the classroom. Whatever a child's preferred type of reading, however, the single most important factor in developing the reading habit is that they should enjoy it.

Building a class anthology can help to motivate some children, as they share the enthusiasm and recommendations of their classmates. We must not underestimate the power of seeing their trusted adults enjoying a good book. This will encourage them to read more, which in turn will make them better at reading and give them the confidence to tackle an ever-increasing range of fiction, as well as useful and interesting non-fictional material. Alongside this, the children will absorb a growing vocabulary, with examples of correct grammar and interesting phrasing, which in turn will increase their ability to express themselves in both speech and writing, and to understand other people's ideas.

In school we ensure that the children have opportunities to sample a wide range of literary genres. Younger and less mature children find picture books, nursery rhymes, fairy stories, folk tales and legends especially rewarding. Older children might prefer adventure, fantasy, mystery or science fiction. Children of all ages enjoy stories based on real life, stories from different cultures, poems, ballads and song lyrics.

Should we continue reading to the children after they become independent readers? Yes, of course we should. As we read to them, and with them, we can demonstrate the higher reading skills and help them to understand what the author is telling them, by reading more difficult and more complex tales than they can manage themselves, by varying pace and loudness to create mood, by using different voices for the narrator and the various characters, and so on, to make the story as interesting as possible.

We can also direct their attention to particular features of the piece – perhaps its structure or the language used – either before we begin reading or through questioning afterwards, with prompts such as:

- Listen out for the different ways the author describes this new character – what do we find out about her?

- Why does the author use this particular phrase?

- Where have we heard about this before in the story?

- Oh-oh, what do you think is going to happen now?

- What function does this character have in the story?

- Why do you think the character did that?

- What else could this character have done to get a better result?

- What were the key events in the story?

Poetry

Poets look at the world from a fresh perspective. They might be describing a scene, an event, a person or a mood, but they are always on the lookout for the best words and phrases, and try to use them in the best possible way. So poetry is full-strength, undiluted writing. Nothing is watered down or padded out. Every word is made to work hard to contribute to the message that the poet is trying to get across.

When children first learn to read, they understand the text at a literal level – if it says that a sweater is blue, then it is blue. As they mature, both as people and in their language ability, they learn more about the subtleties of language and how it can be manipulated to mean more than the individual words might suggest – for instance, they learn that colours can be used to describe moods.

More than this, however, poetry uses rhythm as an active ingredient, and it may use rhyme, although this is not essential. It often conforms to a recognized pattern – it may be divided into verses (or stanzas), it may be limited by the number of syllables (such as haiku), or the number of lines (such as sonnets), or it may have a particular rhyming pattern (for example, limericks or rhyming couplets). Continuing with the idea that a reader's task is to understand what the writer intended, poetry provides some real challenges for the reader, but can also be so rewarding.

Sometimes a particular poem makes such an impression on us that it will stay with us for life. To this end, the children are encouraged to learn a poem, or a section of a poem, by heart, and perhaps recite it before a small audience. This is very much in keeping with the long oral tradition of poetry being performed and shared.

Drama and role-play

Drama and role-play are based on *Let's pretend*.

Sometimes, the children will rehearse and perform a scripted play. The benefits can be enormous, in terms of:

- reading and memorizing lines;
- getting into character and exploring human values, emotions, behaviour and relationships;
- learning about movement, timing, body language, facial expression and speech delivery;
- cooperating and communicating with fellow actors and those working behind the scenes;
- accepting direction;
- the thrill and excitement of performing in front of an audience.

The children are also encouraged to respond to drama, whether this is a piece of group-work in class, a performance in school, a professionally staged play in a theatre, or even a television programme or DVD. With guidance and practice, they become increasingly aware of the characters and events portrayed, the issues explored and the language used, and sharpen their responses to these features.

More often, however, role-play takes place within the normal lessons and is unscripted. The emphasis here is on helping the children to explore a situation through the eyes of other people, imagining what it would be like to be somebody else at that time and in that place, faced with those problems. Of course, the children already do this when they read a story, but with a book they remain *on the outside, looking in*, while drama involves them directly in the plot and draws them further in, so that they can influence what happens next.

This technique can enhance the children's understanding in any subject, but particularly in citizenship, geography, history, Modern Foreign Languages (MFL) and PSHE education. For example, the children might play the roles of various members of a rural community who are discussing the pros and cons of having a wind farm built nearby, or become a group of monks as they learn that King Henry VIII is about to dissolve their monastery, or a French family taking breakfast in Cannes.

In each case, the children take on another person's identity – their gender, age, occupation, family circumstances, personality, hopes and fears, etc. – in effect, becoming that person. In this way, they are drawn into the situation, becoming personally involved with the issues and able to see them so much more clearly than, for example, if they had discussed them in an abstract way in class.

Another important use of drama and role-play is for the children to play themselves as they rehearse their responses to potentially problematic situations that await them in their own lives. These situations often link with their work in PSHE education, for example managing risks ('Mum, can Jack and I go shopping in town by ourselves on Saturday?'), disagreeing (what body language and tone of voice to employ? which words to use?), resisting peer pressure by saying 'no' politely but firmly (again, what words and body language to employ?), opening a bank account (what is the procedure?).

The value of this sort of role-play cannot be overestimated. Incidentally, it can also be helpful to record sessions on video, so that the children can review their actions critically and objectively, with the opportunity to analyse what they could have said, rather than remembering only the words that they did say.

Exploring English

Every subject has its own specialist vocabulary. In Physical Education (PE) we can hit a ball with a *bat*, a *racket*, a *stick* or a *club*, depending on the sport, while in science we use the proper words to describe equipment, substances and concepts. This is because using the right word helps us to discuss ideas clearly and unambiguously, and reach conclusions without misunderstandings.

The same is true when children learn how to use the English language to communicate successfully. Accurate vocabulary helps the children to focus on a specific idea, so that they can develop greater understanding. Technical words the children use to discuss language include:

- noun, pronoun, adjective
- verb, adverb
- preposition
- connective, conjunction
- singular, plural
- regular, irregular

- root, prefix, suffix
- phoneme, grapheme
- digraph
- syllable
- synonym, antonym
- genre

For instance, once the children learn how *adverbs* work, it is both clearer and simpler to use this term when exploring adverbs further, instead of talking about *words that describe how something is done*. When we wish to find words that are related to one another (such as head, behead, headless, heading), it can be useful to be able to refer to *roots*, *prefixes* and *suffixes*.

A useful strategy for exploring the language is for the children to carry out *language investigations*, for example:

- discussing examples of how vocabulary, style and tone are used to accommodate different audiences and purposes;

- making collections of books and stories of a particular genre, or prepositions to do with *time*, or different ways to start a story, or words that always have a capital letter, or puns;

- looking for patterns in what they have collected, and suggesting rules – when are apostrophes used? how do we make the plural of a word ending with the letter 'o'?;

- changing sentences – from the past tense to the future tense, from a statement to a question, from the local dialect to Standard English, and vice versa;

- deleting words or making substitutions – reducing a sentence to its shortest form, but keeping its sense; or changing individual words within a sentence and noting the effect.

The power of language

There is no doubting that language is a powerful practical tool as we go about our everyday business. But it is so much more. Language and communication are the key to learning – we listen to news and read information, we exchange views, we analyse situations, we explore ideas and concepts, both with other people and when we are alone. These are all greatly enhanced when we are confident in our use of language.

On a more personal level, language oils the wheels of our social lives, forging friendships and helping us to share joy and sadness, overcome social barriers and keep in touch – whoever heard of a wedding without promises, speeches, chatter, singing and laughter? More than this, however, we can delight in the richness of our language for its own sake, through conversation, poetry and song.

9

Geography

What is geography really about?

An outline

Geography is about *places* – quite simply, pieces of land, anywhere on the Earth's surface. These can be of any size and any shape, from a field to a continent, from a street to a city, from a beach to a desert.

As a subject, geography investigates questions such as:

- What *physical features* are to be found in different places?
- What *human features* are there – how do we humans interact with, and use, particular places?
- How are different places linked?
- Ultimately, how can we make life on Earth more pleasant and more productive for the human race, while protecting the planet from harm?

Physical features

When we describe the physical features of a place, we usually refer to the *land-forms* and the *environmental conditions* found there. *Land-forms* are features such as hills, valleys, mountains, cliffs, plains, slopes, plateaux and caves. These are basically areas of rocks and soils of different types, such as granite, limestone, sandstone, clay, sand, peat, etc., moulded into different shapes. Where land is covered with water, we might see ponds, lakes, seas, oceans, springs, streams, rivers or estuaries or, in some places, more exciting features such as waterfalls.

The environmental conditions we encounter on a day-to-day basis are the weather and climate (*climate* being the general case – what we would expect to see – while *weather* is what we see at any particular moment). This takes in temperature, precipitation (rain, drizzle, showers, monsoons, hail, sleet, snow, blizzards), wind (breezes, gales, tornadoes, hurricanes), mist, fog and frost. Less common environmental conditions – those that happen only in particular places in the world –

include volcanic activity, earthquakes, waves and tsunamis. Geographers also take note of gases and air pressure.

Interestingly, while we experience these environmental conditions in the here and now, they have also, over thousands and millions of years, played a part in shaping the Earth's surface to create particular land-forms, and then transforming those land-forms into *environments* such as grasslands, heathlands, moorlands, wetlands, woodlands, forests, jungles, bare rock, beaches, hot deserts, tundra, ice caps, etc.

If the children are to extend their knowledge and understanding of the physical features found in different places, and appreciate their diversity and beauty, they need to:

- know what they are looking for, and recognize these *land-forms, environmental conditions* and *environments*, both in real life and on DVDs and television programmes;
- understand what each of them is and be able to describe them;
- know a little about how they might have been formed;
- understand relevant concepts, such as altitude, temperature, erosion.

Human features – the ways in which people use particular places

The second aspect of geography is about how places are used by people – this is sometimes called *land-use*. Whatever we might like to think, we humans do not control the planet – we can't just do whatever we like, wherever we like, because conditions do not always allow us to. So geographers look at what human activities are possible in particular locations, what activities would be difficult or even impossible, and how places are actually used.

The children learn that we use land for:

- housing, in settlements of different sizes (hamlets, villages, towns, cities);
- farming, forestry, fishing, mining, quarrying and power generation – the so-called *primary* industries;
- manufacturing – everything from aeroplanes to zip-fasteners – *secondary* industries;
- shops, offices, hotels, restaurants, banking, healthcare, leisure facilities – *service* or *tertiary* industries;
- education, libraries, information technology and government – *quaternary* industries.

Because people also need to move around and transport goods from one place to another, we also use land for:

- paths, pavements, roads, railways, canals, airports and harbours.

Ways in which places are linked

Places can be linked in lots of different ways, and geographers investigate these links and relationships. First, they identify them, then understand why they have developed, and then point the way to future possibilities. Linked places might:

- have a similar land-form, for example, they might both be in a valley, or on top of a cliff above a rocky shore;
- share an environmental condition – places with similar temperature or rainfall patterns;
- be close together – adjacent classrooms, or villages within a rural area, or towns within a county.

Or they might have:

- good transport links – for passengers or freight;
- economic or trade links – where people do their shopping, places they go on holiday, where the clothes we buy were manufactured;
- educational links – pre-school, schools, colleges, universities;
- cultural links – languages, architectural styles, music, art, sport, town-twinning, or through migration;
- historical links – in any of the areas above.

(QCDA 2010: 40)

Geography is a very broad subject and reaches out in so many different directions. It can focus on the *physical features* and become very specialized indeed, taking in more scientific themes such as geology, vulcanology, meteorology and ecology. Or it can emphasize the *human features*, and overlap with history, citizenship, politics, economics and technology. It can also get personal, for example, when we choose where we want to live, where to go on holiday and the best way to get to granny's house.

Very few places on Earth are untouched by humans, so most places possess both physical features and human features. While some of the topics the children explore will emphasize the physical features of a place, others will highlight the human aspects – most, however, will combine both of these in some way or another.

What do the children actually learn about?

Places

The places that the children investigate in their geography lessons can be big or small, of any shape, close to home or far away, personal to an individual or available to everybody – for example:

- a living room, bedroom, garden;
- a classroom, school grounds, field;
- a shopping street or mall, station;
- a street of houses, housing estate, village, town, city;
- a beach, river, mountain range;
- a region, country.

The children study each place in terms of:

- its physical features;
- the ways in which we humans make use of it.

The children are helped to develop a feeling for the *unique identity* of a place, by considering questions such as:

- What land-forms and environmental conditions exist there (using the correct geographical words)?
- What makes the place distinctive?
- What features does it share with other places and how is it different?
- Is it a pleasant place?
- How do the physical features affect the way people use the area, encouraging some activities and restricting others?
- How do people actually make use of the place?

For example, by investigating Blackpool in Northern England, the children find out that it is in Lancashire, on the coast of the Irish Sea, with sandy beaches. It is located on a low, flat piece of land between the River Wyre to the north and the River Ribble to the south, and has good, fertile soil nearby, on which farmers produce vegetable crops. It is mild in winter, warm in summer and enjoys a good amount of sunshine. It has a well-established tourist industry, with hotels, amusements and parks, and has a railway and a motorway leading right to it. The children might conclude that the climate and the land-forms combine well to allow the holiday industry to flourish.

During the primary years, the children study a large number of places worldwide, learning about physical and human features, and seeking to understand which features are most significant in making a place what it is today.

They may also be asked to think about what might happen, and how the place and its surroundings might be affected, if a particular change takes place. If, for example, a new school opens, or a new road is built, or a new factory or supermarket opens.

Children are helped to appreciate that there is a relationship between the physical and human features found in a particular place. They might think about:

■ What is possible and what is not possible, in view of its physical features. Is it a good idea to build a railway across marshy ground? Is the climate suitable for growing grapes?

■ What is the impact on people's lives and activities when the land-forms and environmental conditions combine to do something out of the ordinary – for example, what happens when there is an earthquake, or an avalanche, or a drought?

■ What are the consequences for the land/plant life/animals when people (that is, humans) change their behaviour? What would be the environmental impact of building a bridge at different places along a river?

■ What are the effects of man-made changes on our own lives? What happens if we make our high street into a pedestrian zone? How does this affect shoppers, shop owners, local residents, bus companies and motorists?

Links between places

The main lesson for the children with regard to *links between places* is that places do not stand alone – each one connects with all sorts of other places in all sorts of ways. These links might extend over a very short distance (for instance, the routes the children take to get to school) or worldwide (buying a shirt that was made in China). Examples the children might investigate include: Where does their family do its shopping? Why there? Where was their family car made? Where does their water come from and how much do they waste? Where are their e-mails stored?

Younger children will be helped to *notice* and then *describe* the links. Older children will move on to try to *understand* and *explain* these links and patterns. They will seek answers to questions such as:

■ What exactly are the relationships between places? How far do these links extend? How often are they made?

■ If the relationship involves transport, by what route and by what means? Why?

■ Why are the relationships as they are?

■ Are the relationships stable, or have they changed over time?

■ What are the positive effects of the link? Are there any negative effects?

■ Is there a better way of getting the same benefits, but without the costs?

■ What might be the effects of any changes? Are these effects likely to be desirable or not?

Using questions like these, the children could explore why we buy flowers that have been grown in Holland and peas from Africa. They could also be used to make judgements closer to home, for example, whether it would be feasible for each class to visit the local library each month, or whether it would be a good idea to extend the number of schools that are involved in the schools' chess league.

In order to carry out informed investigations on a worldwide scale, the children need a background of facts and understanding, such as:

- what the climate is like in different parts of the UK and the world;
- that the air is cooler at high altitudes, including the tops of mountains;
- that rivers flow downhill, from higher land to the sea;
- what species of plants and animals live in different parts of the world and what makes them suited to these places;
- what *raw materials* are, what a factory is and what a warehouse is used for;
- what banks do;
- how far it is from one place to another and how long it takes to cover the journey, using different modes of transport;
- what a monsoon is and what effects it can have;
- which countries share the same language and cultural backgrounds.

Caring for Planet Earth

A key characteristic of geographers is their positive and caring attitude towards the planet, and the plants and animals that live here. The children are taught that the relationship between a place and the people who use it is a two-way affair:

- the physical environment of a place can have a bearing on people's lives and activities;
- humans, and the way they live their lives, can have a profound effect on the place and its environment.

The children are taught that the Earth is a fragile place and that we need to:

- use natural resources carefully, conserving them as much as possible and not wasting them (e.g. gas, peat, trees);
- maintain, manage and protect the environments and eco-systems found in different places, for instance, the school garden or pond, heathland, canal banks, woodland;
- do our best to protect plants and animals and preserve their habitats.

Geographical skills and enquiry

What skills are involved?

Geography provides many opportunities for children to develop the *transferable skills* that underpin the primary curriculum, helping them to make further progress throughout their school career and their whole life (see Chapter 2) – skills such as research and enquiry, problem solving, making and checking hypotheses, and working accurately.

Overlapping these, geography has its own particular set of skills:

- using photographs and video;
- using maps, globes and plans;
- fieldwork;
- enquiry.

(QCA 1998a)

Using photographs and video

The children can learn a huge amount about places and environments by studying photographs and video clips. They are taught to view places from different angles, from different distances (including satellite images) and at different times (of the day, week or season, or over a longer timescale). It is also important that places are considered in relation to other places close by.

Of course, the children will need guidance in interpreting what they see on photographs, but they usually find them fascinating. Aerial photos are particularly useful, as they also provide a link to learning about maps. On photographs, children can see both the *static features* (both natural and man-made ones) and maybe also some *moving elements*, for instance, cars or trains, which may help to demonstrate some of the links between places.

Using plans, maps, globes

The children begin by taking a bird's-eye view of objects in the classroom – perhaps on their desk-top – and drawing a *plan*. They draw a picture of what they can see from this new perspective – that is, the shape of the top of each object (which has no visible height). The shape, position and size of each item all need to be considered very carefully. This task becomes more difficult when making a plan of their classroom or the playground because they can't actually look down vertically on the place, so a certain amount of imagination, and measurement, are required.

This skill is then extended to *maps*. The difference here is that objects are not drawn true-to-life, but are represented by symbols, icons and colours. It is a stylized representation of the picture from above. Things are not exactly as we would see them, so rivers might be coloured blue (even though they are usually brown), roads might be red (although they are grey), houses might be shown as a rectangle, even if they have a conservatory attached, and so on.

The children learn:

- that a map is a flat representation of a real-life place, as viewed vertically from above;
- to take note of the map's purpose (a look at the title is often useful);
- that real-life features are shown as symbols, icons and colours;
- to use the *key* to interpret the symbols, icons and colours on the map;
- about directions – left and right, and the eight major points of the compass;
- to use coordinates (grid references) to identify the location of places or features on a map, reading the numbers or letters along the bottom and up the left-hand side of the map; in the early stages this is likely to be presented as a letter and a number (*the treasure is buried in square B5*), but the children will progress to using two-, four- or even six-figure references for greater accuracy;
- about distances and scales – and, on local plans and maps, matching these to real distances on the ground;
- to interpret the information on a map, so that it can be used as evidence in an investigation;
- to draw their own reasonable sketch-maps of a local place.

The children learn about three distinctly different types of maps, which are used for different purposes:

- First, there are maps and globes that simply show us where places are. For example, we might want to show where in the world Mount Everest is, or which part of the town we live in, or where we went on holiday.
- The second type is used to help us find our way around, for example, road maps, street maps, rail maps, the London Underground map, maps showing ferry links between the UK mainland and the islands around it, or personal sketch maps to show a friend how to get to our house.
- Third, there are maps that are designed to give specific information about places. These often include facts and statistics that can be used to aid decision-making. For example, maps showing:
  - the predicted weather – temperature, wind speed and rainfall – which can help us decide what clothes to take with us on a trip, and gives good advice to climbers and emergency services;
  - the density of traffic flow through a town's high street, as a basis for making changes to the streets, and increasing safety for motorists and pedestrians;
  - where certain animals live – for example, where otters live in the UK – and whether conservation work is being successful;
  - restaurants in a holiday resort and what sort of food they serve, so that tourists can decide where to eat.

The children learn to read and interpret each of these three types of map and to have a go at making their own.

In their everyday lives, the children are probably most familiar with the first two types, that is, showing where places are and how to get from one place to another. To get the best out of them, the children need to learn some reference points – for example:

- where their own classroom is, within the school building;
- where their house is, in relation to other places in their home village, town or city;
- where local villages and towns are in relation to one another;
- where the different countries are on a map of the British Isles, and the key towns and cities;
- where in the world countries, continents, oceans, cities and principal rivers are located.

In the twenty-first century, in-car satellite navigation devices (sat-navs) are increasingly used to find a route from one place to another, but these cannot give a full geographical picture of the journey and the surroundings on the way, and as a consequence maps may be more useful overall.

Fieldwork

First, despite its name, *fieldwork* does not have to happen in a field! Rather, it is about going to a *place* and finding out about it *at first hand*. It is sometimes also called a *site visit*. Through fieldwork, the children can use their five senses to relate to a place – viewing the landscape, feeling the air, soaking up the sounds and the atmosphere, studying the links with other places, and so on – all at first hand. This gives the children far more opportunities to learn about a place than looking at books, maps and webcams alone.

However, fieldwork brings with it a whole new set of skills for the children to learn and practise:

- identifying real-life features, such as hills, valleys and so on, that match the symbols on a map – this is much more difficult than reading a map in the classroom and simply saying what we would expect to see *on the ground*;
- using the correct vocabulary to describe what they see and feel;
- using specialist equipment – direction compasses, thermometers, wind gauges, rain gauges, cameras, video cameras;
- getting a feel for directions, distances and scale;
- drawing sketch-maps;
- keeping observations, records and data in a form that can be used later.

Through fieldwork, children have a chance to respond to the place in their own way – to become absorbed in it, to find their own points of interest, to ask their own questions, to lead their own investigations and to use their specialist instruments in a practical setting – in short, to become real, practising geographers.

Enquiry

The following three stages might appear to be the wrong way around – but it is the way most children develop the skills of enquiry in geography:

- first, they learn to seek out, gather and record information about a place;
- then they learn to communicate their views and findings, and draw conclusions;
- finally, they begin to ask their own questions and follow their own lines of enquiry in a more independent way.

Enquiry – seeking out, gathering and recording information

As we help the children to learn about places, we often use questions as prompts, such as:

- What place is this? How big is it?
- What is it like?
- Where is it? What other places are near it?
- Why is it in this particular location? Why is it here at all?
- Are there other places like this? What aspects are the same and what is different?
- Why is it like this?
- Is it natural, or did humans cause it or create it?
- Has it always been like this? What was it like before? How did it become like this?
- What links has it got with other places?
- How strong are those links?
- What do they mean in practice?
- Is the place staying the same, or is it changing?
- Is this desirable?
- Will a change here affect other places? Will this be positive or negative for them?
- Is the place vulnerable in any way? Does it need protection? If so, how?
- Can it be improved? How? What would be the impact on other places or plants or animals as a consequence?

Some questions are more straightforward than others, of course. Some can be answered by researching secondary sources of information such as books, newspapers, the Internet and asking other people. However, others will require the children to explore artefacts from a place, using any of their five senses, and perhaps carry out fieldwork at the place itself.

ICT devices can prove useful in helping the children to collect information about a place: Global Positioning System (GPS) to find an exact location, a camera to record visible features, a webcam to record changes over time, and data-logging equipment to detect soil types, temperature and wind speed.

As they collect details about the place, the children need to record what they have seen, heard, read and found out, so that information is not lost, but can be brought together and discussed later. This can be done by jotting down notes, taking photographs, making sketches, drawings, diagrams and tables, drawing sketch-maps (with a *key*), making voice-recordings, etc. The children need to build a repertoire of techniques and skills like these, so that they can select the most appropriate ones in their future work.

Enquiry – drawing conclusions and communicating findings

If geography really is to make the world a better place, it needs to be a persuasive subject, not just asking important questions and collecting information, but also suggesting ways forward that benefit mankind, without damaging the environments of the Earth. Of course, the children will need a lot of help, as well as a certain level of confidence, to draw conclusions from the information they have found. At an early age, they can give opinions about what they like and dislike about a place, but as they get older, they are encouraged to justify their views and opinions by referring to the information they have collected.

As in other areas of the curriculum, the preferred means of communicating one's thoughts, opinions and conclusions will depend on the question being discussed, the information and evidence being put forward, the intended audience and, crucially, the children's skills. As this is geography, however, we encourage the children to include geographical techniques wherever possible to present their findings. So, as well as writing, they also use:

- photographs, aerial photographs, video;
- sketch-maps (with a *key*) and drawings (with notes);
- diagrams, lists, tables and graphs;
- three-dimensional models of landscapes;
- multi-media computer presentations.

Enquiry – asking questions

With lots of practice and interesting examples, the older children will begin to ask their own questions about places, to find out about:

- the place itself;
- the physical features found there;
- the way people have transformed places and how they use them now;
- links between this place and others;
- how the place is, or could be, managed and developed in a sustainable way.

Of course, all this does not come to the children straightaway, but by asking and investigating questions like these, the children are well on the way to becoming real geographers. They will also undoubtedly gain so much more from their travels around the UK and the world, both as children and later as adults.

The broader aims of geography

Geography is such a wonderfully broad subject. It covers the whole world, from the patch of ground underneath our feet to the North and South Poles, passing the Equator on the way, and it involves almost every area of human activity, because everything we do takes place somewhere – that is, in a place.

It offers opportunities for the children to become interested in the various physical and human features to be found on the Earth's surface and to appreciate the beauty of the world. It also enables them to make informed comment about the quality of their environment, and to develop a sense of responsibility for the care of Earth and its people, its flora and its fauna.

10 History

What is history really about?

History is about people and societies in the past. It is about what was going on at different times in the past, and about changes that have happened over time – what caused them and what the effects were afterwards. The subject is based on the idea that the way we lead our lives today is the product of all the changes and developments that have happened over the previous tens, hundreds and thousands of years. So history can give us lots of clues about how our society came to be the way it is and why we live our lives the way we do. By extension, historians also believe that we can plan for a better future by learning lessons from what happened, both locally and worldwide, in years gone by (DfEE and QCA 1999: 103).

In broad terms, by studying history, we attempt to:

- describe how people used to live at different times in the past, painting as clear a picture as possible as a background to the lives of individual men, women and children;
- understand events that happened in the past and decide how significant they were;
- explain how societies, and the people who lived in them, came to be as they were and how they moved on towards their future;
- discover how people dealt with problems and situations that arose in the past and, taking note of the different conditions and circumstances between then and now, suggest ways in which we might best go about dealing with similar situations nowadays.

History's scope is enormous – it covers all areas of human activity, from the smallest details of everyday life, to major issues and events. To make sure that the children receive a balanced view of life and events in the past, it has been suggested that each of the following aspects is covered at one time or another:

- *political aspects* – power and government; war, invasion; migration and settlement; beliefs, opinions and human rights;

- *economic, technological and scientific aspects* – trade, jobs, industries; travel; discoveries and inventions;

- *social and religious aspects* – family, heredity and status; living conditions; education, employment and leisure; beliefs, faith, orthodoxy and splinter groups;

- *cultural and aesthetic aspects* – stories, drama, art, music, leisure, fashion, etc.

(DES 1989b: 15)

During the primary years, the children touch on each of these aspects of life several times as they explore different time periods. For example, a unit about the Vikings' invasion of Britain some 1,200 years ago might include:

- invasion and settlement, the power of the king (*political*);

- sea travel (*economic, technological and scientific*);

- houses and villages, monasteries, Viking gods (*social and religious*);

- clothing, sagas (*cultural and aesthetic*).

(QCA 1998b)

Some of the themes addressed in history lessons might be new to the children – for example, the ideas of *trade, democracy* and *class*. History is an ideal vehicle for introducing abstract aspects of society like these.

Of course, we don't want the children to find history remote or dull. We want them to be touched by the events of the past, and to understand and empathize with the people found there. So, by studying a wide range of historical topics, they increase their knowledge and understanding of:

- the lives of ordinary people – men, women and children; rich and poor; local and worldwide; at work, at play and in the home;

- the life and work of influential people – rulers, politicians, religious people, philanthropists; scientists, inventors, explorers; artists, poets;

- significant events – e.g. the Great Fire of London in 1666, the invention of the telephone;

- immigration – by invasion and settlement; by peaceful settlement, as people move from one country to another in search of a better life;

- specific activities – e.g. farming, transport, medicine.

In each topic, the children are encouraged to compare the way things were in the past with their own present-day experiences – for example, the toys that Victorian children played with were very different from the ones children have nowadays.

In order to get a balanced picture, the children are encouraged to interpret their findings in the context of the time – for example, when they think about the poorest people at the time of Robin Hood, they need to consider them as they actually lived in the year 1198, not as if they were alive in the twenty-first century. Values and attitudes in the past have been very different from our own and, while the children need to accept that this is the way it was, they should certainly not be discouraged from voicing their opinions on the events and standards they discover in the past.

What do the children learn about in their history lessons?

Children first gain a sense of the past by investigating their own lives and the lives of their parents and grandparents – where they used to live, what they used to eat and play with, etc. After these personal links are established, the children begin to explore people and events from different periods further into the past, for example, the Second World War (70 years ago), Florence Nightingale (150 years ago), the Great Fire of London (some 350 years ago) and the Ancient Egyptians (some 3,000 years ago).

Another approach is for the children to explore a single topic over several timescales – perhaps *children's toys*: in Ancient Greek society, in the UK in the 1930s and in their own toy cupboard. Or they might explore the development of written messages from the earliest days (e.g. cave paintings) through papyrus scrolls and the invention of the printing press, to the present day (e.g. instant messaging).

As a rule, once we have selected a period or a theme for the class topic, we help the children to:

- seek out factual information, such as names, dates, places and events;
- develop their background understanding, by considering the beliefs, ideas and opinions that existed at the time;
- build the fullest possible picture, by linking together facts, ideas and evidence, and deciding just how significant each piece of the jigsaw might be.

An important aspect of history is the study of *change*. Societies are constantly *on the move* as new ideas come along and new developments take place. Historians particularly look at:

- how things have changed over time;
- who or what caused these changes;
- what were the consequences of those changes;
- how long the changes lasted before they changed again;
- what things did *not* change during this period.

The children might study *change* in any area of life. The subject might be of personal interest (writing implements, fashion) or it could be of national importance (crime and punishment, education). All of these are valid topics for historical study.

The children discover that, when change happens in one area, it usually has an effect on several other areas, too. For example, the invention of television in the twentieth century (a technological change) had a significant effect on so many areas of life: political, social and religious issues were brought into the living room, new jobs were created, family routines changed, advertising showed people a new way of life to which they could aspire and new forms of entertainment became available to the general population.

What skills do the children use to find out about the past?

In general terms, we might say that historians carry out their craft by *investigating traces of the past that have been left behind*. This means that history, as a subject, not only helps the children to learn about the past, but also offers opportunities to develop their *research and enquiry skills* – one of the important *transferable skills* – no matter which period of history or what theme is being studied.

So, using a range of historical contexts, the children:

- ask and answer questions;
- seek out evidence;
- bring pieces of information together;
- draw tentative conclusions.

Asking and answering questions

To begin with, the children seek out answers to questions set by adults. As they gain more experience, they are encouraged to ask their own questions – to set up their own lines of enquiry – and then to carry out the necessary research to answer them. The sorts of questions they ask are:

- What was it like to live at this time in the past?
  - As a background, what was going on – in the world, in the country, in the region and locally? What changes were taking place at this time? How did these affect people on a personal level?
  - How did people spend their time? What would a day have looked like for different people?
  - Why did people behave as they did? What was their motivation? What choices were open to them?
  - What was important to them? What did they believe?
- How was this time in the past different from the present and how was it similar? What has changed in the meantime?

- What is the same, or similar, between the two periods? What is different?
- What do we do now that was not possible then? What do we do now that they did differently then?
- What caused the changes? Were they sudden or gradual?
- What effects did the changes have on the people and their lives? Did all the changes have a lasting effect?

■ What of the future?
- What changes are happening now that will affect people's lives in the future?
- Is there anything to be learned from the way previous changes have taken place?

Seeking out evidence

Of course, historians don't just guess at answers to these questions – they are constantly looking for *evidence*. They do this by carrying out research carefully and methodically – making observations, collecting and recording evidence, and deciding on its importance and relevance to the topic being studied. The children are helped to do the same. Evidence is also called *sources of information*, or *sources* for short.

The children learn that there are *primary sources* and *secondary sources*:

■ *Primary sources* are those that actually existed *at the time in question*, for example:
- objects or fragments of objects – also called *artefacts*;
- paintings, sketches and drawings made at the time;
- buildings and remains;
- archives – diaries, pamphlets, letters, maps, newspaper reports, photographs, advertisements, posters;
- census data, statistics;
- interviews with people who were there;
- art and music that was created, written or performed at the time.

■ *Secondary sources* are those that were created *after the event*, for example:
- television and radio programmes, web pages;
- stories, biographies, textbooks, videos, plays;
- pictures, maps;
- the results of research already carried out by other people.

Primary sources can be found in all sorts of places – not just in museums, galleries and libraries, but also in houses, gardens and sheds, in and underneath buildings, behind walls, in excavations, in caves, in fields, at car-boot sales, through archaeology, through discussion with people who were there. Wherever possible, historians prefer to use primary sources of evidence. However, secondary sources are undoubtedly useful, as they draw on interpretations of evidence made by other historians.

Bringing different pieces of information together

In the early stages, children look at only one *source* at a time – perhaps a picture, an artefact or a story set in the past – and tell us what they notice. As we guide them with prompts and questions, they are helped to make observations, suggest comparisons with the present (or with other times in the past) and interpret the resource – that is, draw information from it and form a hypothesis about it. For example, if they are looking at an object from the past, they would particularly concentrate on:

- describing the object;
- suggesting its purpose and function, and when it might have been used;
- noting how it fits in with other evidence.

We could offer prompts such as:

- What can you see?
- What is it made from?
- Is it real or a replica?
- What do you think it was used for? Do you think it would have been any good?
- What do we use now to do the same job?
- Who would have owned it? And who would have used it?
- When, in history, would it have been used? What makes you think that?
- What was life like at that time?
- How has this survived so long? Where else have these been found?
- Do you think this is an important piece of evidence? Why?

As they gain experience, the children begin to look at several pieces of evidence together. They will need to use the same process for each piece individually, and then the sources will need to be sifted and selected for relevance, and compared together, to decide whether they confirm or contradict each other, and therefore whether the evidence is likely to be reliable. For example, we might compare a piece of armour, a painting of a battle and a story set in the same period – was the soldier's armour authentic in the picture? Or was the fragment from a different time in history?

Drawing tentative conclusions

Once the children have brought their evidence together and analysed it, they need to draw conclusions from what they have found. But how certain can they be? If truth be told, much of the history that we *know* (or think we know) may be little more than an *educated guess*.

Of course, we do have some factual evidence from the past – many objects from the past come to light, and dates and times of events may be beyond dispute. But word-based evidence is far less reliable – which bits of information can we believe and which are best taken with a pinch of salt? We have only to read today's newspapers to understand how opinion and *spin* can distort the truth! So children are helped to distinguish between *facts* and *opinions*, and to be aware that there may be several different versions of a single event. They may also suggest why historical events might have been presented in a particular way – who is telling us, have they got a particular viewpoint, or a vested interest?

At each stage of learning about the past, the children will form a view about *what it was like*. We know that they are constantly learning more – from lessons, of course, but also from stories, television programmes and films. As they come across new evidence, the whole picture needs to be looked at afresh. They need to be encouraged to ask themselves questions such as:

- Does this new evidence fit-in with what I already know, or does it lead me to believe something new?
- Does it come from a reliable source?
- Whose version of the truth is it?
- What are the implications, if this new information is real? What needs to be changed in my thinking?
- What is my new hypothesis about what was happening at the time?
- Is there any other evidence to support my new hypothesis or to counter it?

When a fresh event comes to light they may ask:

- What really happened?
- Who caused it? What were they trying to achieve?
- What were the consequences? Did anything change as a result?
- What would we think if this happened today?
- How important is this new piece of evidence?

Of course, it is likely that many of these questions have no definite answer, so the children are encouraged to employ a *disciplined imagination*, to suggest ways in which the gaps might be filled in. It is very much like a detective game, piecing together snippets of evidence and analysing them, trying to draw conclusions about what actually happened.

It is often a tentative process, which can lead to only tentative conclusions. Seldom do historians jump to conclusions and announce 'I know this to be the truth'; rather, they might say 'In light of this new evidence, I think it likely that . . .'. The children should be encouraged to take this cautious view as well. Sometimes historians offer several alternative interpretations and insights, but these are always based on the evidence available to them at the time.

Returning to the detective idea, historians would say that a cornerstone of historical research is an absolute respect for the evidence presented. This thorough approach allows us to judge the past without prejudice. It also motivates us to preserve parts of the present, so that our descendants might gain an accurate picture of the way we lead our lives. The practice of burying a time capsule in the school grounds has prompted valuable discussions about what items sum up the present day, and might provide evidence of everyday life early in the twenty-first century.

Measuring time (chronology)

Children often find the concept of historical time very difficult to understand, partly because of its vast scale, and partly because there is no hands-on unit of measure like a metre-stick or a kilogramme-weight, against which it can be compared.

We need to remember just how very young these children are – they were all born during the past decade, yet we ask them to think about periods of hundreds or even thousands of years. We might teach them that the Egyptian pharaoh Tutankhamun lived from 1341BC to 1323BC, but what do the intervening 3,300 years or so actually *mean* when you are only ten years old? If King Henry VIII lived *a long time ago*, how should we describe the *distance in time* between the present day and when Tutankhamun was alive?

In history, the *order of events* – the *sequence* – is important:

- What actually happened?
- Why did it happen just then and not before?
- Why did it happen just there and not somewhere else?
- Is it possible that one particular event might have been caused by another?
- Is it possible that a particular event had one or more consequences?
- Did the consequences last a long time? How long? What happened then?

By discussing questions like this, the children develop skills in:

- sequencing events, placing events in chronological order;
- placing events in historical time or periods;
- developing the vocabulary of time – before/after, old/new, past/present/future, ancient/modern, BC/AD.
- using dates and year numbers to describe time (including describing the 1600s as *the seventeenth century*).

Time-lines, covering anything from a day, a week, a century, the duration of an event, or even 10,000 years, can be a good way for children to tackle sequencing.

Local history

Most schools seek to make history more personal by helping the children to find out about local history. This often concentrates on how the local area developed over the past seventy years or so, in terms of an important local industry, or a changing population (and where these people moved from or to). By choosing this sort of timescale, the children can play the role of a professional historian, seeking out and gathering evidence from a whole range of sources, including first-hand interviews with elderly people who have lived in the area for some time, family photographs, objects (artefacts) from people's houses, archived newspaper articles, and local museums.

In a local historical investigation the children might focus on any of the topics covered in their other units – people, social conditions, government, employment, technology, change, etc. – but it is their past, their heritage, their families and, ultimately, their future that they are investigating.

History's breadth

History deals with the whole of mankind, from the beginning of the Earth to the present day. It deals with every aspect of life's rich tapestry – the everyday, the interesting, the magnificent and the awful; love, power and jealousy; genius, strategy and incompetence; vision and selfishness; opulence and squalour. We delve into the lives of both ordinary people and noblemen, the good and the evil, those who changed the world and those who had change done to them. We cannot fail to be moved by much of what we learn, whether this be admiration or loathing, joy or despair. It's a never-ending puzzle, of which we are allowed to see only some pieces, and are then left to guess at what the other pieces might have been in order to build a whole picture. While we are doing this, we are constantly comparing events with our own present-day lives. Have the same problems and questions come round again? Are there any lessons we can learn?

11

Information and Communication Technology (ICT)

What is ICT really about?

ICT in primary schools is not just about computers and the Internet. Rather, it takes in a whole range of electronic equipment:

- computers, laptops, notebooks, tablets
- mice, keyboards, switches, buttons
- radios, TVs
- remote controls
- digital and video cameras
- electronic timers, sensors, scanners
- games, toys, robots
- microwaves
- mobile phones
- touch screens, interactive whiteboards
- CD/DV/mp3 players
- sat navs, GPS equipment
- microphones, voice recorders
- electronic keyboards
- e-book readers
- washing machines, dishwashers

In fact, ICT includes any pieces of equipment that contain microchips that are pre-programmed by the manufacturer to carry out particular functions. Having said that, the emphasis in schools is still very much on using computers and the Internet.

Our job is to help the children to learn how to use these machines (and any others that might make an appearance in the coming months and years) *for the purposes that are important to them*. These purposes might include schoolwork and learning, keeping in touch with friends and family, managing their everyday lives, supporting hobbies, entertainment, playing games and solving puzzles.

Clearly, these everyday tasks have been accomplished quite well without electronics in the past. For example, a message sent by e-mail would previously have been sent by letter, music can be made by playing an instrument instead of using electronics, and calculations now made on a spreadsheet could be made using paper and pencil.

But the fact remains that we are increasingly using electronic equipment. There are many good reasons for this. For example, it can carry out complicated processes quickly, precisely and reliably, and once it is set up, it can be left to repeat actions again and again with unwavering accuracy. Also, it can handle vast quantities of information, which can be readily transferred from one machine to another and from one place to another. And, of course, electronic devices are increasingly portable and are becoming ever easier to control.

If ICT equipment did not have these qualities, we simply wouldn't use it – we would go back to using old-fashioned, low-tech methods to achieve what we want. Perhaps we should be guided by the principle that *we should use ICT when it is advantageous to do so*.

In order to make good use of ICT, the children need to learn what each piece of equipment (the *hardware*) is capable of doing, and how to work it and control it. They also need to learn what each program or application/app (the *software*) is capable of doing, and how to use it to achieve what they want to achieve. Together, these put the children in control of the equipment. But this is not enough – they also need to make some important decisions. Exactly what do they want to achieve through a particular task? Which piece of equipment and which piece of software should they use to achieve the desired result? Finally, they need to carry out the procedure, while at the same time making further decisions about the quality of the result.

ICT is valuable in every subject in school, helping the children to:

- find things out;
- develop their understanding;
- explore situations and try out their ideas;
- make things happen;
- exchange and share ideas (communication).

ICT also offers opportunities for the children to refine and improve their work in all subjects as it progresses, both swiftly and effectively (QCA 2003: 6).

Finding things out

ICT is an excellent research tool. It makes it possible for the children to find out about everything from song lyrics to weather forecasts, from pictures of baboons to family histories – the breadth is limited only by their curiosity. They learn to seek out facts, statistics, information, views and opinions – in the form of words, pictures, photos, diagrams, sounds, music, video, tables, charts, graphs, logos, post-codes, prices, etc., – using television, video, sat navs, computers, indexes, contents pages, menus, favourites, bookmarks, hyperlinks and key-word searches. Then they learn to save the information they have found, categorize it, file it in folders and, of course, retrieve it later.

In order to become skilled in this, the children learn to:

- talk about, and be clear about, exactly what they want to find out;
- ask the right questions;
- decide on the best place to find that information;
- carry out searches to find the information they want;
- classify and organize what they find;
- decide whether it is relevant to the original question;
- interpret it;
- draw conclusions.

They are also taught to be aware that, although the Internet is akin to having a whole library in their own home, crucially, it has no *quality control* – what is written may be true, but equally it might be biased (in terms of politics, racism, sexism, etc.) or simply wrong. So the children also need to learn how to carry out checks and make good decisions. Is this information reasonable and reliable? Is it accurate? Are there any mistakes? Is anything missing? Is it biased?

Electronic equipment is particularly good at holding large amounts of information in the form of *databases* – lists of contact numbers on a phone, play-lists on an mp3 player, personal and financial data held by banks, and so on. In essence, a database is just a collection of information, rather like a set of card-index files, where individual items of data can be added, changed or removed.

In the classroom, the children learn about databases by carrying out question-naires among their friends and then constructing their own databases from the information they have assembled. This might, for instance, include the children's name, birthday, address, and method of transport to school – in each case the same pieces of information (called *fields*) are held for each child.

The value of a database program lies in its ability to search through data to find *matches*. It can carry out thousands of searches each second. In our example here, it could find all the children who travel to school by bus. Or it could find all those born in a particular month, by responding to the instruction 'find all the records that contain the word *November* in the *Birthday* field'. The program can even collate the information, and produce charts and graphs to display it clearly. But – and it is a big *but* – if the data is faulty or incomplete, the result of the search will also be faulty. So the children will need to judge whether the results they obtain are reasonable and reliable, and check that they did, in fact, *ask the right question*.

One type of database is worth a special mention – the *branching database*. This is used when the children are trying to identify something that they cannot name, such as an unknown bug found in the school garden. To find out what it is, they will need to consult an *animals* branching database and, by asking questions with *yes* or *no* answers, they can narrow down their search by eliminating groups of animals at each step:

- Is it an insect? Yes.
  - *The computer will now search through all the* animal *data entries and eliminate those without the word* insect *in them.*
- Has it got wings? No.
  - *The computer will now search all the* insects *left in and remove all those with the word* wings *in them.*
- Has it got spots? Yes.
  - *The computer will now search through all the* wingless insects *not yet eliminated, and remove all those without the word* spots *in them.*

This continues until only one bug remains. And that's our bug!

This is all done by *matching*. The children learn about the principles of this process, so that they can use databases for all sorts of reasons. They will also have experience of creating their own databases on a computer, often making a paper version beforehand.

Understanding things better

A key feature of the microchip is its ability to handle a lot of information, of different sorts and from different sources, very quickly. This means that the children can find a range of words, tables, images, animations, speech and music about a single topic, then bring them all together and, crucially, link up bits of information and ideas that were previously separate, thereby gaining new insights and new understanding about the topic

For instance, when the children learn about the solar system, they can search through any number of sites on the Internet and bring information together, organizing and refining their ideas as they prepare their own *multi-media presentation*. Skills the children use in this process include:

- exploring sources of information, as described in the 'Finding things out' section, above;
- collecting information together, and checking it;
- deciding which bits to use;
- organizing it;
- importantly, refining their ideas, as each new piece of information comes to light;
- amending and editing at each stage;
- finally, composing a coherent piece of work that demonstrates their *updated* understanding of the subject.

Groupwork is particularly effective in this context, as it provides opportunities for the children to *try out* ideas and hypotheses, and discuss the relevance and importance of each new piece of information before reaching a conclusion.

Exploring situations and trying things out

When we need to make a decision, and it is not clear which of the available options is best, we can sometimes use ICT to test out ideas *in a virtual world* first, before we commit ourselves to making choices and decisions that might prove time-consuming, expensive or even dangerous. This is called *modelling*. It is based on the principle of *trial and improvement* – we can keep changing individual elements until we like what we see.

In the classroom, the children use programs like this in the context of music-making, photo editing, drawing and painting, doll dressing, word processing, desk-top publishing, and even playground designing. In each case, they can try out ideas, answering the question 'I wonder what it would be like if I did this . . .?' They can test out different colours, shapes, fonts, clothes, layouts, and so on, before committing themselves to a final decision. (It is useful to save each version with a different file name, so that they can return to a *quite good* version, when later variations lead down a blind alley.) They might ask: 'I wonder whether this photo would be improved if I were to zoom-in like this?' or 'I wonder whether my tune would sound better with this chord in the background . . . or this one?' or 'I wonder which is the best way to get to the concert hall?'.

Where only numbers, sums of money or time are involved, older children can use a spreadsheet program to try out options. They might ask: 'With a budget of £40, I wonder what is the best combination of fruit, snacks and drinks for our party?'. The children learn that this technique is an established part of the professional design process – for example, engineers try out their ideas on computers before spending millions of pounds on building cars and bridges.

Simulations like this are intended to be used *before the event*, to try things out and clarify our thoughts and ideas before we make our decision about what we should actually do. After all, the program only offers advice – we have to make the decision ourselves in the end.

Another way to explore ideas and theories (hypotheses) is for the children to analyse their own scientific or mathematical data after they have collected it – for example, 'I wonder how the growth of my seedlings was affected by being given different amounts of water and fertilizer?'. Here, they have moved on to explore *relationships*. By collecting data and entering it on to a spreadsheet, the children can use the mathematical functions of the spreadsheet to help them analyse the results – rates of growth, life spans, heights, and so on – producing charts, graphs and tables of numbers for individual plants or any combination of plants they wish to compare. It is important that the children realize that the program only does the arithmetic – they are making all the decisions and doing the maths themselves.

Making things happen

All electronic devices work in the same way:

- the software receives an *input* consisting of instructions or data;
- it processes this;
- it then produces an *output*.

Many devices receive their instructions and data through buttons, which are properly described as *switches*. Each switch tells the machine, through its pre-programming, to do something specific – on a microwave, for instance, we can set the power, the cooking time, and so on.

However, electronic equipment can respond to a much wider range of inputs than this, to *make things happen*. Other inputs that trigger an output include:

- *light* – cameras, security bulbs;
- *heat* – thermostats;
- *movement* – burglar alarms;
- *sound* – verbal instruction to mobile phones, microphones;
- *time* – alarm clocks, video timers;
- *location* – sat nav, GPS equipment;
- *bar codes* – shop tills, library cards;
- *magnetic swipe cards* – bank cards, locks;
- *pressure* – scales, interactive whiteboards, touch screens, touch pads, keyboards;
- *money recognition* (both coins and notes) – vending machines.

Not forgetting the click of a mouse on a computer, of course. The children learn about the ever-increasing number of ways to make digital equipment do their bidding.

Some equipment is designed merely to log the data it receives, perhaps display it on a screen, and then store it so that it can be retrieved and interpreted later. Electronic thermometers, light meters and sound meters fall into this category. The children use these in their science lessons, but could also use them to monitor how loud passing traffic is, or how hot the sausages are at lunchtime. While the equipment does the measuring, the pupils do still need to interpret the data in the context of the investigation taking place.

Other equipment has a more active output, following an input:

- an image on a screen (monitor, phone, camera, watch);
- movement (a programmable toy, unlocking a door, water flowing into a washing machine);

- sound (music keyboard, mp3 player, phone);
- heat (a microwave).

The children learn that, in many cases, an operation involves more than a single input and more than a single output. When withdrawing cash from an ATM, for example, we swipe our card and push buttons (both inputs) and the machine gives us cash, a receipt and an entry on our next statement (all outputs). Information is often stored electronically as well, so that it can be retrieved at a later date, for instance, on cameras, computers and phones.

The children are introduced to many different pieces of electronic equipment and are shown what each is pre-programmed to do. They learn that programs are made up of several steps, which need to be carried out in the correct sequence, in order to make things happen. They might compare a washing machine cycle (the ICT method) with the series of steps needed to wash a shirt by hand (the low-tech way). This sort of sequencing is an excellent way to introduce the idea of *programming*, that is, controlling a machine through a number of steps (or *routines*), so that it does what we want it to do, every time and without fail.

The children first learn to give instructions that produce an immediate response (that is, just one step), and then move on to plan and give instructions that achieve a delayed or automatic response (requiring several steps). For instance, they learn to record a television programme by pressing the red button on the remote control, before moving on to recording a programme later in the day. They also learn to instruct a programmable toy (such as a floor turtle) to move through a series of movements one at a time, moving forwards or backwards a particular distance, and turning through a number of degrees left or right, before moving on to programming a journey for the turtle through a model town.

Many instructions are based on the phrase *if . . . then* – this is similar to real life, when we tell a child '*If* you are good, *then* you will get a treat'. On a computer, perhaps as part of a game, it might be '*If* the word is spelled correctly, *then* play a trumpet fanfare'. We can also tell the program to *repeat* an action a particular number of times, for example, a series of instructions to *draw a 5 cm line, turn 90 degrees, repeat 4 times* will produce a square.

Now, we are not intending that the whole class should become computer programmers, merely that they have some appreciation of how programs and applications *work*, so that they understand how to control the machines' functions for their own purposes.

Exchanging and sharing ideas (communication)

When using ICT to exchange and share ideas (that is, to communicate), the children should, as always, take due consideration of the *audience* (one person, a particular group of people, or the whole world) and the *purpose of the message*, and only then decide on the presentation (see pp. 73–75 for more on this).

The children learn that e-mail and text messaging are ideal for people in a hurry, who wish merely to give information or ask a simple question – they can send the message when they are ready to do so, and the recipient can pick it up at their convenience. This avoids the frustration of missed calls on a telephone, and is a much quicker process than writing and sending letters. On the other hand, when discussion is needed, a face-to-face meeting or a phone call is likely to give a better result, and if participants are geographically separated, video-conferencing is possible, or we can combine a webcam with a voice-over-Internet connection.

The Internet has undoubtedly brought the world closer together. We can often exchange messages over several thousands of miles more quickly than popping next door to speak with a neighbour. The children learn to use trusted websites, where news arrives instantly. They have access to the ideas, interests, cultures and languages of millions of people across the whole world, people whom they have never met, and may not even have heard of before; and they can post their own comments, thoughts and opinions on the Internet for those same millions to see, read and hear.

On a technical note, it is important for the children to understand that, in the world of ICT, when words, pictures and music are stored, they have no *form* of their own – they are just a set of data (although they do carry with them an additional piece of data, which will tell the receiving equipment what it is supposed to be). This means that a picture, for instance, can be sent from computer to computer, or from a camera to a screen, quickly and easily, and then *unpacked* at the other end, when the equipment receiving it recognizes the *extra bit* and opens it in its proper form, using an appropriate program. This is completely different from non-digital words, images or sounds, which retain their format from sender to receiver.

Children are frequently asked to use presentation software in their lessons to communicate with their audience – for instance, they may be asked to make an anti-bullying poster in a PSHE education lesson. We need to be clear that the purpose of using ICT in this situation is to enhance and clarify the message. It is not enough to design and create an eye-catching poster that does not convey a convincing anti-bullying argument. However, there is no doubt that ICT allows the pupils to try out different layouts, so that they can communicate their message as clearly as possible. Without ICT, they might have used felt-tip pens, and their first draft would probably also have been their final version.

Refining and improving work in progress

People sometimes talk about the *provisional* nature of ICT, because it is so easy to edit and improve work through several versions – drafting and redrafting pieces until it is as good as it can possibly be, using a process of *trial and improvement*.

This feature is certainly useful for correcting mistakes, but it has the far greater benefit of enabling the children to be ever more inventive when creating:

- *text* – for example, stories, letters, poems – trialling vocabulary, ideas, the order of words, sentences, paragraphs, etc.;
- *images* – pictures, photographs, animations – varying line, colour, shape, size, shading, cropping, distortion, symmetry, rotation;
- *sounds and music* – modifying rhythm, sounds, tempo, melody, arrangements;
- *video* – editing, adding sound;
- *posters* – combining text and images;
- *multimedia presentations* – combining text, pictures and photographs, moving images, sounds and music in different ways;
- *web pages* – combining text, pictures and photographs, moving images, sounds and music, and making links to other pages or other websites.

An invaluable feature of this technology is the speed with which children can bring their ideas to fruition. For example, once they understand how graphs are constructed, and have drawn a number of them using squared paper, pencils, rulers and crayons, they can use ICT programs to create not just a single graph but, in an instant, many graphs of different sorts from the same data. Importantly, this allows them to spend more time on the higher-order skills involved in investigating the information shown on the graphs. This is a real bonus, providing more opportunities for children to develop problem-solving and thinking skills.

ICT – a subject in its own right?

In the past, ICT has straddled the divide between being a subject in its own right – with its own areas of knowledge and understanding and its own set of skills – and being an essential element in other subjects. This second approach is gradually overtaking the first in primary schools, so we are increasingly teaching ICT knowledge, skills and ideas alongside geographical ideas, historical knowledge, design and technology skills, and so on. This may rob some time from the other subjects, but the equipment and functions offered by ICT provide wonderful opportunities for children to extend their knowledge, understanding and interest in the other subjects far beyond the level that would be possible without it, supplementing the first-hand experiences we are able to offer, in exciting and enjoyable ways.

We do need to remember, however, that, as with any skills, the children need time to practise using ICT, so that it can be used effectively and efficiently in all situations.

Access and inclusion

The huge range of equipment and programs available through ICT means that children with learning difficulties now have many more opportunities to be included in lessons and take part in the activities enjoyed by their classmates. ICT can help in so many ways, no matter where the child's difficulties show themselves – speech, vision, hearing, communication, literacy, physical, emotional, social, and so on. This can involve:

■ using specialist equipment;

■ using specialist programs and applications/apps;

■ using everyday equipment and programs in less usual ways.

Examples include:

■ large, high-definition monitors, for those with visual difficulties;

■ interactive whiteboards, touch screens and joystick mice, for children whose difficulties include motor control;

■ specialist programs that convert words to symbols and back again, for those with limited language skills;

■ programs that focus on interpreting body language and facial expression, for children with an autistic spectrum disorder;

■ speaking word processors, which read the children's work aloud, and can also be used to read aloud the content of websites;

■ word processors with word banks, for those with severe spelling difficulties.

In addition, ICT activities allow children greater independence in their learning, which can be a boon for children with communication difficulties and those with emotional or social difficulties, as there is a reduced need for the children to approach a member of staff to ask for help.

Physical and personal safety

ICT lessons are an ideal time for the children to learn about safety procedures when using electrical and electronic equipment. These include avoiding trailing cables, keeping the volume down when using headphones, making sure seats and monitors are at the correct height, turning monitors to avoid glare and reflections, leaving space for others to walk behind their chair, and keeping food and drink away from the equipment.

But the children also need to learn about other dangers inherent in using the technology:

■ phone-calls and text messages are not always sent from a fixed, identifiable place, so children are susceptible to harassment and bullying;

■ unsavoury strangers may be using false personal information in chat rooms;

■ websites with familiar-sounding names can display offensive material;

- some websites are set up with the sole purpose of obtaining users' personal information;
- the Internet is largely uncontrolled as far as belief and bias are concerned;
- some websites allow, and even encourage, children to carry out acts such as gambling, copying music, and even self-harm.

(Becta 2009: 7–8)

We need to make the children aware of these dangers (in ways that do not cause undue alarm) and teach them how to avoid harm, develop sound judgement and be willing to seek adult advice if they suspect they are being targeted.

Flexibility

National guidelines do not prescribe any particular hardware or software that the children should learn about or use. So, as well as becoming skilled in the use of the particular equipment and programs they use in school, the children also need to learn the principles of how these work, so that they will be able to make use of other electronic equipment as well, wherever they meet it, both now and in the future.

For example, it is particularly useful to know why passwords are so important, how to save and retrieve data, how to find their way around menus, how to access *help files*; and to appreciate that these are just machines – they can go wrong, they are not intelligent, they just perform routines, and they cannot make our decisions for us – that is our responsibility.

12 Mathematics

What is maths really about?

If you ask mathematicians what maths is about, they will tell you that it is a creative subject, and that it is based on patterns, relationships and reasoning. They will probably add that it allows us to explain the world around us, and to communicate our thoughts and findings to other people. It can also be used to solve problems, providing practical and sometimes *elegant* solutions.

From a more practical perspective:

- maths allows us to be precise (without numbers, we could not even be sure how many children we have in our class – we would only have *some* or *a few*);
- maths helps us to understand and control the world – we describe our lives in terms of numbers, distances, weights, ages, times, shapes and sizes of all sorts;
- complex architecture and engineering would be impossible without maths;
- numbers are international – when we go abroad on holiday, numbers are perhaps the only writing we understand;
- maths helps us to cope with a vast range of everyday situations, such as working out value for money in a supermarket, deciding whether a new settee will fit into our living room, judging how long a journey will take, calculating how much interest we can expect from our building society account, etc.
- maths helps us to organize the larger elements of our lives, such as whether we can afford a particular house and calculating our body mass index.

In a nutshell, we can say that maths is a *life skill*, without which we would stumble through life, making hit-and-miss guesses instead of informed decisions. We want the children to be comfortable with numbers, measures and all the other mathematical ideas and skills, so that they can use maths in all these ways.

The subject is usually divided into:

- number and calculations;
- measures;

- shape and space (geometry);
- handling data (statistics).

This is only half the story, however. The children also need to learn how to use the knowledge, skills and understanding they gain in each of these areas.

Maths is all around us

Maths is everywhere and we are not always aware of it. For example, even a box of lasagne sheets offers opportunities to learn about:

- shape – faces, edges, rectangles, cuboids;
- length, area, capacity and weight;
- number – estimation and counting;
- time (for cooking);
- money and change.

Of course, the children will not think of all these ideas as *maths* – they are just interesting facts. This is when *maths* becomes *common sense* – not a school subject, but a part of everyday life. This is an important step in gaining numeracy.

Understanding is the key

Every school subject has a key set of knowledge, skills and understanding that the children need to learn, and maths is no exception.

Knowledge includes any facts that need to be remembered, for example, the names of the numbers and how to write them, mathematical vocabulary (such as *degrees*), how many pennies make a pound, how many millimetres in a metre, and so on.

Mathematical *skills* include how to set out *sums* and the procedure for carrying them out, how to use mathematical equipment (such as rulers and protractors), how to tackle complex problems that involve more than one step, etc.

The key to maths, however, is *understanding* (Ofsted 2009: 3). That is not to say that knowledge and skills are unimportant – facts, rules and methods do need to be remembered and practised, as they provide both accuracy and fluency. But it is our *understanding* that helps us to decide what maths is needed to solve a problem. Some examples of mathematical understanding include:

- knowing what numbers actually mean and how big they are;
- what particular calculations (addition, subtraction, multiplication, division) can tell us;
- what a decimal point is;

- how fractions work;
- understanding what our measures are actually measuring (weight, capacity, time, etc.);
- the scale of amounts, e.g. how much a gram is or a litre;
- what a *turn* is and why it is important in the study of *shapes*;
- what information is presented in different sorts of graphs and how reliable it is likely to be.

Our aim is to help the children to understand the world and solve problems by using mathematical principles. The secret is to introduce the key ideas in contexts that the children relate to and are genuinely interested in and then, when their understanding is more secure, to use these to explain other contexts. Many situations begin with 'Let's imagine', or 'Let's pretend', or 'It's a bit like'. For example, we might introduce the *take away* aspect of subtraction with 'Let's imagine we've baked twelve buns and put them in a tin. At teatime we take four of them out.' Once the children understand that something *has gone*, that some *are left where they were* and that we can calculate how many *are left*, we can move on to other stories where different things are *removed*, such as bursting balloons, switching off lights, extracting teeth, and so on. The children are helped to identify other everyday events that follow this pattern and to describe them using numbers.

In order to develop their understanding, children need to discuss their work with an adult, considering options, and explaining both their reasoning and their methods. Only in this way will we know whether they are on the right lines, or on the wrong track altogether, or just guessing! Remember, making sense of maths can help us to make sense of the world; equally, if we don't understand maths, it can leave us confused and dispirited.

What do children find so difficult?

There are so many different ways to misunderstand maths, but if we recognize why a child finds something difficult, then we have a better chance of helping them overcome their problem. Discussion with the child can reveal which bits of the problem they *have* understood. They may, for instance, fully understand the problem and be able to tell you how to go about solving it, but *get stuck* when actually doing it by themselves (so often a child's *partial understanding* remains hidden because they cannot provide a *complete* solution).

Difficulties with maths include:

- not understanding the idea – or not understanding the step before this one, so that the new idea isn't based on anything substantial;
- not understanding the signs and symbols (including numbers and letters);
- failing to appreciate that a *sum* has anything to do with a real situation;

- not remembering what to do in order to carry out a procedure;
- not understanding the mathematical vocabulary or jargon.

Clearly, each of these difficulties will require a different response from us.

Using and applying maths

Maths is so much more than just manipulating numbers. This section outlines the understanding, skills and attitudes the children will need, to make the best use of maths in their everyday lives. These are necessary whatever the situation and whatever the problem – whether we are working out when we should take the scones out of the oven, or how much luggage we can take on holiday.

Problem solving

Problem solving involves the following stages:

- being sure of what the problem is;
- recognizing when we can use maths to solve a problem and when we can't;
- identifying what information is needed to answer a question or problem and what information isn't relevant (consider this: 'A farmer who was born in 1970 owns 12 sheep and 5 cows; how old is the farmer?' – clearly, only one of the three pieces of information is needed to answer the question);
- making any necessary calculations, being sure to use the right *scale* (for instance, *metres* and not *millimetres*);
- following a line of enquiry in a logical way;
- building a repertoire of mathematical *tactics*, which can be applied to a wide range of everyday problems and questions;
- being prepared to try a different way if the first-choice method does not work;
- solving a problem that requires more than one step, by splitting it into smaller parts;
- choosing suitable mathematical equipment, including ICT, and using this accurately;
- making reasonable estimates of answers, so that we know when we are a long way out;
- checking results;
- relating the results of our calculations back to the original question;
- being willing to use maths to aid learning in other subjects.

Each stage here requires logical thought and action, and uses mathematical knowledge, skills and understanding (whether we recognize them as *maths* or see them as *common sense*).

Communicating

The children learn to communicate through maths, by:

- using mathematical language correctly;
- using mathematical signs, symbols, graphs and diagrams appropriately;
- organizing written work clearly for others to read and interpret;
- being clear about how the answer relates to the question.

Reasoning

They learn reasoning skills, such as:

- understanding what a *hypothesis* is;
- making hypotheses (for instance, *I think that my classmates who are taller are also heavier*);
- carrying out investigations to test hypotheses;
- thinking logically and explaining reasoning;
- solving mathematical problems, puzzles and investigations;
- using letters to describe *the general case* (this is *algebra*, but it is not at all complex at this level – for example, we might just describe the number of matchsticks needed to build triangles as *3x*, where *x* stands for the number of triangles we assemble).

General strategies

And they learn and practise general strategies, such as:

- using the process of *trial and improvement*;
- simplifying difficult tasks, for instance, rounding numbers up or down, so that we can work with easier numbers – after all, it is not usually so important that a tree in the garden is actually 1 m 89 cm tall rather than 2 metres – *roughly* or *approximately* is an important tool in maths;
- working with smaller numbers first to see whether a particular approach works;
- looking for and recognizing patterns in number, shape, and so on;
- being systematic;
- making connections between pieces of information;
- coming to a reasoned conclusion.

These strategies can't be left to chance – the children need to be taught the benefits of using these approaches, and then helped to develop them. They are likely to need plenty of time, plenty of examples, and plenty of prompts to use them.

These ideas, skills and attitudes are introduced gradually, through whatever mathematical topics the children are learning at the time. For example, the children will look for patterns, carry out investigations, solve problems and so on, while they are learning about weight, graphs, percentages or whatever.

Numbers

Numbers are at the heart of maths. They attach themselves to every other area of the subject – and indeed, to every part of our lives. They let us describe our environment with precision, explain what we see and exert some control over our lives. However, they are by no means straightforward. While they are everywhere around us, they keep shifting their meaning, depending on what they refer to and how they are set out on the page.

Let's imagine an investigation leads us to the answer '9'. We need to ask ourselves whether, in this particular context, 9 is ordinary and expected, or in some way significant and to be taken note of. For example, if it refers to a person's weight, then 9 stones is perhaps rather heavy for a primary aged child, perhaps average for a woman, but light for a man. But what if it indicates a child's weight of 9 kg? What then? How old is the child? How tall? As you can see, every number needs to be interpreted in the context of the topic being discussed. And in the classroom we, as adults, need to lead that discussion.

Numbers come in all sorts of formats:

- integers (that is, whole numbers);
- single digit numbers (0–9);
- 2-digit (10–99) and 3-digit numbers (100–999);
- larger numbers (thousands and millions);
- negative numbers (numbers below zero, usually used to describe temperatures below freezing, or a poor *goal difference* in football league tables);
- simple fractions (e.g. ¼), improper fractions (e.g. ⁵⁄₄), and mixed numbers (e.g. 1¼);
- decimal fractions (using a decimal point to indicate tenths and hundredths);
- percentages (the number of parts per 100).

Unfortunately, being able to read and write these numbers is not enough – it is essential that the children develop a sense of their size as well:

- What does *5 things* look like?
- What does *100* look like?
- What does ¼ look like? (pizzas are useful for demonstrating fractions).
- What does *a whole one* refer to?
- Is *89 a lot* more than *24*?
- Is my answer of *25* likely to be right, or should it be *250*?

It is also useful to understand which numbers are near others – either just above or just below, so that the children learn that:

- 92 is just less than 100;
- 12 is a bit more than 10;
- ⅓ is a bit bigger than ⅕;
- 43% is nearly a half.

We use ideas like this to give information with just the right amount of precision, using words and phrases such as *about, nearly, a little over* and so on (there are *just over* 300 children at our school). This is both sensible and useful, as we can avoid getting bogged down in unnecessary details. However, it is a matter of judgement, and the children need both guidance and experience when making those judgements.

The children also learn that numbers that look different might have the same value:

- ¾ is the same as ½, which can also be 0.5 or 50%;
- 0.2 is 2-tenths, which is also ⅕;
- 25% is the same as a quarter, which is also 0.25 in decimal format.

This understanding – for it is understanding, not mere knowledge – can only be gained by actively trying to get a *picture* of numbers. Bearing in mind that numbers relate to real things and that these real things can be of any size, this is no small task.

Number lines are invaluable as a visual aid to understanding numbers. They usually begin at zero: 0–10, 0–20, 0–100, 0–1,000, or even 0–1, which can show fractions, decimals or percentages.

A key feature of our number system is that it is a *decimal* number system, that is, it is based on the number *ten*. Each *column* becomes *full* with 9 items, and any more need to be packaged as a *ten* and placed in the next column to the left. This principle works not just for *tens and units*, but also for *hundreds and tens, millions and hundreds of thousands*, and even *tenths and hundredths*. It is crucial that the children understand this principle and understand that the position of a digit governs how much it is worth – this is called *place value*.

In terms of knowledge and skills, the children need to be able to:

- read numbers, and write them down;
- count on and back (starting and stopping at any number);
- count on and back in regular-sized jumps, e.g. twos, fives, hundreds;
- identify odd and even numbers, square numbers and prime numbers;
- use numbers in everyday conversation;

- put numbers in order, both when they are consecutive (such as 4, 5, 6, 7) and when there are gaps (such as 34, 190, 202, 7,005);
- find factors (numbers that multiply together to make a larger number).

The children also learn to deal with ratios and proportions, solving problems such as *scaling up* and *scaling down*, for example, to cook more or fewer buns than stated in a recipe.

Calculation

An introduction

Often, we use numbers to describe a static situation (for example, *I have 4 pets*). However, calculations are used to describe an *action* – items are *brought together*, or *taken away*, and so on.

Calculations are also used as an aid to planning, to find out what is feasible. For example, 'I have already got two rabbits in my garage, but the children have asked for another two – the present run covers 4 square metres of floor space – have I got enough room to house another two?'.

The children learn that some of the numbers in a *sum* refer to *counted groups of objects* (for instance, *4* might be a group of 4 sausages, or a distance of 4 metres, or 4 points in a game), while other numbers are part of the instruction that tells us what action to perform (e.g. +4, –6, ×3) – they should be encouraged to engage with the story in which the calculation takes place and understand what we are trying to find out by carrying out the calculation.

In the early stages of learning about calculations, the children draw pictures or diagrams, perhaps with arrows, circles and crossings out to demonstrate the actions taking place. This enables them to use both visual cues and discussion to clarify exactly what is going on in the story. Diagrams also provide a fall-back position when the children are faced with more complex stories and situations, and help them to sort out what is relevant and what is happening. It is important that the children estimate *roughly* what the answer will be, so that an error does not lead to an answer that is blatantly ridiculous in the context of the story.

What do our calculations actually tell us?

Only four types of calculation are taught in primary schools – addition, subtraction, multiplication and division.

At a basic level, **addition** is about bringing groups of objects or measurements together, to see how many objects there are altogether, or what the total measurement is. For example, we might physically move things to be together, such as emptying two packets of sweets on to a plate. Or we might just think about objects being included in a new group – for instance, as long as we know how many chairs there are in each classroom, we would not need to move them all into the hall to find out how many there are. Or we might tot up distances to see how far we will travel on our proposed tour of Wales.

Subtraction has two distinct forms. In its first form − the familiar *take away* form − we take some objects out of the group to find out how many are left. In real life (or in more exciting imaginary situations) they might have been lost, eaten, cut off, flown away, etc.

In its second form, called *comparison* or *difference*, we compare the size of two groups of objects to find out how many more there are in one, and how many less (or *fewer*) there are in the other. This is a popular topic of conversation in our everyday lives − Who can run faster (and by how much)? Which price is cheaper (and by how much)? Whose waist is smaller (and by how much)? − we humans are so very competitive!

Although these two forms of subtraction are totally separate in terms of their *story*, they share their methods of calculation. This is because, in both cases, we can *ignore* some of the objects. In the first story, they have been *taken away*, and we just need to count the objects that are *left over*. In the second story, there are the objects in the larger group that match the whole of the smaller group, and these can be ignored when we count how many *extras* there are in the larger group (and therefore *how many more*).

It is worth noting that the children have far more difficulty explaining *how much smaller* (in all contexts) than *how much bigger*. Therefore, they might carry out a calculation and find out that one runner bean is 3 cm longer than another, but then have trouble converting this same information into *the second bean is 3 cm shorter than the first*.

Multiplication is simply adding together groups of the same size (or the same measurement) over and over again to see how many there are in total. It is merely a quick way of adding, which is itself a quick way of counting. It could be counting up the value of the 5p pieces in our pocket, or counting the number of seats we have set out for the school play (we have 20 seats in each row and we now have 8 rows). Interestingly, we can calculate 20 eights or 8 twenties, and we still find out that we have 160 seats.

Division is about subtracting the same number over and over again, until there are not enough left to make another whole group. We might hear the *number sentence* $13 \div 3 = \square$ expressed as *how many 3s are there in 13?*, but it is probably more helpful to read it as *how many times can I take 3 from 13?* The difference between these two sentences is subtle, but the second version more closely describes real-life situations and will therefore make better sense to younger children.

Division has two distinctly different *stories* − *grouping* and *sharing*. In *grouping*, we have a number of objects (perhaps 25 eggs) and we wish to find out how many groups of a certain size we can make (in this case the groups would be sixes, enough to fill an egg-box, so we take six eggs at a time from the pack, and find that we can do that four times). We then have the bonus of finding out how many eggs are *left over*, which are not enough to fill another box (this is the *remainder*).

In *sharing,* we have a number of objects (perhaps the same 25 eggs) and we want to share them out equally among a known number of people (perhaps 6) to find out how many they will each be given. In this case, we could distribute the eggs on a *one-for-you, one-for-you, one-for-me* basis – or, to be more efficient, we can take six eggs out of the pack and give out one each. The number of *rounds* tells us how many each person will get. Again, there might be a remainder that tells us how many objects are left, which cannot be distributed fairly.

The calculation needed for these two stories is the same. However, the answer – *four and one left over* – needs to be interpreted carefully in the context of the question. Was the question:

- How many boxes will be filled? (answer 4), or
- How many boxes will I need? (answer 5), or
- How many eggs did they each get? (answer 4), or
- How many eggs were left undistributed? (answer 1).

If we use a calculator to work out 25 ÷ 6, we would get an answer of 4.1666. Whatever does that mean in the context of each of these questions?

Carrying out calculations

Whenever possible – and wherever this is reliable – calculations should be carried out *in the head.* When they cannot be dealt with in this way, however, the children will need to use *pencil-and-paper methods* or, as a last resort, a *calculator* or *computer.*

Children often make up their own *calculation strategies* – and clearly some of these are better than others. Our aim is to ensure that all the children have methods at their disposal which are effective, reliable, can be generalized to all numbers (or can be developed in a straightforward way to do so) and are efficient (they don't take too long).

Mental methods

Mental methods have the advantage of speed. They include:

- memorizing addition and subtraction facts (*number bonds*);
- counting on and back, using fingers where necessary, usually starting with the bigger number first;
- adding the tens first and then counting on the ones (or subtracting in the same way);
- adding a whole 10 or 100 to any number (or subtracting them);
- memorizing multiplication and division facts (*tables*);
- doubling and halving (actually multiplying and dividing by 2, of course);
- multiplying and dividing by 10 and 100;

- using knowledge about addition to carry out subtraction and/or multiplication;
- using knowledge about subtraction and/or multiplication to carry out division;
- using known facts and making minor adjustments (adding 9 can be achieved by adding 10 and subtracting 1; finding 9 × 7 can be achieved by knowing 10 × 7 and then subtracting 7);
- and *always* checking our answer against our initial estimate and deciding whether it is *reasonable* in the context of the question.

Pencil-and-paper methods

Pencil-and-paper methods include any occasion when we write something down to help us with our maths. Of course, this includes *sums*, but it could also take the form of very informal notes, both in the early stages of learning and later on.

Informal pencil-and-paper methods include:

- drawing pictures of the objects in the story – if the question is about rabbits, a young child might draw rabbits;
- drawing counters (circles, crosses, marks) to represent the objects (or rabbits);
- drawing diagrams, arrows, circles, crossings out to demonstrate the action taking place in the story (the *four rules* are all actions);
- number lines, drawing *hops* along them, forwards or backwards;
- number squares;
- notes and jottings, to remind ourselves of *where we are up to* in longer tasks.

More formal pencil-and-paper methods include traditional *sums* and *expanded forms*.

While traditional sums are undoubtedly the most efficient method of carrying out a written calculation – and they work very well for many people – it is all too easy for the children to forget what the numbers represent, what they are trying to find out, or exactly how to carry out the calculation. If this happens, they need to be able to start again, this time following a logical *transparent* series of steps, without any shortcuts or tricks. This is the so-called *expanded form* of calculation.

This *expanded form* is not an optional part of maths, but a fundamental stage of learning. Some children pass through it very quickly, while others will rely on it for years. Consider this example:

$$\begin{array}{r} 9\ 7 \\ \times\ 2\ 6 \end{array}$$

Our *expanded* method is to say:

So, we've got twenty-six lots of 97, have we? That's:
   10 lots of 97
   and another 10 lots of 97
   and 6 lots of 97.

Then each part of the calculation can be worked out in the best way the children can:

- perhaps they know that 10 lots of 97 is 970 . . .
- and then 6 lots of 90 . . .
- and then 6 lots of 7 . . .

If the children find this too difficult, should we perhaps be asking ourselves why we are using such difficult numbers – why have we not engineered a more straightforward example using 1s, 2s, 3s and 5s?

Yes, this method is slower than the original sum in its *compact* form, but it will work. Furthermore, the children can check back and see what they have done, where they are up to and what they still need to do. That is the beauty of the *expanded form* and why the children should learn it, for each area of calculation. Quite simply, they will not be *stuck* any more – or, at the very least, we will be able to see where their errors and misunderstandings lie and can teach these parts specifically.

To deal with calculations effectively, the children should ask themselves:

- Can I estimate the size of the answer? What is my estimate?
- Can I do this in my head or do I need a written method?
- Will the written method I know be helpful and reliable?
- What do I need to write down to help me calculate an answer and to keep track of my working?

Only then should they decide how to go about it.

Using a calculator or computer

Some calculations are so difficult that even written methods are too complex. These are best carried out using either a calculator or a computer. This is often the case when the children are solving real problems, and we have not been able to arrange for the numbers to be neat and manageable. When the children have sorted out the essential maths of a problem – they know which numbers need to be combined and how, and all that is left is a complex calculation involving difficult numbers – there is simply no point slogging away at the numbers and perhaps making mistakes. They should use a calculator or a spreadsheet to help them. Incidentally, the children also find these useful to check answers they have worked out mentally.

A word of caution here. Calculators and spreadsheets each have their own very precise procedures, which the children must follow if they are to get the answers they want. Then, of course, calculators have no way of dealing with *time* or *angles*, and they certainly don't offer a *remainder* when doing a *division* calculation.

There is a lot to remember when using spreadsheets, too. For example, how to make the multiplication and division signs; to begin formulae with the = sign (so we type in = 5 + 6, where we would normally write 5 + 6 =); to write the formula either in a cell or on to the formula bar; to tell the computer how many figures to show after a decimal point, and so on. Children need to be actively taught how to use calculators and spreadsheets, otherwise they won't appreciate the limitations and will therefore fail to make best use of them.

Measures

An overview

Much of the maths we use as we go about our daily lives involves *measures*:

- we *describe* objects and people (he is 1 m 32 cm tall now, and still growing);
- we *organize ourselves* (we've got half an hour left in the pool before Mum picks us up);
- we *compare things* (my onion is heavier than yours, so I win the prize);
- we *solve problems* (how much paint will I need to buy for the living-room walls?);
- we *are creative* (I think the cake will taste better if we add just 3 ml of almond essence).

The children are shown how to use measures for each of these purposes, as they learn about:

- length (distance)
- weight (mass)
- capacity
- time
- money
- area
- volume
- temperature
- angles

As adults, we generally use both a *number* and a *unit of measure* to describe a measurement, for example, 31 centimetres, 4 litres, 70 miles per hour. However, the children have a great deal to learn and understand before they get to this stage. First, they need to understand what *quality* we are talking about when we speak of measuring something. For example, they need to learn what *heaviness* is, before they can discuss *weight*; they need to learn what a *surface* is, before they can talk about *area*, and so on. These concepts can only be learned through experience of handling objects and discussing what things look like and feel like. When it is well directed, *playing in the sand-pit* can become *learning about capacity and weight*.

Once the concept of a measurement is established, the children also need to develop a sense of what heavy, hot, long, etc. are *in the context of the object being considered*. For instance, a cat is only *big* or *small* when we have some sense of how big a cat usually is, because in comparison with a horse, all cats are small!

At the same time as they develop this understanding, the children learn to compare items, describing them as *heavier, lighter, hottest, coldest*, etc. This can be done without numbers, *by direct comparison* – putting objects next to each other to see which is longer (or shorter), or filling one container with water from another to see whether it overflows, and so on. We can probably say that the children truly understand the idea when they can place three or more objects in order of weight, length, heat, etc.

This next problem is more difficult – *is the desk at school the same length as the table at home, or is it longer or is it shorter?* This needs to be answered through *measuring*, because the desk and table cannot be pushed next to each other, so we can't use the *direct comparison* method. Young children can use any *unit of measure* they like – for instance, they can count how many toy cars fit along each of the distances to be measured when they are laid bumper to bumper without any spaces in between. Any small objects could be used – pencil sharpeners, hand-spans or spoons would all fit the bill. However, the children need to appreciate that they should use the same unit (e.g. toy car) for both the desk and the table in order for their results to be meaningful. We cannot make a valid comparison if we find out that the desk is *5 big cars long* and the table is *9 small cars long*.

The next stage is to introduce the idea of a *standard measure*, which is *the same every time* and which everybody understands. For example, we can use *centimetres* because these are always the same size – in any context, anywhere in the world. However, these standard measures are not like real objects – they are only imaginary. While there are items that hold a litre of liquid and items that are a metre long, there is no such thing in real life as a *litre* or a *metre*. This is a very difficult idea indeed.

So, what does a *kilogram* feel like? What does a *litre* look like? What does a *square metre* look like? The children need to get a *feel* for these units. Have they got an example in their head of what a gram feels like? And 10 grams, 100 grams, 1 kilogram, 10 kilograms? And have they got an appreciation of how heavy a 5-year-old child is? And what is normal for a tin of beans? To make this even more difficult, a kilogram can feel heavy or light, depending on whether the object is made of polystyrene or metal, and a litre (of a liquid) can change its shape, depending on the shape of its container.

Children will already have learned to use numbers to describe a quantity of objects, for example we might ask them to get *4 spoons* out of the drawer for breakfast. Now this ability needs to be extended to working with these imaginary units of measurement and working in two or more scales at the same time, such as metres and centimetres, or kilograms and grams.

At its heart, this system is simple enough – it is similar to the 10-base number system. So 100 small units make a larger one (for instance, 100 cm is one metre). However, some measurements only work using 1,000 (for instance, 1,000 ml is one litre) and this is obviously difficult if the young children are not confident when using numbers of this size.

For each measurement, the children learn:

- to decide which *unit* is best suited to the measurement that is required;
- to estimate quantities – for instance, how tall a tree is, or how hot their bath-water is;
- to choose appropriate equipment to take the measurement;
- to use that equipment carefully and take measurements as accurately as possible;
- to read and interpret the scale on the measuring equipment, paying particular attention to the spaces between the numbers (for instance, when the pointer is between 600 grams and 650 grams);
- to make decisions about how accurately something needs to be measured for the purposes of the particular question – for example, in a swimming gala, times are measured to the nearest hundredth of a second (32.45 seconds for 50 metres), but the nearest 10 minutes or so is sufficient when we ask Mum when tea will be ready.

As well as being able to measure accurately (whatever quality is being measured), the children need to be able to discuss their findings, and draw conclusions from the information they have gained. This might include phrases such as too much, enough, not enough (e.g. *the oven is hot enough/just a bit too hot*); roughly, about, approximately; just over, just under.

Length (or distance)

While we usually call this topic *Length*, it is much broader than this, and answers the general question 'How far is it from one place to another?'. So perhaps it should be called *Distance*.

We talk about length, width, breadth, depth and height when we answer questions such as 'How far is it from the top of an object to the bottom?' or 'How far is it from one side of an object to the other?'. But we also measure the distance from one place to another – for instance, when marking out a football pitch, or travelling from one town to another.

Of course, distances are not always made of straight lines – bends and curves can be treated in the same way. In terms of our bodies, we talk about *waist measurements*, meaning *how far is it all the way round, starting and finishing at the same place?* We might do this with regard to objects, too – in a Design and Technology lesson, we might need to cut a coloured band of the correct length to decorate a papier-mâché vase we have made.

When we describe *distances*, the words we use normally indicate the direction of the measurement, whether it is up (tall/short, high/low), down (deep/shallow), or across a horizontal surface (long/short, wide/narrow, broad/narrow, thick/thin, far/near). The children learn how to use all of these appropriately, as well as the -*er* and -*est* forms (longer, longest, further, furthest, and so on).

Children also learn about *perimeter* and *circumference*, which are both special types of distance. Many children stumble over these, but they can usually avoid confusion when they link them to a concept they already understand well.

In the early stages, the children can use informal body measures, such as finger-widths, hand-spans, strides, and so on – a desk might be 8 hand-spans long, or 3-and-a-bit spans wide. Later, they might use any small items, such as pencil sharpeners or wooden rods, always making sure they touch nose-to-tail without any gaps.

The metric measurements used are millimetres, centimetres, metres, kilometres. In order to have a *reference point* for each of these, it is useful to know that a millimetre is about the thickness of a fingernail (or a piece of thick card), a centimetre is about the *depth* through a child's finger from the nail to the fingerprint, and a metre is a very long stride (or the length of a metre-stick). The children may need to walk from school to a significant landmark in order to gain a sense of how far a kilometre is. The children also learn a little about imperial measures – miles, yards, feet and inches.

It is debatable whether, as adults, we use rulers more often than measuring tapes. But in schools, children usually use rulers and metre sticks to measure straight distances, and tapes for curved distances. The children need to be shown that they start measuring from *zero* and not necessarily from the end of the ruler. There may also be times, perhaps when measuring around a particularly wiggly or bumpy object, when they need to use a piece of string, and then match this up to a ruler or tape afterwards.

In general, the longer the distance, the less accurate we need to be in our estimates and measurements. For instance, the distance from Manchester to Paris is 378 miles or 608 kilometres, but we might be happy to call this *just under 400 miles* or *about 600 km*. However, when working on a delicate piece of craftwork, the children might need to measure to the nearest millimetre.

At other times, we may need to know different levels of detail for different purposes about a single event. In the case of a sunflower competition, we need to know who grew the tallest flower (which may actually need no measurement at all – we may be able to judge this *by eye*), but the winning flower would certainly need to be measured, probably to the nearest half-centimetre, ready for an entry in the record books. Children need to be encouraged and helped to make decisions like this for themselves. Some find this very difficult indeed and are unwilling to accept anything other than complete accuracy.

Older children also learn that distance is one of the elements needed when we talk about *speed*. Speed is measured as:

- miles per hour (for vehicles);
- metres per second (for children running);
- centimetres per minute (for snail racing).

In each case, we measure how far an object (or person) travels in a set amount of time.

Weight (or mass)

In some textbooks, the topic of *Weight* is referred to as *Mass*. For the record, *mass* describes *the amount of matter in an object*, while *weight* describes *the downward pressure of an object, as caused by gravity*. In a scientific sense, they are very different. However, while we are on planet Earth, their effect is the same. So we can safely continue to use the word *weight* to describe how heavy things are as we go about our daily business.

While children usually learn about things being heavier/lighter than others quite quickly, they need a lot of varied practical experiences to gain an appreciation of what a *normal* weight is for a particular object. Only after this is established can they make the more subtle judgement as to whether an object is heavier or lighter than expected.

Children also need to take account of the material from which an object is made, as this can distort their estimate – for example, a bag of uncompacted shredded paper will tend to feel lighter than it actually is, while a small metal ball is likely to feel heavier than it is.

There is a limited range of words we use in this topic. These are:

- weigh, weight, balance, heavy/light;
- gram, kilogram, tonne;
- ounce, pound, stone, ton;
- scales.

The children learn that the standard unit of measurement is the *gram* – this is a very small amount (about the weight of a large paper clip). The next standard unit, the *kilogram*, is equal to 1,000 grams, and is the weight of a bag of sugar or a litre of water. The next unit is the *tonne*, which is equal to 1,000 kilograms, and is the weight of a small elephant or a small car. It seems strange that we should describe the weight of a horse in terms of *bags of sugar*, but in everyday conversation we just don't use any other measures before reaching a tonne. The implication of this is that the children will need to be confident in their use of numbers to 1,000, even to deal with everyday items such as packet of butter (250 grams).

Because of the big gaps between the standard units, the children will need plenty of *markers* to be able to estimate weights. This is probably best done by linking weights to particular activities, such as cooking (where weights usually range from 30 g to 200 g) or the children's own weights (which might range from 25 kg to 60 kg).

In shops and on market stalls, items are still sometimes weighed out in pounds and ounces, so the children will need an acquaintance with these terms and have some idea of how heavy these are. Again, some *markers* would be useful, perhaps pointing out that an *ounce* weighs about the same as a tablespoonful of sugar, while a pound is about half a kilogram. Stones are still commonly used for people's weight, and the children will need to learn their personal weight both in kilograms and in stones and pounds.

The children will use both pan-scales and spring balances – the skills required to use these are very different from each other. When comparing two objects, pan-scales clearly demonstrate heavier/lighter and can also be used to weigh single objects by placing standard *weights* on one side. This is a good, reliable way of finding the weight of an object, where the children can feel confident about reaching a correct result through a process of *trial and improvement*.

Spring balances are more difficult to use, as the child needs to figure out which number the finger is pointing to and also interpret the dial when it points to one of the spaces between the printed numbers. If the needle is pointing to a space between 300 g and 350 g, some fairly sophisticated maths needs to be done. Digital scales are much easier.

The children rarely need to be absolutely accurate when weighing objects. In everyday life it is more important to understand *roughly* how heavy things are than to weigh them – for example, they might need to know whether it is safe to lift a heavy object, or whether their own weight is increasing as they grow, or whether they are buying the correct sized box of breakfast cereal. Few recipes require absolute accuracy when weighing out the ingredients.

Capacity

Capacity describes how much of a substance (usually a liquid) a container will hold. So a bucket that will hold 10 litres of water has a *capacity* of 10 litres. This is not to be confused with the *volume* of water which is actually in the bucket, which might be only 2 litres or 4½ litres, or whatever.

However, in primary maths classes, the topic called *Capacity* usually deals with both of these together – the capacity of the containers and the volume of liquids held in them (and I shall do so in this section).

The words used in relation to this topic are:

- container, measuring cylinder, measuring jug, measuring spoon, pipette;
- full, empty;
- holds, contains;
- litre, centilitre, millilitre;
- pint, gallon.

The *litre* is the largest metric measure of capacity we use – we do not use kilolitres (like kilometres), so an oil-tank might have a capacity of 10,000 litres. This can result in very large numbers, which the children can find hard to picture. We also do not use centilitres as often as we use centimetres for lengths. However, we do use millilitres (ml), for example, to describe a quantity of soft drinks or medicines (where extreme accuracy is needed). We continue to use litres and millilitres in the kitchen (using a measuring jug), in the science lab (using a measuring cylinder) and in the garden (variously using pipettes, jugs and buckets).

However, when we go shopping, we seldom look carefully at labels to find out the capacity of bottles or the volume of liquid contained in them. Unless we are calculating *value for money*, we are more likely just to buy a *large* bottle or a *small* bottle of drink, shampoo or sauce. The children will need to learn to make judgements about how accurate they need to be when making decisions about capacity and volume.

Time

Time – an introduction

Time is probably the most difficult topic to learn because:

- It is *invisible* – unlike all the other *measures* we can't see it, touch it or feel it.
- There are two distinctly different measurements of time – one answers the question 'when?' and the other answers the question 'how long?' (these are often used together – 'What time is Granny coming round to visit?' 'How long have we got before she gets here?').
- There is a huge vocabulary associated with the idea of time.
- It is sometimes very precise (at the Olympic Games in Beijing, Usain Bolt won the 100 m in a record time of 9.69 seconds), but for much of the time it can be rather vague (I'll be across *later*) or ambiguous (I'll be there *in a minute*).
- Our perception of time differs, depending on what we are doing – sometimes it seems to fly by (especially when we are enjoying ourselves) and at other times it can drag unmercifully.
- It is never still – just when we think we've pinned it down, it's already moved on.

Time is also one of the most important topics in maths. It is the one we use to organize ourselves and our activities.

Time – when?

In this part of the topic, the children learn to describe a point in time. In everyday life, there are lots of ways to do this – the *point in time* can be as precise as *to the second* or as general as *to the century*, and everything in between.

The children learn to:

- organize their days – around mealtimes and sleeping, in the first instance;
- organize their weeks – through days and weekends, and reciting the sequence of days;

- know when significant dates occur during the year – months, seasons, birth-days and holidays – this is particularly difficult when a child has experienced only five or six years during their lifetime;

- tell the time of day using analogue clocks – o'clock, half-past, quarter-past and quarter-to, knowing that the short hand on a clock-face tells us the approximate time, and that this is fine-tuned to the nearest 5 minutes or minute by the minute hand;

- tell the time of day using digital clocks and watches, and understand the significance of the read-out – 6.58 is very nearly 7 o'clock;

- read timetables and displays in 12-hour and 24-hour formats, understanding am and pm;

- know that we turn the clocks forwards in spring and backwards in autumn, and the implications of this;

- use calendars;

- use the words before/after, earlier/later, now/soon, today/yesterday/tomorrow;

- describe regular events as daily, weekly, annual;

- compare frequency, using the words always, usually, often, sometimes, rarely, never.

Our lives seem to be controlled by time. We set alarm clocks to get out of bed in the morning, we begin and finish work at particular times, TV programmes begin at set times, and so on – we use time to plan our lives and coordinate them with those of other people. Because we refer to it so often, the children need to understand not only the scale of time, but also how accurate they need to be – again, this is a matter of judgement and is gained only through experience.

Time – how long?

This aspect describes the amount of time that passes between one point in time and another. In our everyday lives, we estimate, measure and calculate the passage of time so often – finding out how long it is until playtime, making sure our boiled egg has just the right consistency, racing and competitions, planning a project so that all the jobs get done in time, etc.
The children learn:

- to use clocks, watches, stop-watches and calendars as an aid to measuring and calculating the passage of time;

- to estimate, measure and calculate how long an activity will last (when we know the start time and finish time), when it might finish (when we know the start time and how long it takes), or when it would have started (when we know the finish time and how long it took);

- to describe a person's age (from being born to the present) and how much older or younger one person is than another;
- the relationships between time periods, for example, how many days in a week or seasons in a year. Confusingly, we use 4, 7, 10, 12, 24, 28, 30, 31, 60, 365, 366, 100 and 1,000 for different time relationships;
- that we cannot use a calculator to calculate *how long*?

Time is the measurement that we use more than any other, by a long way.

Money

Money is a man-made invention. Far back in history, people would exchange items directly, for instance, swapping a chicken for a bag of carrots. When money was invented, the person with a chicken could exchange it for some money and could then choose what to buy, rather than being tied to what his neighbours had available at the time. So money has no value of itself – it is just a *purchase waiting to happen*. The children learn that a *fair trade* happens when we exchange money for an item of the same value.

In terms of buying and selling, the children learn:

- to read price labels and write their own;
- to buy single items, or several items, offering the correct money;
- that we can also give the shopkeeper more than the cost and receive *change*;
- to calculate change from all reasonable amounts.

An early concept is that a 5p coin is worth the same as 5 pennies. There is no logical reason why the little silver coin should be worth more – it just is, and this needs to be remembered.

Linking with other parts of the curriculum (particularly PSHE education), we also guide the children to gain an appreciation of the value of money and to make good purchases, that is:

- how much things cost in relation to one another;
- what is a reasonable price to pay for an item;
- whether we can afford a particular item.

When they are young, children see no real difference between buying a packet of sweets and buying a bicycle, but we want them to appreciate that, for instance, a pair of shoes might cost as much as a week's food shopping at the supermarket. So we talk about things being *dearer* or *cheaper*, we talk about *discounts* and *bargains*, and teach the children to calculate the actual cost of *half price*, or a *BOGOF* (buy one, get one free), or a *20% discount*. We teach them to be wary of advertising that offers a new car for *only* £12,000, and to make their own decisions about value and worth.

As adults, we often use a calculator to help us keep track of our money, and it is very well suited to the job, just so long as we remember to take care with the decimal point. The children learn to interpret the figures on the screen carefully – for example, 2.4 as £2.40, and not £2.04. Errors of this sort can largely be avoided if the children always enter zeros on to the calculator. So, for example, 24p is entered as 0.24 and 9p is entered as 0.09 – it helps them to be *on the lookout for zeros*. Older children begin to use spreadsheets for budgeting, perhaps planning, and then tracking, the costs and the income from a mini-enterprise or a class visit.

Area

Area describes the size of a surface. It can be the surface of a two-dimensional shape, such as a wall, a table-top, a piece of paper or a field. Or it can be the *outside surface* of a three-dimensional object, such as the roof of a building, a ball or a box. We might be interested in the whole surface or only a part of it. The surfaces might be perfectly flat or rough, and the shape of the surface could be geometric or very irregular indeed, such as a leaf or a hand.

The children learn that our standard unit for measuring *area* is the square. We could have used rectangles, triangles or hexagons – in fact, any shape that *tessellates*, that is, they leave no gaps when laid out side-by-side to cover a surface. But we could not have used pentagons or heptagons or stars, because they would leave gaps. So the standard is the square. We can count squares to find out how large a surface is (that is, to find its area). We use square millimetres (mm^2), square centimetres (cm^2) and square metres (m^2) in the classroom, although there are also square kilometres (km^2) and hectares (a 100 m × 100 m square), as well as square miles and acres.

The children learn that, to *calculate* the area of a rectangle (for example, one that is 7 cm by 5 cm), we find out how many centimetre squares are in one *row* (this might be 5 or 7, depending on which way we are looking at the rectangle), then decide how many rows there are (that will be 7 or 5), then calculate 5 sevens or 7 fives, to see how many centimetre squares cover the surface of the rectangle. Some shapes (for example, a capital H-shape) can be split into smaller rectangles (two upright ones and a horizontal one), and each section dealt with separately.

The children deal with triangles, curved shapes and irregular shapes by covering them with a transparent grid of centimetre squares and then counting the squares that cover the surface. They are taught to deal with half-squares and part-squares by matching a *big-part* with a *small-part* to make a whole square.

In real life, we do not calculate *area* very often, although we might talk in more general terms about a *geographical area* (to mean a region) or we might say that some autumn leaves have been caught by a gust of wind and blown over a wide area. However, we might use the mathematical version of *area* to decide how much paint to buy when decorating the living room – calculating the area of the walls and ceiling, and matching this with a chart on the tin telling us how many square metres of wall each litre of paint will cover.

Volume

Volume is about the amount of *three-dimensional space* an object takes up. The object can be either gas, liquid or solid. If it is a gas or a liquid, we usually deal with it through the *Capacity* topic, measuring it in litres (l) or millilitres (ml). If it is a solid, we usually deal with it here, measuring it in cubic metres (m^3) or cubic centimetres (cm^3).

The children learn to calculate volume from *distance* measures. For example, how much space is there inside a cuboid (that is, a rectangular box) which is 5 cm by 8 cm, and 4 cm tall? Answer: we can find this out by filling the box with centimetre-cubes. The first *layer* of centimetre-cubes will contain 8 rows of 5 cubes (that is, 40 cubes), and then we can see that there will be 4 layers like this, so the box would contain 4 lots of 40 cubes, that is 160 cubes. So the volume of the box is 160 cm^3. Of course, it is also useful if the children recognize a cubic metre, which is about the size of a bag of gravel delivered by a builder's merchant to a neighbour who is up-dating his drive.

Temperature

Most of us will talk about the temperature at least once every day, in terms of the weather, our cups of tea, the water in our bath, and so on. In many cases, we do not measure the temperature with a thermometer. Rather, we develop a sense of what is *normal* and comment that it is hotter or colder than we would have expected – 'It's warm for this time of year', or 'Drink up your tea before it goes cold'.

When we need to be precise, we measure temperature using *degrees Celsius* (for instance, 23°C). The children learn to read air thermometers and medical ones. Measuring temperature is mostly dealt with in science lessons, but it strays into maths, first because the children do actually measure the temperature, and second because, in their *number* lessons, the children learn about negative numbers and temperature is an ideal context for this study – 'Tomorrow, it will be minus two degrees – that's very cold'.

Angles

An angle is a measurement of how much something *rotates* – that is, how far it *turns round*, without moving its basic position. Examples of rotation are:

- the hands on a clock turning;
- a door opening on its hinge;
- a key turning in a lock;
- an ice-skater spinning round on the spot.

In each case, the *core* of the object stays in its original position (except that it turns), while another part moves around it. For example, the *shaft* of a key stays still as the *blade* moves around it.

The *angle* is a measure of how far round a thing has turned. The measurement is based on a full turn being 360 degrees (360°). In our example, we might need to turn the back-door key a half-turn, or 180°, to unlock it.

Children often confuse angles with distance. If we think about the minute hand moving from 20-past to 25-past on a wrist-watch and then on Big Ben's face, the *ends* of the pointers will have moved different distances, but they will have turned through the same angle – that is, 30°.

The children probably first learn about turning in PE warm-ups and games, where they *turn a ¼ turn to the right* and so on, or in geography games, where a child guides a programmable toy around a route, using instructions such as *forward 3 paces – right 90° – forward 4 paces*.

The children will need careful teaching to master the protractor – the tool we use to measure the amount of turn, because:

- they need to match the *zero* line on the protractor to the starting direction;
- they need to match the centre of the zero line to the point where the turn originates (like the spindle on the clock).

The main use of angles in the primary classroom is when the children learn about *shapes*.

Shape and space (geometry)

Shape

Two-dimensional shapes

Two-dimensional (or 2-D) shapes are flat ones. In the classroom, we often use plastic shapes that the children can handle, but these are not strictly two-dimensional, as they do have *thickness*. Real two-dimensional shapes have no thickness and are therefore only *true* in drawings or perhaps in a laser image. We can measure how long they are, and how wide they are, but we ignore any thickness.

In real life, things can take on all sorts of weird and wonderful shapes, and the language learned in maths lessons can help the children to describe them, whatever they are and wherever they meet them. How would we describe a hand print, or a print from an oak tree leaf?

However, most of the maths teaching about shapes is carried out in the context of just a few *geometric* shapes:

- circles and semi-circles;
- triangles – in *equilateral* triangles, the sides are all the same length; in *isosceles* triangles, just two sides are the same length; and in *scalene* triangles, all the sides have different lengths;

- quadrilaterals – these all have four sides, and include squares, rectangles, rhombuses, parallelograms, kites and trapeziums;
- pentagons, hexagons, heptagons and octagons – 5, 6, 7 and 8 sides respectively.

The children also learn the word *polygon*, which is a general word for any two-dimensional shape.

The children learn to:

- recognize these shapes (in lessons and in real life) and name them;
- sketch them;
- draw them accurately, using rulers, protractors, curves, compasses and set squares.

They learn about their properties and how to describe them:

- lines or sides – how many? how long are they? are any of the same length?
- vertices (corners) – how many? and angles – how many degrees?
- centres, diagonals, the radius and diameter of circles;
- intersections – where lines cross, from vertex to vertex (corner to corner).

They learn whether lines are:

- straight or curved;
- parallel;
- perpendicular (at right angles to each other).

They learn about individual shapes being:

- regular (with lines and angles all the same size) or irregular;
- symmetrical – reflective symmetry and rotational symmetry.

For example, when considering the *rhombus*, the children will learn to describe it as *a quadrilateral, with four straight sides and four vertices, where all the sides are of equal length, opposite sides are parallel, and opposite angles are equal in size. The angles at the vertices add-up to 360°. Lines drawn from opposite vertices intersect at the centre.*

Angles

When describing geometric shapes, we often talk about *angles*. However, as we have already seen, an angle is a measure of *turn*, so how can it be used to describe a shape? First, the children are taught to recognize the point at which two lines touch (the *vertex*). When we measure the *angle* between two lines, we pretend that one line used to lie on top of the other and then measure how far the top line appears to have turned.

The children learn that a quarter turn is 90°, which is also called a *right angle* – this is a key idea in geometry, which will crop up again and again throughout the children's school career. A half-turn is a turn through 180° and looks as though it is a straight line, although it is, in fact, two separate lines, joined at the vertex.

Using 90°, 180° and 270° degrees as *markers*, the children develop the skill of estimating the angles on a whole range of geometric shapes. A protractor can be used to give a precise measurement.

Symmetry

The most common type of symmetry in two-dimensional shapes is *reflective symmetry*. This is where a shape could be folded along a central line, so that the two sides would sit exactly one on top of the other. Young children are often introduced to this idea by painting half a butterfly and then folding the paper – wet paint produces a whole, symmetrical butterfly. These patterns have just one line of reflective symmetry.

Squares have four lines of reflective symmetry: one vertical, one horizontal and two diagonals, while rectangles have only two lines of reflective symmetry – the vertical and horizontal lines, because when we fold along the diagonal lines the two halves do not fit exactly on top of each other.

The children also learn about *rotational symmetry*. This is where we stick a pin through a shape and fix it to a board, and then turn it around slowly. If, before it completes a whole turn, the shape looks the same as when it started, then we can say that the shape has *rotational symmetry around the position of the pin*. If the pin is in the middle:

- a square will show rotational symmetry three times (after 90°, 180° and 270°);
- a rectangle once (after 180°);
- a circle an infinite number of times.

Three-dimensional shapes

Three-dimensional (or 3-D) shapes are *solid shapes*. For each shape, we can measure its *distances* in three directions – its *height*, its *width* and its *depth* (from front to back).

The most common 3-D shapes used in the classroom are:

- cuboids and cubes;
- spheres and hemispheres;
- prisms and cylinders;
- pyramids and cones;
- five regular polyhedrons, where all the faces are the same shape and size; the children meet five of these: the tetrahedron (4 faces), the cube (6 faces), the octahedron (8 faces), the dodecahedron (12 faces) and the icosahedron (20 faces).

Rather like the 2-D shapes, the children learn to recognize each of these shapes (both in maths lessons and in real life), name them and describe them, in terms of their faces/surfaces (how many? are they flat or curved? what shape? are they all the same, or different? regular or irregular?), their edges or sides (how many? straight or curved? how long? are any of the same length?), their vertices (how many? what angles? how many degrees?) and their base (one of the faces, which we conveniently think of as being *at the bottom*). The children also learn to sketch them and to build them, using kits of various sorts, and by folding along the lines on a sheet of paper where their *net* has been drawn.

Although computers can show three-dimensional shapes really well, this is one area where it is vital that the children handle the shapes themselves, turning them around in their hands and investigating them fully. In the early stages, the children might sort the shapes into those that will roll and those that will not, or those with six faces and those with more, as they seek out their properties.

Space

In terms of maths, *Space* is about:

- position – where things are;
- direction – where they move to;
- movement and angles – how they move to their new position (sliding or turning).

Position

Position is one of those topics that the children are quick to learn and then transfer to *common sense*. The words usually tell us where things are *in relation to something else* – for instance, 'the kettle is *on* the worktop'. We always need a reference point and we assume that the position is static (at least at the moment when we describe it). These words might follow the phrase 'It is . . .':

- on, on top of, above, over, under, below, underneath;
- in, inside, outside;
- in front of, behind, beside, next to;
- in between, opposite;
- near to, far away from;
- parallel to, perpendicular to;
- to the N, NE, E, SE, S, SW, W, NW . . . of.

Also included in this topic is the use of *coordinates* to describe a position on a grid, using letters and numbers (for example, the treasure is in square D3), and progressing to use only numbers (the treasure is in square 4, 3). This is then extended to describe positions on a graph.

Direction

When things move, or are moved, we might use words such as these to follow the phrase 'It went . . .':

- to, towards, away from;
- onto, over, under, up, down;
- into, out of;
- forwards, backwards, sideways;
- left, right;
- along, across, through;
- clockwise, anticlockwise;
- horizontally, vertically, slanting, diagonally;
- N, NE, E, SE, S, SW, W, NW . . . wards.

Movement

In maths, we talk about things moving in three different ways, and, of course, each has its own special name:

- A *translation* is just a regular movement from one place to another. We usually talk about how far it went and in which direction. So something might *translate* 3 metres to the south.
- A *reflection* is when something flips over. It might *reflect* horizontally or vertically.
- A *rotation* is when something turns on the spot, as though on an imaginary pin, either through its centre or through one of its vertices. We might say that an object *rotates* through a whole turn, a half turn, a quarter turn or through a right angle (90°), an acute angle (less than 90°), an obtuse angle (more than 90°), or a reflex angle (more than 180°), or through a particular number of degrees.

The children learn to draw these different sorts of movements on grids. This allows them to count squares as an aid to measuring distances and directions.

Handling data (statistics)

Handling data

An introduction

In the greater part of maths, we deal with individual pieces of information – things tend to be either counted or measured, and we can use calculations to answer questions or solve problems about those things.

However, information does not always come to us in bite-size chunks like this. Sometimes, in order to answer questions or solve problems, we need to analyse many more pieces of information (or *data*). A key feature of *handling data* is the principle that *a picture is worth a thousand words* – by investigating data through pictures, tables, charts and graphs, we can simplify large quantities of data, making it easier to identify patterns and therefore reach conclusions. Mathematicians speak rather grandly about *interrogating* data.

A common approach is for the children to investigate a question using a survey or a questionnaire, perhaps 'Who likes which toys best?'. They learn skills such as:

- classifying (e.g. soft toys, construction toys, games);
- preparing and asking questions clearly;
- collecting, recording and organizing responses;
- displaying their findings, using ICT where it is helpful to do so;
- drawing up, reading and interpreting lists, tables, diagrams, charts and graphs.

Older children might investigate how the temperature changes throughout the day. They would, of course, need to take readings at regular intervals through the day, but a single day might not yield enough information to reach any valid conclusions, so they would need to decide how often to take the temperature each day, for how many days, and whether they need to repeat the process in spring, summer, autumn and winter.

Presenting information on graphs and charts

Clearly, when carrying out an investigation, the children could end up with a large amount of data, which would be incomprehensible if it were just listed. They need to decide:

- What sorts of charts or graphs they will use to help them to analyse the data.
- How they will organize and present their findings.

In the early stages, the children draw pictures and talk about them. Later, the pictures become more stylized and develop into diagrams, before moving on to constructing and interpreting a range of charts and graphs, including:

- *Tally chart* – used to record data when information becomes available one piece at a time, for instance, when counting different coloured cars passing the school; usually collected in fives, like a *five-bar gate*, so that the five-times table can be used to count up the total.
- *Block graph* – each block represents one object; the scale is numbered.
- *Bar chart* – all the *blocks* are joined together to make a single bar; bars are usually separated from each other and may be vertical or horizontal; the numbered scale does not show all the numbers – it may be set out in 5s or 10s, for example – so bar-lengths in between need to be judged.

- *Histogram* – a bar chart, where the bars touch each other, to show that data is *continuous*; used for measurements, rather than objects (e.g. how many children are between 1 m 10 cm and 1m 19 cm; 1 m 20 cm and 1 m 29 cm, etc.).

- *Pictogram* – a picture represents a number of objects, so a picture of a car might represent 10 cars in a car park; half a picture may also be used to represent 5 cars.

- *Line graph* – we start with a series of dots showing verified information over time – for instance, how tall a child was on each birthday. By drawing a line joining the dots, we can estimate the unmeasured height between birthdays.

- *Pie chart* – a circular *pie-shaped* chart that may be divided into segments, like a pizza; the size of each segment represents the proportion of the whole number that matches a particular criterion – e.g. the number of cars of each colour; the bigger the portion, the more cars, but it does not show the actual number of cars in each section.

- *Scatter graph* – here we are looking for patterns using two variables – for example, we might investigate whether there is a relationship between our height and how long we take to read 100 words of text, so we ask many children to take a test; on a graph, we show the two variables along the X-axis (horizontal, left to right) and the Y-axis (vertical, bottom to top), and then we plot all the times against the height of each individual; we see a scatter of points. Now, does the pattern show a relationship? Children do, after all, grow taller as they get older and therefore taller children might have had more experience of reading? But not for adults? And what about for children of the same age?

- *Carroll diagram* – this is a grid that is used to sort objects according to two criteria; we might sort two sets of information, such as *girls/boys* and *left-handed/right-handed* into a 2-by-2 grid, to give 4 groups: l-h-girls, r-h-girls, l-h-boys and r-h-boys.

- *Venn diagram* – used to explore objects using two or more criteria, where each object might possess one criterion, or the other, or both, or neither – for instance, when investigating the cars on the car park, there may be Fords, and there may be yellow cars, and one might be a *yellow Ford*; there might also be a motor bike.

(DfEE 1999: 90–3 and 114–17)

The children learn to include a title, describing exactly what the chart shows. Where applicable, graphs should also have their X-axis (the horizontal one) and Y-axis (the vertical one) named. Numbers showing the *scale* should be clearly marked.

However, drawing graphs by hand can be both complicated and time con-suming, so the children usually practise using simplified data and then move on quickly to using computer programs, which are usually straightforward to use, to bring together sets of data that are larger or more complex. In each case, the children learn to interpret the information depicted on the charts and graphs, and to answer questions based on that information. They also need to recognize when there is not enough information to reach a conclusion.

What is an average and a range?

We use the word *average* quite a lot in everyday conversation – we might say 'This coat is about the average price for coats of this type'. However, mathematicians have identified three different meanings for this word, which are similar to each other, but are quite distinct. So the sentence could mean:

■ this price is the one that comes up most often (called the *mode*), or

■ if we place all the coats in order of price, this one comes exactly in the middle – that is, it is the 4th in a line of 7 coats, or 6th in a line of 11 coats (called the *median*), or

■ we add up the cost of buying one of each of the coats and divide the total by the number of coats (called the *mean*).

Our purpose in using an average is to use a single number to *summarize* a larger group of numbers. The three versions of *average* are likely to give similar results, but they may differ – in this example, it would depend on the balance of cheaper and more expensive coats. The older children will learn to use these three ways of comparing groups of numbers.

The *range* is less complicated – it is simply the distance between the highest number and the lowest number. In our example, it would be the difference between the highest and lowest price. We might write it as *the range is £23.49*.

Chance, uncertainty and probability

Generally, young children have the idea that the world is a place built on certainties – it's just that they haven't found out exactly what these facts are. As adults, we know differently.

The children are asked to estimate the likelihood of something happening in the future, for example, that all the girls in the class will get all their spellings correct, or the local football team will win on Saturday. Of course, before they can make a reasonable estimate they will need either experience of these situations, or additional information about past performance. For instance, they will need to have some idea of how well the girls have performed in their spelling tests in the past, and perhaps, how difficult the words are likely to be.

In the early stages, the children describe the probability as: impossible/unlikely/ not very likely/possible/evens/probable/very likely/certain. They often need a lot of help to differentiate between events that are *impossible* and those that are *unlikely*, as wishful thinking occasionally creeps into the discussion.

The children progress to using numbers to describe the probability on a scale ranging from zero (impossible) to one (certain) – we normally use decimal fractions or percentages for this. So, for example, the *one-in-four* chance we have of picking a heart from a well-shuffled pack of cards could be described as a 0.25 chance, or a *25%* chance. A weather forecast predicting *a 0.9 probability of rain* means the same as *a 90% chance* – either way, it is very likely to be wet!

Some probabilities can be *calculated*, such as how likely it is that a coin will come up heads, or that a green sock will be drawn from a drawer (when we know what socks are inside). The children also learn how probability is used to assess risks – how likely is an accident to happen and how serious is it likely to be?

Summary

Maths touches on most areas of our lives in one way or another. So how can we tell when the children are making good progress in the subject? Well, they are making progress when:

- they extend their knowledge, or facts are *recalled* more quickly;
- they learn a new skill, or improve a skill they have already learned;
- they understand something they did not understand before;
- they apply their knowledge, skills or understanding in a new, unfamiliar situation;
- they grow in confidence;
- they deal with problems more easily;
- they improve the way they set about tasks.

Of course, a child does not have to complete a full task in order to make progress – often improvements can be just a small step in any one of these areas – but that is still real progress.

13

Modern Foreign Languages (MFL)

What are modern foreign language lessons really about in primary schools?

As people move ever more easily from one country to another, we can't be sure just which languages our children will want, or need, to learn in the future. So, while most adults who have been to school in the UK have learned either French, Spanish or German as a second language, twenty-first century children might want, or need, to learn Mandarin, Russian, Arabic, or any other language, either to help them in their job, to keep in touch with friends and family, or because they wish to holiday or live abroad (DfES 2002: 5). With this long-term view in mind, the focus for children in primary schools is to get a feel for foreign languages in general, rather than concentrate on perfecting a single language. This is done by acquiring knowledge, understanding and skills that can be *recycled* when learning any foreign language in the future.

Consequently, the goals for children at primary level are to:

- improve their general listening skills, but particularly to develop an *ear for languages*;
- understand how languages *work* – the sounds, rhythms and patterns, how words and phrases are built up into sentences, the grammar and rules;
- communicate at a basic level in a foreign language – speaking, listening, reading and writing;
- become comfortable with foreign languages and cultures;
- learn a little about how people live in other countries and show respect for their way of life;
- and, importantly, learn how to learn a new language.

It is a fact that more than a million children in UK primary schools already speak two or more languages – children living in London use more than fifty different first languages between them. These children can bring such a lot to the lessons, because they already hear and use different sounds and already use differing language structures to build sentences. In addition, they have some appreciation of the culture of places where their first language is spoken (or, at least, they can find this out from their parents).

These children represent a valuable resource for investigating and exploring languages in the classroom. For example, if the language being taught is French, then children with English as their first language can compare French and English, while children with Polish as their first language can compare French with both English and Polish, and can pass on their observations to the other children and to the staff in the class.

In most primary schools the children are extremely positive about learning a new language (Ofsted 2011: 6) – they are keen to repeat words, greeting adults enthusiastically with *bonjour* and *ça va?* whenever they think it appropriate throughout the day, and asking how other words and phrases would be expressed in French and what it is like to live in France.

In summary, then, learning a modern foreign language at primary school is basically a general language course – it builds on the children's previous literacy lessons, adds a cultural element and provides a starter kit for future language learning. The approach is one of exploration and investigation – the children explore languages and the way they work, and investigate the culture and way of life of the people for whom they are the first language.

Learning the language

Just as when learning a first language, the foreign language course begins with *speaking and listening*, and progresses to *reading and writing*. However, these last elements can often be introduced quite quickly, because the children have already gained a good understanding of the link between the spoken and written forms of language in English.

Because we want the children to be able to apply their learning to any number of languages in later life, they learn so-called *core language structures*, which can be reused in different contexts. For example, the phrase *I would like . . . please (Je voudrais . . . s'il vous plaît; Ich möchte . . . bitte)* can be adapted in many ways. By inserting a noun, we can be quite precise in our shopping:

- *I would like an ice cream please.*
- *Je voudrais frites* (chips)*, s'il vous plaît.*
- *Ich möchte Kaffee* (coffee) *bitte.*

As soon as the children understand the way a language structure works, they can create their own phrases and sentences – most nouns can be dropped into this structure to make a new sentence. So the children can ask for food or drink, or even pester their parents for a pet: *Je voudrais un chiot* (a puppy)*, s'il vous plaît, maman.*

This method of learning allows the children to move on to creating their own sentences very quickly. Moreover, it is a very efficient way of learning, because they do not need to memorize each individual sentence they might wish to use. For example, the holiday phrases *my tyre has burst* and *my kettle is broken* can both be conveyed with the phrase *my * does not work (mon * ne marche pas; mein * ist kaputt)*.

In this way, the children get a feel for the way the language works. By comparing languages, they realize that, while languages might sound different, and go about things in different ways, each one has its own set of structures or conventions, and is fairly consistent within itself.

Some of the most common words, phrases and structures that can be reused and recycled in all languages, include:

- greetings: hello, goodbye, how are you?
- please, thank you
- a, the
- I, you, he, she, it, we, they
- verbs: tenses – past, present, future
- verbs *to be* and *to have*
- nouns: singular and plural
- possession: my, your, his, her, our, their
- the order of words
- numbers, age, money, how many?
- the alphabet: letter names and sounds
- titles: Mr, Mrs, Miss, Ms
- what is this? this is, that is
- yes, no
- verbs: endings change for different people
- verbs: negatives
- I like, don't like, prefer
- nouns: masculine, feminine, neuter
- adjectives: big, little, colours
- asking *where is the *?*, prepositions
- times, days and months
- unfamiliar sounds and letters to match

(CILT 2009)

Of course, the children use more words than these in their lessons, particularly words that relate specifically to the topic being discussed. For example, if the children are learning about colours, they might also learn the word for *balloon*, but the main attention will be focused on the colours, which can be reused again and again in different contexts.

A note on negatives: learning to change a sentence from a positive (*I like*) to a negative (*I don't like*) effectively doubles the number of sentences the children can use!

At first the children copy the good model of language given to them. Later they substitute words into the structures to make their own phrases and sentences. With more experience, they will be able to link phrases together, perhaps even making a presentation to the class:

Hello. My name is Max. I am ten years old. I live in Manchester.
I live in a house with my mum, my dad and my little brother.
He is called Thomas and he is five years old. We have two cats.

Or perhaps they will prepare and rehearse what they would say if they became detached from their parents while on holiday abroad.

It is vital that the children have frequent opportunities to hear the language spoken fluently as it is spoken by native speakers, even if it is slowed down to make it more accessible. In this way, the children hear (and can mimic) new sounds and rhythms – for example, the bouncy delivery of Spanish, where the accent in most words lies on the second-to-last syllable – _uno muchacho_ (a boy), rather than _uno muchacho_ or _uno muchacho_. The key thing here is that the children *develop an ear* for the new language, so that they can reproduce the patterns when they bring words, phrases and sentences together. This mirrors the way the children learned their first language – they were exposed to the sound of the language when they were babies, before developing their own language skills, beginning with single words and progressing to more complex language structures.

While the children might have been using their first language for seven years or more, and therefore speaking fluently in everyday situations, their *understanding* of it might be less well developed than their *knowledge*. A fresh approach, through a new language, gives them opportunities to revisit and reinforce some of the language structures they have been learning in their first language – things like the function of an adjective in a sentence, how words are made up of syllables, verb tenses, and so on, and we can also remind them of the correct vocabulary when discussing language.

On top of this, the children are also introduced to the idea that language is constantly changing. Many English words originate from our multicultural heritage – as people have moved to the UK, they have brought with them words and phrases that have become part of the general vocabulary. And as travel and communications have increased in scale and speed, hundreds of international words are added to our language every year.

Listening and speaking

Here, we include all four aspects of spoken communication:

- listening and understanding;
- speaking, but not interacting – activities such as reciting a rhyme, or singing;
- talking with somebody, which involves both listening and responding to them;
- body language and gesture such as shaking hands in more formal situations.

The stages of development are very similar to the stages children pass through when they learn their first language: listening is followed by speaking, which is followed by talking and gesture. The big advantage when learning a second language is that the children already know a great deal about the way communication works. They know, for example, that the things we say and hear are supposed to make sense, that we take turns when speaking, that questions are followed by answers, and that foreign languages sound different, so we might need to use a particular accent and rhythm. Importantly, they also know something of the way the world works, which makes it easier to predict what a speaker might be saying in any particular context.

Probably the most important thing we can do to aid listening and speaking is to provide a good model of the language for the children, so that they can *tune in* when listening and *mimic* when speaking. Ideally, this is provided by staff in the classroom, but we can also make use of visitors, webcams, Internet websites and recordings.

Through listening carefully, the children learn to:

- pick out unfamiliar sounds in the new language, such as the *j* in French and Spanish, or the *ch* in German, and perhaps discuss which sounds they like, and which are easy or difficult to reproduce;
- identify individual words within the flow of speech;
- recognize how set phrases and language structures are adapted for use in different circumstances.

Then they can move on to:

- understanding and responding to classroom instructions (for example, *sit down*, *come here*, *quiet please*), and playing games such as *Simon Says*;
- understanding a story being read to them, first with picture prompts and then without;
- joining in with singing or with repeated phrases in a story;
- recreating authentic sounds and using correct pronunciation in the new language;
- describing pictures and scenes with single words and short phrases;
- using language for a wider range of purposes, such as expressing likes and dislikes, or speaking about their work, by substituting fresh words into set phrases and structures;
- telling a short story, after preparation;
- taking part in dramatic pieces that involve two or more people talking together socially;
- taking part in question-and-answer sessions about a particular topic, using set phrases;
- generating their own language to hold a very short conversation that they have prepared beforehand;
- holding a short, real conversation with a native speaker.

Children hear their own language every day, at home, on television and at school, but they probably hear their new language only at school, and the weekly MFL lessons are not really long enough to allow them to develop their ear for the language. Consequently, regular short sessions, in addition to the main lesson, are extremely beneficial.

Reading and writing

The children use many of the same skills when reading in a foreign language as they do when reading in their first language. They read common words and phrases *by sight* – words such as *the, a, I, he, she* and phrases such as *there is a . . .*, or *my name is . . .*

They use *phonics* to read unfamiliar words. They already know a good deal about English phonics and now add in new sounds, new letter combinations, and perhaps written accents and other marks attached to letters.

They also know that the words, phrases and texts they read should make sense. So they might be able to predict what particular words might mean by noticing their position in the sentence and the way they are used (for example, does the flow of the sentence suggest that a particular word is a noun or a verb, or a person's name?), from the context of the piece (are we talking about a train journey or a family having their breakfast?), or by noting whether a particular word looks a bit like an English word.

In the early stages, the children learn to read individual words and set phrases (the *core language structures* referred to earlier). They then move on to reading short sentences where a new word is substituted into the language structure – for example, they might see a picture of some children and read speech bubbles that tell us how old they are: *j'ai cinq ans, j'ai neuf ans, j'ai sept ans* – the size of the children in the picture might give an additional clue as to how old they are.

Although it is not strictly necessary in terms of understanding the text, the children are often encouraged to read aloud, frequently as a group, as this gives additional opportunities to practise the sounds and the accent they have been learning through listening and speaking activities.

Later, the children read longer pieces, with the aim of understanding both the general idea of the piece and some of the detail. Texts that contain familiar topics give the children the best chance of success. Fairy stories are particular favourites, because the children already know the story – for example, in the French version of *The Sleeping Beauty* the characters are recognizable and perform the same actions, even if they have different names, and a good number of unfamiliar words can be read by noting similarities with English words – we see words such as *forêt, prince* and *beau*.

Writing is the last of the skills to be learned. However, English literacy skills are still useful, even when learning to write in another language:

■ words and known phrases can be copied – perhaps to label pictures in the first instance;

- some words can be spelled *by sight*;
- others can be built up according to the phonic rules of the new language;
- phrases can be built up around core language structures;
- phrases and longer sentences can be composed using word-banks, posters and dictionaries;
- with the help of a writing frame, older children might write three or four sentences about a familiar topic.

ICT can be a great help when learning to read and write in a foreign language – for instance, the children can read comic-type stories from DVDs or from the Internet, in which the on-screen text can be played back at the click of a mouse, with an authentic accent. Programs also exist that allow a child to have their own writing read back to them, again with a good accent. And, of course, individual words and whole sentences can be translated on-line.

Carrying out activities such as these helps the children to appreciate that people in different countries tend to say much the same things as we do – it's just the words and the phrasing that are different.

Learning about other people's lives

Learning another language provides an excellent opportunity for the children to explore other cultures. The multicultural nature of the UK society means that the exploration can often begin within the school and maybe even inside the classroom itself. They can find out which languages, other than English, are spoken by classmates and their families. They can compare names – both first names and family names – and learn about the way names are borrowed from one language and culture to another, for example, *Madeleine* was originally a French name. They can also compare traditional and contemporary clothing and food, and explore festivals and special days.

In this way, the children establish the principle that there are many different languages and cultures in the world, and that many of these can be found within the UK. They might be surprised to learn, for instance, that English is a second language for some Welsh people.

The next step is for the children to focus on the target language itself and find out where in the world it is spoken. For example, French is spoken not only in France, but also in Canada, and Spanish and Portuguese are national languages in South America as well as in Europe. Using photographs, video, songs, rhymes, art, stories, story books, magazines, the Internet, visitors to school, food, and so on, they research these places in terms of their major cities, climate, houses, family life, work, sport, fashion, traditional festivals and celebrations, games, etc. In short, they investigate how people live in these places.

Importantly, at each step, the children also compare their findings with their own lives and communities, thereby learning more about culture in the UK at the same time – for example, as they research flower festivals (which possibly take place in every country), they might also learn about the tradition of well-dressing in the Peak District of England.

As far as possible, the children learn about the new language and the culture of the place where it is spoken at the same time – not just *breakfast*, but *a French breakfast*; not just *a car journey*, but *a journey from Calais to Paris*.

The children may be surprised to discover that the lives of children in other countries are often very similar to their own. As they gain knowledge, understanding and experience, they feel increasingly comfortable with the differences and embrace them – perhaps running a French café and singing a selection of traditional French songs for a parents' evening, or learning how to make Spanish paella in their technology lessons.

They also learn that, as people move around the world, they bring features of their culture with them and adapt them for their new lifestyle. So people might add particular spices to English recipes, or wear a mixture of traditional and ordinary clothing, or they might translate traditional stories into their new language.

Looking at this from the other side, the children should be encouraged also to consider how a person from another country might feel when coming to live in the children's own community, and to develop empathy for classmates and others who have moved to the UK with their parents and find themselves immersed in a new language.

The children are encouraged to take an interest in all manner of things from abroad, and to develop an open mind to new ideas – leading to respect for foreign people, their values, their customs and their way of life.

Useful strategies

Learning a new language is not easy, so there needs to be plenty of variety, plenty of repetition, plenty of successes and lots of fun! The ideal is where the children throw themselves into the new language while engaged in thoroughly interesting activities such as rhymes and songs, story books and story telling, videos, dance, games, puzzles, computer games, matching activities, reading and writing, e-mail, puppets, drama, meeting visitors, rhythm activities, displays, and so on – in fact, anything we would use for language development in the children's first language. Additionally, ICT activities provide excellent opportunities for learning and practice, especially for more timid children who lack the confidence to *have a go* in public.

Some strategies that have proved useful in class include:

■ learning new vocabulary and structures in a memorable way – aiming for a remark such as 'Oh, I remember, that's the phrase we learned when we all dressed up as clowns';

- using actions and gesture with words – for example, waggling a finger back and forth rhythmically when learning *ne . . . pas* (to make a negative statement in French);

- giving picture cues to new words to help recall;

- making sure that *core language structures* and basic vocabulary are revised and reused in each new topic;

- comparing the new language with English (or other first language) and looking for similarities and differences, using the children's strength in their own language to overcome a difficulty in a new one;

- separating out individual syllables in new words and creating a recognizable rhythm in the way they are said;

- reinforcing the sound of the language by encouraging the children to experiment and play with words, perhaps making up their own words which sound real or preparing lists of pretend words that rhyme with a real one;

- carrying out language investigations – for example, how many girls' names end in an *a*, and how many in an *o*? Why might this be?;

- compiling a personal list of words and phrases they have learned, and watching the list grow;

- discussing with the children how they learned a particular element and how they made it easier for themselves.

However, we don't have to wait for the MFL lessons to practise – the new language can be used at any time of day, in any context, wherever and whenever the children find it interesting and stimulating to do so. This could be, for example, when greeting visitors to the classroom, or when counting objects or people, or singing songs in a music lesson, or naming colours in art lessons, or answering the register, etc.

Similarly, the culture of the countries where the new language is spoken can be learned through other subjects – for example, the physical landscape in geography lessons, traditional dishes and ingredients in food technology lessons, cultural events in RE lessons, and so on.

14

Music

What is music really about?

If there is something called *the visual arts*, which includes pictures, sculptures, and so on (and there is), then I suppose there should also be something called *the auditory arts* or *the art of sounds*. The subject that fills this space in schools is called *music*.

It includes music in a traditional sense, but also takes in speech, natural sounds (animal noises, the wind, breathing, flowing water, and so on) and what we might call industrial sounds (vehicles, machines, computers, fans, kettles, etc.). Then there are also sounds that are designed to give us information – usually electronic bleeps and buzzes that come from computers, phones, door bells, pedestrian crossings, scientific and medical equipment, etc. In our own lives, depending on our job, our interests and our mood at the time, we actively listen out for some of these and desperately try to filter out others.

So, I guess that a broader definition of music could be *sounds that have been actively composed and performed to communicate ideas or provide entertainment*. Using this definition, music is everywhere around us and would be difficult to escape, even if we wanted to. For instance, it can be:

- the main event at gigs, concerts and recitals;
- available on CD and mp3 players;
- the basis of many radio shows;
- a way of marketing products;
- in the background in lifts and restaurants;
- on computer games;
- the soundtrack for television programmes and films.

It is even supposed to motivate us to work harder at the gym!

Too often, however, we let music wash over us, and are aware only of its general effect, rather than having a sharper focus on the finer points and really feeling its power. But how much better could we appreciate it and enjoy it if we knew more about it, such as:

- What was the composer trying to convey?
- What techniques was the composer using?
- Why were the ideas presented in this particular way?
- What should I be listening out for?

People who make music, in whatever form, can become passionate about its role in their life – it provides opportunities for self-expression, sensitivity, imagination, creativity, cooperative effort, pleasure and fulfilment – all of which are difficult to measure, but are just as important as those things we can quantify.

While music lessons in schools do not aspire to turn children into virtuoso performers (that needs to be pursued out of school hours, with specialist tutors), it does aim to give them a sound basis for understanding music of many types, so that they come to appreciate and enjoy it more deeply, when listening to it, dancing to it, playing it or even composing it.

Obviously, music has strong links with dance, ICT and science (which explores how sounds are made), and these should be exploited so that all children have as many ways as possible of accessing music and responding to it.

The final point here is that music in schools should be a practical subject. Yes, the children must listen, and listen carefully, but for the majority of the time, the children should be exploring and making music in a hands-on fashion.

Musical genres

Music lessons can include everything from ring-tones to Tchaikovsky, and from babbling streams to African drums. Although it is an artificial and inexact exercise, we tend to categorize music into styles or *genres*. Most genres have their origins in, or are associated with, a particular geographical location, social group, period in history, instrument or rhythm. For example:

– classical	– Gospel	– jazz	– punk
– country	– Gregorian chant	– music hall	– rap
– flamenco		– opera	– reggae
– folk	– heavy metal	– pop	– rock

If we add in both *natural* and *industrial* sounds, and the songs and tunes especially written for children, *genres* provide a convenient and interesting starting point for children to learn about music.

Musical elements

When reading a novel, we follow the plot, but we also take notice of the setting and the characters, the particular vocabulary selected, the length of sentences and the word order and punctuation. The author makes these decisions to help us understand the story and feel the mood of the piece and the emotions displayed by the characters.

Music is very similar in its composition – the composer and performer make use of a range of *musical elements* to help us understand the *story* of the piece, appreciate the mood of the music and generally understand the composer's intentions.

Like all subjects, music has its own specialist vocabulary, and as the children learn about each musical element, they also learn the words associated with it:

- *pitch* – high notes and low notes, and moving up and down;
- *interval* – how big the changes in pitch are, sliding or jumping;
- *melody* – the order of the notes to produce a tune;
- *pulse* – a steady beat; this often links well with movement and dance – usually two beats for marches, three beats for waltzes, four beats for rock music; the children tap their fingers, recognize what a *bar* is and count beats in a bar;
- *duration* – the length of notes, how long or short they are;
- *rhythm* – grouping and ordering the long, short and same-length notes to build the tune, repeating patterns;
- *phrasing* – grouping a run of notes to show, for example, where to take a breath;
- *dynamics* – loud or quiet, becoming louder or quieter and how quickly it does this;
- *silence* – the spaces between notes, often important for the feel of a piece;
- *tempo* – the speed at which music is played, often measured in beats per minute – slow, walking pace, running;
- *timbre* – the quality of the tone, whatever instrument is being played; when playing a drum, the difference between striking it with wooden sticks, rubber beaters and brushes; when using voices, the difference between whispering, speaking, singing, calling and shouting;
- *texture* – the *arrangement*, the overall effect of *layers* of sound, played by different instruments or voices;
- *harmony* – sounds that go well together (or don't), chords;
- *structure* – the way sections of the piece are arranged one after the other, which might be fast – slow – fast, call and response, cumulative songs, verse and chorus, round.

(DES 1992b: 5, 7)

These musical elements are the essential building blocks of music and the children are taught about them explicitly in their lessons. They will need a great deal of personal exploration before they understand how they work and what contribution each element can make to a piece of music.

So the children learn that the way music sounds is no accident, but rather, the composition is carefully planned. As their experience grows, they learn to:

- recognize these elements when they appear in music;
- name each element;
- understand how each one plays its part in helping to fulfil the composer's intention;
- take note of them when they themselves perform and compose.

As these elements are common to all musical compositions, understanding them will be of benefit to the children in the future, whatever genre captures their interest and enthusiasm, and whether listening, singing, playing an instrument, arranging or providing background support (such as recording or acting as a DJ).

Knowledge, understanding and skills

As the children learn about the *musical elements* through particular *genres*, they also develop knowledge, understanding and skills in the areas of *listening*, *appraising*, *performing* and *composing*.

Although these can be listed and described separately, the children make best progress in any one area by drawing on their knowledge and understanding in one or more of the other three. And by getting involved in making music themselves, of course.

Listening

Perhaps *listening* should really be called *active listening and responding*; certainly, it should not be confused with *passive sitting and hearing*. Without listening, the children won't recognize the musical elements and will therefore never be able to discuss the effectiveness of a piece of music, nor refine their own performances, nor create their own compositions with conviction.

Listening includes:

- listening attentively – this needs to be built up, as the children mature;
- recognizing, and then naming, sounds – starting with everyday natural and industrial sounds, moving on to single instruments and then instrumental music;
- identifying sounds, melodies and rhythms, and repeating them back;
- recognizing the different musical elements and noting how they are combined and organized to create mood, expression and effects;
- following musical instructions;
- understanding and using correct musical terms, remembering that, as in all subjects, the children understand new ideas best by discussing them in their

own familiar language, and that the proper word is merely tacked on as a *label*, after they have shown that they understand the idea; this grows only gradually;

■ recording their own sounds and music – listening carefully, deciding which sounds and pieces are required, and then replaying, to aid appraisal.

Appraising

This is about evaluating and making judgements about the effectiveness of pieces of music – both commercial pieces and the ones the children have made themselves. They:

■ say whether they liked a piece of music or not, without being swayed by friends;

■ say what they liked or disliked about it, and how it affected them – this involves using the language of musical elements, as well as the language of style and mood;

■ respond to the music, appreciating the composer's intention and understanding why the composer used particular elements in particular ways; clapping and dancing are acceptable ways of responding to music, of course;

■ build a repertoire of sounds, songs and techniques, both for pleasure and as a foundation for further learning;

■ recognize and understand the context of music – its genre, and its cultural, social and historical background;

■ improve their own work – individual or group work – evaluating how well it turned out, and then drafting and redrafting to improve it.

Of course, the children won't be able to appraise music unless they have listened carefully in the first place.

Performing

Performing includes singing, playing instruments (including body parts, for example, when clapping) and dancing. Performances should be delivered with control and expression, and with a sense of audience. Children's performances are always improved by active listening, appraising, amending and, of course, rehearsing.

When performing, the children:

■ use their voices – speaking, chanting, rapping; singing rhymes, choruses, verses, parts, descants; staying *in tune*, both individually and in a group; controlling breathing, shape of mouth, clarity, quality of sound;

■ use body parts – clapping, clicking, slapping, rubbing, tapping; body drumming, tongue clicking, toe tapping; dancing (responding to pulse, rhythm, mood and emotion);

■ use instruments – tuned instruments (these have notes of different pitch), e.g. recorder, keyboard, guitar, xylophone; untuned instruments (no variation of pitch), e.g. drum, kazoo; the correct way to hold and play the instrument by blowing, striking, plucking;

■ control the *musical elements* to achieve the expression and effects intended by the composer;

■ play or sing individually, unaccompanied or with an accompaniment; play or sing as part of a group, listening to each other and understanding how the parts fit together;

■ follow musical direction from a conductor, understanding and following hand signals such as ready, start, stop, louder, quieter, higher, lower, faster, slower;

■ follow written musical direction – that is, reading music – in various formats (see Composing, below);

■ hopefully, show enthusiasm and confidence.

Composing

Composing is about:

■ creating and developing musical ideas from a stimulus – a place, a person, a story, an event, an emotion, an atmosphere, a product, and so on;

■ deciding on a format – a song, a jingle, a dance, instrumental, enhancing a story with sound effects and atmospheric musical phrases, etc.;

■ deciding on a structure for the piece – its *shape*, for instance whether to use repeats, verses, and so on;

■ choosing sounds – first, knowing what sounds are available from which instruments and then selecting from among them;

■ organizing sounds and musical elements to achieve the desired effect by making decisions about what qualities to use in respect of each *musical element*, e.g.:
  – how high or low should the sounds be?
  – how loud should they be? should changes from loud to quiet, and from quiet to loud, be sudden or gradual?
  – should the notes be long or short? what rhythm patterns should be used?
  – what sounds should be heard at the same time? *harmony* or *discord*?
  – should there be any silences? how long? where?
  – how should the notes be sequenced and phrased?
  – what pulse should be used, and at what tempo?
  – what *timbre* (tone) should the music have? how can this be achieved?

In order that the piece might be performed again at a later date, the children also need to learn how to record their thoughts and decisions in some way, starting with informal signs and symbols, such as wiggly lines, stars, splashes, etc., and moving on to more formal ways, such as:

- the sol-fa scale (doh–ray–me);
- letter names (A to G), with sharps (#) and flats (*b*);
- stave (each symbol shows the duration of a note, while its position on the stave shows its pitch);
- drum music written on a stave;
- chords and tablature for guitar;
- Italian words to describe elements such as speed and volume, for example, allegro (quickly) and forte (loudly).

Composition is the most complex of the skills, as it brings imagination together with the knowledge, skills and understanding that come from listening, appraising and performing.

How are lessons organized?

Units are often based on a particular genre, so that the children get a feel for that genre and learn to describe its essential features, whether these are the melodies or rhythms used, or the instruments, or whatever.

The children tend to concentrate on just one or two musical elements in each unit. For example, when learning about *intervals* (jumps in *pitch*) they might:

- *listen* – to a variety of pieces which exemplify wide or narrow intervals;
- *appraise* – discuss when particular intervals might be appropriate for particular topics (they might suggest small intervals when playing snake music but larger intervals when describing a child playing with a yo-yo);
- *perform* – sing songs and play instruments to demonstrate various intervals;
- *compose* – in response to suitable stimuli.

In this way, the children get a feel for *intervals* from several different angles. They might then be encouraged to listen out for examples of wider and narrower intervals when listening to music for their own pleasure.

A note on singing

It is common in schools for singing to be the main musical activity when the children are very young. This is how it should be. In order to be able to sing in tune, the children need to be able to shape the sounds in their head (developing what musicians call the *inner ear*) before releasing them through their mouth. It is all done in a split second, of course. The piano plays and they're off, remembering what they did the last time they sang this song, listening to the piano (or to their friends) to match their tempo, rhythm, pitch, dynamics, tone and clarity. It doesn't always appear in the sweetest or most tuneful form, but it is excellent practice for learning about and internalizing the ideas, which together make music what it is. The *output activity* of singing helps the children to focus on the *input activities* of listening and appraising, and vice versa (Department of Education Northern Ireland).

Experimenting and performing with instruments, keyboards and computers

Instruments largely fall into two groups – tuned and untuned:

■ tuned instruments are those which can play different *notes* and therefore a melody – pianos, recorders, chime bars, violins, saxophones, and so on;

■ untuned instruments are those that have only one note in terms of *pitch*. These include many percussion instruments – drums, shakers, triangles, and so on, as well as instruments like kazoos and whistles.

Unfortunately, children often regard untuned instruments as inferior, because they can't play a tune (a melody) on them. However, a look down the list of musical elements reveals that this is the only contribution untuned instruments cannot make. In all other areas, they can contribute as much as any tuned instrument.

All instruments require knowledge, understanding and skill to be played effectively – high quality blowing, shaking, plucking, striking, scraping, pressing valves and switches depend on the shape of the mouth, the touch of the fingers, and so on. And, of course, the performer needs to know about the variations that can be made in respect of each of the musical elements and how to achieve these variations on their instrument. Some elements are controlled in a similar way on different instruments – pulse and rhythm, for instance – but producing high and low notes, and creating variations in the *timbre* (the tone of the notes) is different for different instruments, and will require both technique and practice.

Remembering that music is a practical, and therefore inherently noisy, subject, the classroom can appear rather chaotic at times as the children develop their ideas and practise their skills. However, one instrument stands out as easier to control in the classroom when the children are practising – the keyboard; it has a volume switch and can be used with headphones. It is also the ideal instrument with which to explore musical elements, as it has buttons to control *tempo*, to play a preset beat (*pulse*) and to mimic other instruments. The children can be as inventive as they like, pursuing lines of inquiry purposefully with *I wonder what it would sound like if I . . .* and experimenting with effects such as *echo* and *reverberation* to extend the range of their musical repertoire.

Computers can extend this even further, by allowing multi-layered composition, on screen, with instant audio feedback, so that the children can hear whether their experimentation has led to something they would like to keep. This encourages them to explore the elements of *texture*, *harmony* and *structure* in a way that could not be achieved by any other means when working alone.

Group performances

I believe that musical performances made by groups of children can be breathtaking – they certainly bring a lump to the throat of many parents in the audience. It's not so much the individual performances, but the cooperative pursuit of excellence, when there is no competition and no winner – there's just a sense of a group achieving, together.

Non-musical benefits to be gained from music lessons

Clearly, it is enough to learn about music for its own sake, for its importance as a leisure pursuit and for its cultural value. Nevertheless, we should not forget the transferable skills that the children practise and develop through this subject:

- *personal skills* – perseverance, creativity, making judgements, exploration of emotions, self-confidence, self-expression, self-discipline, taking care of instruments;
- *social skills* – communication, introduction to world cultures and languages, cooperation with others;
- *learning skills* – memory, hand–eye coordination and nimbleness of hand, reading codes, following instructions, making and understanding patterns, problem solving, developing ideas by exploration, trial and improvement;
- working skills – concentration, attention to detail.

(DfEE and QCA 1999:122)

So, while musical activities have value in their own right, the spin-offs from them can be enormous.

15

Physical Education (PE)

What is physical education really about?

In the past few years, a great deal of effort has gone into persuading us all to adopt an active and healthy lifestyle. In schools, many aspects of this are dealt with through PSHE education, for example urging us to eat more fruit and vegetables, and alerting us to the dangers of smoking.

However, physical education (PE) also has an important role to play – by establishing physical activity as a central part of the children's lives, so that it gives them pleasure when they are young, and then stays with them as a recreational activity throughout adulthood.

Clearly, regular exercise has physical benefits in terms of:

- *health* – the effect on the heart and lungs, etc.;
- *fitness* – increase in muscular strength, endurance, etc.;
- maintaining a satisfactory *body weight*;
- improved *posture*;
- *safety* – better balance and coordination.

Other positive effects include:

- *personal and emotional benefits* – self-esteem, a positive mood, the ability to relax;
- *social benefits* – inclusion in group and team activities;
- *intellectual benefits* – thinking skills and an appreciation of aesthetics.

The benefits seem beyond doubt. However, we also have to recognize the many pressures that might draw children away from physical activity, such as the availability of television and computer games, increasing traffic and a growing belief that it is dangerous to play outside.

In the face of such obstacles, in school we need to:

- provide a wide range of activities that the children can sample, so that they might find one or more that they enjoy and want to pursue;
- help them to build and improve their physical skills and make good use of them in all sorts of ways;
- help them to appreciate the physical, emotional, social and intellectual benefits of taking part in sport and exercise;
- help every child to feel successful in their chosen activities.

As adults, we can choose from a vast range of active pursuits, for example, aerobics, cycling, fell walking, fencing, football, golf, line dancing, racket games, skateboarding, swimming, tap dancing, volleyball, etc. Each presents a different challenge from the others and requires a slightly different way of thinking – individual or team, physical or creative, indoor or outdoor, cooperative or competitive.

For children in school, PE lessons routinely include gymnastics, dance, athletics, games, swimming and water safety, and outdoor and adventurous activities. There are also other opportunities for physical activity at other times:

- at breaktimes – playing informal ball games, chasing games, clapping and skipping games, hopscotch, and so on;
- at after-school clubs – following the enthusiasm of individual members of staff;
- in other lessons – drama (English, history and modern foreign languages), field-trips (geography), collecting data (maths and science), etc.

If we are to succeed in getting every child active, we need to make the most of these opportunities to find out what activities they enjoy, and then help them to build their skills and enthusiasm further, so that these activities become an important part of their lives. If games need to be modified or adapted so that everybody can be included, then that's fine. What is important is that every child is taken seriously, whatever their preferences and whatever their initial level of skill, so that they can be helped to experience success, feel a sense of personal achievement and have fun.

Fitness, safety and health

While the children are offered a wide range of physical activities, it is natural that they should show a preference for some rather than others – after all, they are all very different in their appeal. For example, hockey vs. dance, throwing a discus vs. orienteering, swimming vs. composing and performing gymnastic routines.

Interestingly, though, all these sports, games and pastimes rely on the same four physical qualities – *strength*, *stamina*, *speed* and *suppleness* (taken together, these give a good definition of *fitness*).

However, each sport and activity requires a different mix of these qualities – *rowing* requires strength and stamina, some speed, but little suppleness; *fencing* requires suppleness, stamina and speed, but perhaps less strength; *gardening* demands strength, stamina and suppleness, but rarely speed.

Of course, we are all different from each other in terms of our shape and size – some people seem to be naturally stronger than others, while others are faster or more supple. These qualities inevitably make us better suited to some activities than to others. However, with guidance, training and practice, each of these qualities can be improved, making our life both easier (we can do the things we need to do more easily) and more fulfilling (we can also do more of the things we would like to do).

In PE lessons, the children learn how the body is affected by exercise and how to exercise safely. So, for example, younger children:

- change into their PE kit before the lesson;
- follow an adult's warm-up and warm-down;
- learn how to avoid bumping into each other;
- describe the feelings in their body as they take part in different activities;
- wash or shower themselves after the lesson.

Older children learn:

- to choose suitable clothing and equipment;
- to handle apparatus and equipment safely;
- how different activities make different demands on the body;
- just how warm-ups and warm-downs are good for the body;
- how diet can affect energy levels;
- that different events require different combinations of strength, stamina, speed and suppleness;
- to pace themselves in different types of event, so that they can keep going steadily and maintain the quality of their performance;
- what happens to their breathing, heart and temperature during exercise;
- why a shower after exercise is necessary, for both hygiene and social reasons;
- what the longer term benefits of regular exercise are, in terms of fitness and health;
- about opportunities for participation in sporting and physical activities in the local community (dance troupes, rugby teams, swimming clubs, etc.).

Clearly, the best time for children to learn about these things is during their PE lessons, when their body gives them immediate feedback. At the same time, we do not want to interrupt the activity too much – a balance needs to be found – and additional follow-up might be needed in PSHE education lessons.

Transferable qualities, skills and attitudes

Physical activity and sport have the ability to bring out some wonderfully inspirational personal qualities such as:

- a sense of fun and enjoyment;
- willingness to *have a go*;
- concentration, determination and perseverance;
- willingness to take responsibility and make decisions;
- willingness to work for the benefit of the team as a whole, self-discipline;
- being competitive – against oneself, against standards and against others;
- playing fairly and working safely, considering the activities and movements of other people;
- cooperation and teamwork.

Alongside all this, most amateur sportsmen would agree that there is great satisfaction to be gained from playing well, even if we don't win (although there is always that extra frisson of excitement if we do manage to beat an opponent).

Similarly, there is much self-esteem to be gained from playing in the school team and being an ambassador for the school. In many schools, older children are encouraged to lead sporting or playground activities, setting a good example for the younger children.

Some children, especially those who are heavy or small, can feel very exposed during PE lessons – they know that they can't run or jump as well as their classmates, and feel that there is no way to escape comparison. It is easier for these children to maintain their motivation if the whole class is clear about the reasons why they do PE:

- to increase each individual's strength, stamina, speed, suppleness and skills;
- to compete against themselves and work towards achieving a personal best;
- to develop a wide range of personal qualities, attitudes and social skills;
- to improve their health.

In order to make progress in these areas, the children first need to describe their own actions and those of other people, identifying differences in the way different people carry out the same movements or skills. They can then suggest how improvements might be made, before setting themselves realistic personal challenges.

Improvements might be made in terms of *quantity* (things we can measure – distances, times, repetitions, and so on) or *quality* (style, accuracy, smoothness, fluency). However, improvements in quality and technique will often also lead to improvements in quantity, so this is where we should direct our teaching.

Of course, it is very difficult to see exactly how we are performing a movement while we are actually doing it. So cameras and video (operated by staff or children) are useful in allowing the children to evaluate their performances and make instant improvements – 'My legs should have been straighter', or 'My run-up wasn't fast enough', or 'I didn't notice my team-mate on the other wing', etc.

This emphasis on analysing movements and performances is clearly invaluable in terms of improving the children's performance. But it also helps them to develop a sporting vocabulary so that they can discuss activities knowledgeably, and encourages them to gain enjoyment from watching other people, including professionals, play sport. After all, we don't have to be experts in rugby to enjoy watching it and sharing in the excitement. The physicality, the skill, the tactics and the teamwork can be breathtaking!

Activities

An overview

The core activities that every child experiences in primary PE are gymnastics, athletics, dance, games, swimming and water safety, and the so-called outdoor and adventurous activities (DfEE and QCA 1999: 130–3). Other activities may be added at the discretion of the school.

While some aspects of PE can be measured ('I swam 100 metres today', or 'We won 3–2'), each of the activities also has an *aesthetic quality* (think of the delight when completing a smooth forward roll in gymnastics, or achieving the perfect synchronization between stroke and breathing when swimming), and offers opportunities for *imagination and creativity*, for example, planning choreography in dance, linking movements in gymnastics, outwitting an opponent on the netball court, or finding new ways to pass the ball in rugby. PE in school offers so much more than a weekly visit to the gym!

As the children move from one activity to another, they:

■ develop different aspects of their physical fitness;

■ acquire and refine the skills particular to each activity;

■ learn and apply the strategies, tactics and compositional ideas they need in order to be successful;

■ understand what makes a performance effective and strive to achieve it;

■ enter into the particular mood and spirit of the activity.

Whatever the activity, we would hope that the children will extend their personal qualities and social skills, *give it a go*, and enjoy it as much as possible.

Like all activities in school, the children are taught to approach their PE work in three stages – prepare by thinking about how to approach the task or activity, practise it and do it, and then evaluate the quality of their performance, asking 'How did it go?', 'How could I do it better next time?'.

·*Space* is an important element in all aspects of PE and perhaps needs a special mention here. Through their PE lessons, children become increasingly aware of their personal space, and how they can control it and use it. They also become more conscious of the wider space around them – Where are the other people? How are they moving? Quickly or slowly? In a straight line or in a curved pathway? Where are they moving to? Will this lead to a collision? Does it present an opportunity to make a good pass?

These ideas help the children to be successful in all PE activities – knowledge of their personal space is especially helpful in dance and gymnastics, while the broader view helps in games where passes and tackles need to be made, and opponents need to be outwitted. They are also very helpful outside the realm of PE and sport, such as road safety.

Warming up and warming down

A good warm-up should prepare the children, both physically and mentally, for the activities that follow. Warm-ups usually include:

- jogging or some other aerobic activity, starting gently and increasing speed gradually – to raise the pulse, and warm the muscles and blood;

- a gradual increase in the intensity of movement – for example, skipping, hopping over a line, arm circles – to gently stretch the muscles that will be used in the activity to follow;

- practising movements that will be used in the main activity, but at half-speed – getting the body used to the demands that will be made on it during the lesson;

- moving around the work-space, stopping and starting, and becoming increasingly aware of the work-space and the other people using it.

(Members of Primary Curriculum Support Programme
(Ireland) 2008)

Warming down takes place during the last few minutes of each lesson, as the children gradually reduce their pace, stretch out their muscles and discuss what they have done during the lesson. The more demanding the physical exercises, the more important is the warm-down afterwards.

Gymnastics

Long before the children start school, they have learned many *gross motor skills*, such as rolling over on the floor, crawling, standing, walking, running, jumping and turning.

In gymnastics lessons, the children explore these same actions in more detail, with the aim of:

- increasing their awareness of the ways in which they can move their bodies (or body parts), with a heightened sense of what it feels like when they do;
- increasing their *movement vocabulary* – that is, the range of actions they can perform;
- developing more control over their bodies as they carry out this ever-increasing range of actions.

So, in a way, gymnastics is about pure movement.

The children learn about and experience:

- *stillness* (maintaining a position) – in many actions, we want the whole body to be still for some of the time; in others we want a single part to remain still while other parts move;
- *travelling* (also called *locomotion*) – for example, crawling, rolling, stepping, running, hopping, skipping, sliding, climbing, doing cartwheels;
- *flight* – jumping, vaulting, leaping, taking-off and landing;
- *balancing* – on large or small parts of the body: back, bottom, one foot, hands and feet, shoulders, etc., as well as counterbalances with a partner;
- *turning* – while on the floor, while upright, rolling;
- *body shape* – making the body wide, small, long, thin, curled, twisted, spiky;
- *body tension* – relaxed, stiff, stretched.

The children combine these elements in various ways, by carrying them out:

- at different *levels* – near the floor, at body height, or reaching up;
- using different *directions* – left, right, forwards, backwards, up, down, towards, away, clockwise, anticlockwise;
- using different *pathways* around the room – straight, curved, zigzag;
- at various *speeds*.

Each of these actions can be performed:

- on the *floor* – the most versatile piece of PE apparatus;
- on, around and through *apparatus* or obstacles – for example, a bench, climbing frame;
- with *equipment* – for example, a hoop, ball or ribbon, or without any of these;
- with a *partner* – or without one.

To begin with, the children learn actions by copying the leader or their class-mates. Later, they use their creativity and imagination as they combine gymnastic skills and actions in a series of challenges:

- to form *movement phrases* (for example, *move slowly, backwards, staying low*);
- then longer *movement sequences*, which might include a clear beginning, middle and end, with defined starting and finishing positions (showing stillness and balance), a range of body shapes and balances, interesting ways to *travel* (move), thoughtful use of different levels, speeds, directions and pathways, individual work or partner work, rhythm, flow and continuity from one element to the next.

Gymnastics plays a central role in PE, because these same movements are used in particular ways and for particular effects, in each of the other areas of PE and games.

Athletics

Athletics is basically about:

- *running* – including walking, jogging, running, sprinting, hopping, skipping, rope-skipping, hurdling;
- *jumping* – for height, distance or accuracy;
- *throwing* – for accuracy, distance, height, power.

The children refine their *running* skills by making decisions about:

- Whether their style (their *gait*) is efficient – Should the foot fall on the heel, ball or toe? Should the stride be longer or shorter? Should the knees be high or low at each step?
- How the arms can help to increase speed and maintain balance.
- What pace they should run at to complete the distance as quickly as possible, without losing technique or becoming exhausted.
- Adjusting the stride and speed when approaching an obstacle.
- How best to change direction at different speeds – side to side, and stopping and turning.
- How best to follow different pathways – straight, curved, zigzag, over or around obstacles.
- How to pass a baton when running relay races (shuttle races and wheel races).

There is much to learn if the children are to *jump* safely, with control and coordination:

- the best way to take off;
- how to make a safe, controlled and comfortable landing;

- different sorts of jumps – hops, two-foot jumps, one foot to two feet, jumps with a run-up;
- combination jumps – for example, hop, step and jump.

Variations in *throwing* include under-arm, over-arm, over-head, two-handed push, roll; balls of different sizes, as well as bean bags, quoits, hoops, mini discuses, foam javelins; a direct throw or with a bounce; with or without a run-up; from sitting, kneeling, standing. Throwing can be a difficult skill for some children, particularly techniques such as *turn sideways, opposite foot forward and rotate the body to generate power.*

Many of the techniques learned in athletics are used in other areas of PE. For example, stopping, starting and changing direction are invaluable in tennis, throwing skills become bowling and fielding in cricket and rounders, and jumping needs to be elegant when used as a part of dance.

Dance

Dance makes use of all the elements learned in gymnastics lessons:

- stillness, travelling, flight, balancing, turning, body shape, body tension;
- levels, directions, pathways, speeds.

Dance then uses the movement and control to tell stories, describe scenes, and communicate feelings, ideas or relationships. It is an art form, in the same way as painting and sculpture are. Of course, it is usually linked to music and can be an excellent way to introduce the children to styles of music they would not normally take notice of.

In the primary school, the children encounter two types of dance:

- Formal dance styles – which are made up of prescribed steps, pathways and gestures, and usually have a name, for example, folk dances, maypole dances, line dances, jive.
- Creative dance – where the children respond to music to tell a story or express an idea, making up their own sequences of steps and movements.

In both of these, the children learn about:

- creating and composing;
- practising and performing;
- evaluating and appreciation.

The interesting thing is that when we compare very different dances – for example, a maypole dance and a creative dance (which might, for instance, portray sailors on the high sea fighting against a storm) – we see that they both require decisions about the same *qualities*:

- *Body shape and size* – how to hold our legs and feet, and our arms and hands; should the trunk be tall or small, wide or crouched?

- *Body tension* – strong or weak, tensed or floppy, what facial expression?

- *Action* – how should we move in response to the music – creeping, stamping, scuttling, slithering, skipping, arm-waving?

- *Dynamics* – heavy or light, fast or slow, rhythmic or jerky, sudden or sustained?

- *Continuity* – how to start, how does one action flow into the next, how to finish?

- *Space* – how to move our body parts within our own personal space (twisting and turning, rising and falling, what gestures should we employ?), and what patterns and pathways should we use across the shared space – which direction, straight, curved, zigzag?

- *Relationships* – should we work alone, with a partner, or as part of a larger group? If working with others, should we move in unison, or in canon (making the same movement, one after the other), or should our movements take the form of question and answer (action and reaction)? How should we stand and move – should we make a pattern? How should we relate to objects in the work-space (scenery etc.)?

When a *formal dance* is introduced, the children learn not just the steps, but also how these *qualities* are used to reflect the mood and style of the dance. They learn a realistic and achievable number of steps and movements, with which they might experiment later to create their own dance routines in that particular style.

When the children perform *creative dances*, they explore different movements, discussing how they relate to the story, poem or character and how they match the music being used, referring to the same seven *qualities* listed above.

By discussing these qualities, the children develop a sense of what makes a performance effective:

- Did the dance have a clear beginning, middle and end?

- How did the dance develop, and were the transitions between sections of the dance smooth and elegant?

- Was it clear what was being portrayed?

- Where could the quality of movement be improved?

- Was the dance interesting and worth watching? Which parts of the dance stood out, and why?

As the children gain greater understanding of these elements, they move on to compose their own movement sequences in response to a stimulus such as music, poems, stories, traditional rhymes and art work – or even a visit to the zoo, or a football match. However, dance is also an intensely aerobic activity, promoting both fitness and health, so pupils will need plenty of energy!

Games

Games bring together many of the elements from other areas of PE:

- fitness – strength, stamina, suppleness, speed;
- stillness, travelling, flight, balancing, turning, body tension;
- levels, pathways, directions, speeds;
- running, jumping, throwing.

Some new elements are then added in:

- cooperation with members of your own team and, at the same time, competition against your opponents;
- game skills and ball skills – while many skills are shared among a number of games, each game also has its own distinctive skills, such as particular ways of hitting, throwing, kicking or catching;
- rules and conventions;
- tactics – how to outwit the opponent.

The games played at primary school can be grouped into:

- *Running and chasing games* – variations on *tig*, such as stuck-in-the-mud, bulldog.
- *Invasion games* – where we try to defend our own territory, but invade our opponent's territory and score a *goal*; these games include handball, netball, basketball, hockey, football, rugby.
- *Striking and fielding games* – for example, rounders, softball, stoolball, cricket.
- *Net games* – tennis, short tennis, table tennis, badminton, volleyball.

There is a lot for the children to learn:

- understanding the object of the game – this is fairly straightforward in games with a goal or a net, but is more difficult in games such as rounders;
- understanding the scoring system – goals, baskets, tries, points – how many points are needed to win a game of badminton?
- recognizing who might be winning or losing when part-way through a game of rounders or cricket;
- understanding and remembering the rules;
- understanding and interpreting each game's particular jargon;
- recognizing the limits of the playing area, and regions within it – who is allowed in which regions on a netball court, and when is a player off-side in football?;
- appreciating the direction of play – and remembering to change ends at half-time;

- identifying their own team, and the emotional confusion of competing against friends instead of cooperating with them;

- understanding particular roles within the team, such as attack and defence, and playing in different positions to fulfil these functions;

- marking opponents and tackling – what is involved? what is fair? – is it the same as on television?

- understanding and applying strategies and tactics to get the better of an opponent.

To cope with this, the children build up to playing a full game only gradually, moving through a number of stages beforehand:

- First, full cooperation, such as counting the number of passes or hits or catches – this is usually used to build skills and familiarize them with the game's jargon.

- Then, simplified games, with limited rules and easier equipment, e.g. bigger balls, shorter sticks, a smaller playing area, and perhaps only two-, three- or four-a-side.

Games like this encourage maximum participation by all the children, as well as getting a feel for the game.

Three skills are fundamental to playing most games successfully:

- Being aware of the space within the playing area and of where team-mates and opponents are likely to be; then we can, for instance, pass the ball to team-mates accurately, mark opponents effectively, and get away from opponents marking us and, hopefully, hit the ball into a space.

- Judging the ball's speed and direction accurately – we want the ball to move fast enough to evade opponents, but we don't want to over-hit passes, or make weak shots at goal.

- Running – purposefully, stopping and starting, and varying the direction, pathway and speed.

In *running and chasing games*, there is no ball. With that exception, these same skills are all needed, along with:

- tigging other players gently;
- avoiding trips and pushes.

Additional skills required to play *invasion games* include:

- Running with the ball – sometimes dribbling.
- Sending balls – throwing, kicking, heading or hitting with a stick; over different distances, in different directions, with different power, directly or bouncing; to pass or shoot.

- Receiving balls – stopping and catching a moving ball (it might be rolling, bouncing or in the air); trapping it, using feet, hands, body or stick, as allowed for within the rules of the game.

- Intercepting the ball and tackling opponents.

When playing *striking and fielding games*, additional skills include:

- Striking – holding the bat efficiently (left- or right-handed) with a good grip, hitting the ball (this is easier when using a bat with a large face and a short handle and when the ball is fairly large), controlling the direction and force of the ball into spaces, away from fielders, high or low.

- Bowling – variously, according to the rules of the game, under-arm or over-arm, straight or bouncing, fast or slow, from a stand-still or with a run-up.

- Fielding – stopping a rolling or bouncing ball, catching a ball (again, larger balls are generally easier than smaller ones), returning a ball to base, controlling power and accuracy, combining the skill of chasing after the ball, stopping it, turning, and throwing it back to base.

- Using tactics that involve bowlers and fielders working together.

When playing *net games*, particular skills include:

- hitting a ball on the fore-hand, on the back-hand and overhead;

- using a variety of bats and rackets;

- playing rallies – cooperatively and then competitively;

- serving according to the rules of each game.

However, these skills come to nothing if they are not used tactically. Clever tactics help a player or team that is weaker in one area of the game to overcome a stronger opponent, by making best use of each player's skills and by players combining their skills. The children need to ask themselves questions such as:

- How can I make it hard for my opponent to make a pass?

- How can I communicate with my team-mates?

- Where should I position myself?

- How can I make it less likely that my pass will be intercepted?

- Who should I pass the ball to, if it comes to me?

The games in PE lessons are not like darts, where players take turns to have the oche to themselves. In each of these games, our opponents are on the pitch or court with us, trying to play the game in their own way, and trying equally hard to prevent us from playing as we would want to – their gain is our loss and vice versa. It is this direct competition – and the combination of fitness, skills, understanding, mental attitude and tactics – that can make games so intriguing.

Swimming and water safety

Swimming is not only a potential life-saver, it also contributes to personal health, develops all-round fitness and has become a life-long hobby for many people, as they play in the water with friends, swim competitively, sail, snorkel or scuba dive – or swim lengths alone for their own satisfaction.

In most schools, the children's swimming lessons have two main aims:

- to be confident and safe in water;
- to swim a decent distance on their front and back, using recognized strokes.

An important message for the children is that, while water can offer fun and excitement, it must be treated with respect – the best way to get out of trouble is not to get into trouble in the first place!

To a great extent, confidence comes from feeling safe in the water, so the children wear armbands or carry flotation aids whenever necessary, as they learn how to:

- get into the water safely – using the steps, sliding in over the poolside, jumping in using a pencil jump, star jump or straddle jump, or diving in (much later, of course);
- get out of the water safely – using steps, or over the poolside.

Then they progress through:

- hopping, walking and jumping in the water, getting a feel for the water and the buoyancy it provides;
- ducking under the surface and blowing bubbles;
- performing a *push and glide* from the side wall, remaining balanced;
- floating on the back and on the front;
- performing a surface dive;
- rolling and turning somersaults, both on the surface and underwater;
- touching the bottom of the pool at various depths;
- swimming underwater, keeping eyes open to locate and pick up objects;
- treading water, keeping hands and feet moving to stay afloat.

The children also learn about the less obvious dangers of playing in, or falling into, open water – the temperature of the water in and around the UK, underwater obstacles, the strength of the waves, and the strength of tides and currents.

They move on to learn survival skills to increase their chances of survival in life-or-death situations:

- swimming in clothes;
- using objects to help keep them afloat;

- curling up to retain body heat;
- resting in the water to minimize the amount of energy used;
- using ropes and poles to leave the water when these are offered from the bank (or poolside).

Alongside these confidence and survival skills, the children also develop swimming technique in each of the basic strokes:

- on the front – crawl, breast-stroke and basic butterfly;
- on the back – sculling and full back-stroke.

They use skills such as:

- using arms and hands, and legs and feet, in a particular way for each stroke;
- coordinating arms and legs;
- attention to body shape, streamlining and body tension – e.g. stretch out, with high hips for backstroke;
- balance;
- breathing rhythmically in a stroke, and coordinating breathing with arms and legs.

Some children seem to learn these skills very quickly indeed, while others need a lot of coaxing to get started. This last group will need a great deal of help, support, encouragement and patience from the adults working with them.

Outdoor and adventurous activities

This might seem to be an *add-on* to the traditional areas of PE in primary schools, but it provides the sorts of activities that, in later life, might lead to hiking, orienteering, mountaineering, camping, pony-trekking or any of those other sports that take place in the countryside, outside the controlled confines of a hall, court, pitch or stadium. These are activities that combine physical fitness and skills with well-developed personal qualities, as participants attempt to overcome obstacles that the surroundings (including the weather and the landscape) put in their way (English Outdoor Council).

People taking part in sports and pastimes like these need to be in touch with nature and to recognize that the outside world is forever changing – according to the time of year, the amount of light available, the temperature, the likelihood of rain, the strength and direction of the wind, etc.

In the school context, most children take part in group challenges, based on *route-following* – that is, following a trail while overcoming problems and setbacks on the way. More adventurous activities might include rock climbing, abseiling, canoeing or camping. These are often incorporated into residential experiences and led by professional outdoor pursuit leaders. Of course, the children need to build up to these, so practice activities (which are often set in the context of exciting stories) might include challenges such as getting the whole team, with their bags, across the stream without getting wet (using ropes on the school field to represent a stream and carpet tiles to represent stepping stones), or finding a range of objects around the school grounds, and plotting their position on a plan (a *scavenger hunt*).

The key areas of learning are:

- map-reading skills and following a route;
- planning skills;
- working effectively as a member of a team;
- developing personal qualities;
- appreciating the health benefits of being outdoors.

When learning to *follow a route*, the children first need to develop their observation skills by describing and sketching the main features of particular locations. The next step is to match features on the ground with photographs, diagrams and symbols on plans and maps. They can then use these skills to follow a route around a known area, and then a less well-known one.

Planning skills are needed in order to think through problems before they happen and plan solutions. The children learn that they first need to identify the problem and state it clearly. They can then generate ideas about how to solve it, expressing them logically, before making decisions – preferably team decisions – by selecting from among those ideas. They also learn the value of varying and adapting their ideas according to changing circumstances.

Teamwork is a key element in outdoor and adventurous activities. But high-quality teamwork does not just happen – the children need to develop a number of skills and attitudes to become good team members. They need to understand that different aspects of the challenge require different skills, which can be provided by different people. They need to join in decision-making discussions, both giving and receiving ideas in a spirit of cooperation. Once a decision has been made, they need to be willing to take responsibility for their part in putting other people's ideas into practice. They also need to encourage and support other members of the team, both physically and mentally, and recognize their contribution to the outcome.

Outdoor challenges inevitably carry a certain amount of risk – this is what makes them adventurous. In order to complete challenges successfully, the children will need, in the longer term, to develop a particular set of *personal qualities*, including a positive outlook, initiative, a realistic appreciation of their own strengths and limitations, perseverance even in activities they find physically challenging, working and playing safely when outdoors, recognizing and managing risk in a sensible way, and being willing to abandon an activity if the risks are too great.

In terms of all-round *health*, outdoor and adventurous activities build fitness, particularly strength and stamina, offer opportunities to find out how the body reacts in different environmental conditions, and open up a whole range of physical activities and challenges that might tempt the reluctant dancer, athlete or games player.

The knowledge, understanding, skills, qualities and attitudes learned during outdoor and adventurous activities will be invaluable to the children in all areas of their future lives, not just in this context – map-reading on holiday or when visiting somewhere new, planning skills when preparing for a DIY project or planning a day out, working as a member of a team at work, in the family, with friends and in hobby groups and, of course, we want the children to remain safe and avoid accidents wherever possible.

Well-thought out and well-run activities can be both exciting and challenging, and the benefits to the children in both the short- and the long-term can be enormous.

Other activities

Many schools organize additional physical activities such as karate for the children, often through after-school clubs. These can be invaluable in attracting pupils who are reluctant to become involved in the usual fare offered in PE lessons.

Many schools also encourage the pupils in *active travel* – that is, walking or cycling to and from school, either with or without their parents. Some offer cycling proficiency courses.

In the spirit of the PE curriculum, any physical activity – as long as it is safe for the children – is better than no physical activity. When we catch the children's imagination and enthusiasm, we can never know what the spin-offs might be in later life, but there will always be benefits in terms of health and fitness.

16

Personal, Social, Health and Economic Education (PSHE Education)

What is PSHE education really about?

An introduction

Personal, Social, Health and Economic Education (PSHE education) focuses on helping the children to play a role in developing and maintaining their own personal health and well-being. This includes:

- keeping themselves physically clean and healthy;
- eating a healthy diet and getting plenty of exercise;
- looking after their mental, emotional and sexual health;
- managing risk so that they keep themselves safe, both from accidents and from people who might wish them harm;
- developing and maintaining good relationships with other people;
- enjoying, and benefiting from, new challenges;
- lending a hand when it is needed;
- looking after their personal finances;
- making the most of their abilities;
- leading confident and independent lives.

(Macdonald 2009: 10–11)

However, we need to remember that parents are usually the key people in shaping their children's development in these areas. They have much greater knowledge of their children than we do, and set their own aspirations for them. Our role is jointly to support the parents in this, and to act as part of the back-up team if things go wrong.

How can we measure children's success in PSHE education?

Children demonstrate their progress in PSHE education in a number of ways:

- by acquiring knowledge, understanding and skills;
- by cultivating and expressing positive values;
- by the way they behave in everyday situations.

However, in PSHE education, probably more than in any other subject, there is the potential for a gap to develop between the *learning* and the *doing*. After all, how many intelligent people do we hear about, who drink more than is good for them, even though they understand that it isn't healthy?

It is probably fair to say that each child is the product of their genes, their up-bringing and their experience. They exist in the context of their families, and each family is different, in terms of their values, behaviour, interests, and so on. Should we, then, expect the children to revise their behaviour immediately when we teach them something new, when this might be different from what they see at home? Realistically, we may have to accept a delay in the take-up of new ideas, and that delay could be several years.

Personal education – personal development, and emotional and mental well-being

Who am I?

If we are to take control of our lives, we first need to understand ourselves:

- Who am I? Where do I belong?
- What personal qualities do I possess?
- What am I good at? What do I need to develop further? How can I do that?
- What do I want out of life?
- What are these emotions that I feel? Are they normal? How can I control the *negative* ones?

By answering questions such as these, we can develop a sense of ourselves as unique human beings and learn to value who we are. We learn about our abilities, our limitations and our potential. We learn to take more control of our lives, which has a positive effect on our mental health, and helps us to increase our feelings of contentment and fulfilment.

Our task is to help the children along this path, by providing opportunities for them to explore personal qualities, emotions, relationships and everyday situations, so that they might reflect on and clarify their own values and attitudes, and refine their ideas on how they should live their lives.

Of course, we can't expect the children to make once-and-for-all decisions – their ideas will continue to develop as their needs change, as they see more of the world, and as they discuss what they see and hear. However, we can set them off on the pathway to taking responsibility for their own lives, as far as they are able.

Personal qualities

There are a great number of personal qualities that we admire and would want our children to acquire. These include:

- self-respect, self-esteem, self-belief, assertiveness;
- respect for others, sensitivity, humility, compassion;
- a sense of right and wrong, willingness to take responsibility;
- honesty, trustworthiness, loyalty (but not naivety);
- the ability to deal with change without undue worry;
- ambition, high aspirations;
- patience, persistence, the ability to maintain focus;
- interest, enthusiasm, optimism;
- politeness, friendliness, kindness, generosity; and so the list goes on.

Qualities like these are so important. They help the children to build and maintain positive relationships, they accelerate learning in the classroom, and they make them and everybody around them feel good.

Our job is to help the children both to understand what these qualities mean in practice and to appreciate their value. We also need to help them to recognize these qualities in themselves, to cherish them and develop them further, and to recognize and value them in others.

Emotions

We humans encounter a huge range of emotions, both positive and negative. These include positive feelings such as:

- love, affection, fondness;
- cheerfulness, delight, joy, happiness, satisfaction;
- excitement, enthusiasm, exhilaration;
- contentment, pleasure, pride, optimism, hope;
- relief, surprise, amazement, astonishment.

And they include negative feelings such as:

- annoyance, frustration, anger;
- jealousy, bitterness, vengefulness;

- sadness, unhappiness, disappointment;
- hurt, upset;
- regret, guilt, sorrow, shame;
- loneliness, insecurity;
- nervousness, anxiety, worry, fear.

The children learn that these feelings have names, that most of us have felt them at one time or another, and that they are all legitimate. They also learn that some feelings (or emotions) are to be celebrated, while others need to be controlled.

In class, a group discussion might focus on just one emotion (for instance, *anger*) and cover areas such as:

- Can we name this emotion?
- Is it normal?
- Is there more than one sort of *being angry*? Are there any other words for it?
- Do we recognize this emotion in ourselves?
- Can we recognize it in others? Can we tell from their face, their voice, their behaviour?
- Can we see who is angry in this video clip?
- What causes us to feel this way?
- Do we enjoy feeling like this?
- If it is a negative feeling, how can we control it, or get over it and make ourselves feel better?
- What would we like other people to do or say when we feel like this?
- How should we behave when someone close to us is feeling like this?

The children learn about emotions from a wide range of sources – in PSHE lessons, of course, but also in Circle Time and individual tutorials, and when discussing characters in stories, videos and television programmes.

They consider situations in which people have experienced negative emotions – a bereavement, changing school, being let down by a friend, feeling threatened or bullied, a personal failure (measured against their expectation of themselves) – and are encouraged to consider how these situations were dealt with and to suggest other ways in which they could have been resolved to deliver a better outcome.

They also learn that even negative emotions can be turned to advantage, for example, if they break a friend's toy and feel shame and regret, they can decide to be more careful with other people's possessions in the future. If they feel unable to control negative emotions by themselves, they learn that it can be helpful to talk to a friend or a trusted adult, at home or in school.

In any classroom, there may be a small number of children who have encountered rejection, violence or abuse in their lives. While PSHE activities are undoubtedly valuable for these children, in the same way as they are for all children, they may need additional assessment and support in order to maintain their emotional well-being.

Social education and social development

This is about how the children relate to other people – their family and friends, other children they know, other adults they know, and all the people whom they have yet to meet.

Communication

Communication is a key factor in all relationships. In the English chapter of this book, there is a list of reasons why people communicate, and in PSHE activities, the children have opportunities to learn more about the various sorts of communication, and to practise sending the messages they want others to receive and receiving messages in the way they were intended. They refine their skills in:

■ speaking – choosing vocabulary, tone of voice and gesture;
■ listening – understanding the words, and interpreting facial expression, eye contact and body language;
■ the way they behave towards other people.

Understanding other people's emotions and being supportive

As well as understanding their own feelings and emotions, the children learn to read the clues about how other people are feeling, from their behaviour, facial expression, voice, and so on. They learn that people can show emotion in different ways, for example, disappointment might lead to crying or to anger, whereas joy might be shown by jumping up and down and squealing, by smiling or even by tears. If they are to mix well in society, the children need to be able to read these signals and interpret them as accurately as possible.

Leading on from this, if they are to support their friends and family as well as they would like, they need to know how to behave around them when they are experiencing strong emotions. There are no definitive answers to this, but there are some useful pointers, especially about what *not* to do and what *not* to say. The children need to be able to judge when they need to accept a person's behaviour and when it would be better to help them manage their mood in a more positive way, at all times maintaining consideration and respect towards them. They also need to be aware of the effect of their own behaviour on others, particularly their friends, classmates and family, and use this to create harmony and happiness.

Television programmes provide valuable opportunities for the children to discuss emotions and relationships. However, *soaps* are not always instructive in showing how to control emotions in a positive way.

Respecting and valuing other people

It is easy to get on with people we like. It is much harder to get along with people we don't much care for (for whatever reason – real or imagined), or people we don't know well. The children learn that everybody deserves to be shown respect and patience, and to be valued for who they are, and not just for what they can do for us, irrespective of their age, gender, race, ethnicity, religion, skin colour, disability and so on. In the classroom setting, this includes:

- following the class and school rules, thereby respecting others;
- waiting quietly until everybody is ready to begin an activity;
- listening to ideas put forward by others, without dismissing them out of hand;
- showing kindness and integrity to everybody;
- helping others to feel comfortable in the group;
- accepting responsibility for making the classroom and the school a safe and fair place for everyone.

The children learn how the *common good* is enhanced in all communities by paying attention to ideals such as justice, freedom, collective effort, and support for those who need help to reach their potential.

Developing and maintaining personal relationships and friendships

There are certain people with whom the children have a closer relationship – their family (the immediate family and extended family), their friends, members of their school and class (including the adults), members of clubs they belong to, people they meet through friends and family, etc.

We want the children to feel comfortable and confident in each of these relationships – for example, chatting easily with grandparents, and playing games at their football club fairly and in a spirit of friendly competition. The children are taught that, within these groups, they have both rights and responsibilities. The children learn that they need to:

- look out for each other, both on a day-to-day basis, and through difficult times such as accidents and illnesses;
- spend time together on cooperative activities and ventures, taking turns nicely;
- be aware of the needs of others and accommodate these needs;
- be loyal (but not blindly so, because that may not be supportive in the long term);
- be generous with their possessions and their time;
- put others first on occasions, before satisfying their own wants and needs;
- help others to feel good about themselves and develop new qualities and talents.

However, we can't assume that everybody will act towards the children with the same degree of consideration as they give to others, so they also learn strategies to look after themselves emotionally, and to deal in a self-assured way with unkind comments, insults, teasing and bullying, differences of opinion, arguments and temporary falling out.

Importantly, they learn to distinguish between different kinds of close relationships and to understand what might reasonably be expected of them in each – identifying different types of *love*, distinguishing between *good* and *bad* secrets, and learning what to do if they feel uncomfortable in a relationship. And recognising that some behaviours are just wrong, for instance, physical and emotional bullying, and inappropriate touching.

Working together

Through discussion and by practising in group tasks, the children are helped to appreciate that they can sometimes be more productive when they cooperate and collaborate with others than when they work alone. While many of the skills they need overlap with those needed to play together nicely, new skills are also required. These include:

- accepting ideas and opinions with an open mind, asking for clarification when needed, and showing appreciation;
- making suggestions diplomatically;
- agreeing and prioritising actions;
- taking on particular roles reliably, even when they were somebody else's idea;
- showing high moral standards – for example, with regard to cheating.

Resolving disagreements

Even in the closest friendships and relationships, there can be disagreements. These can either escalate into arguments or they can be resolved peacefully – and there are definite skills to be learned and attitudes to be developed if the children are to learn this latter path. They are taught:

- that all decisions have consequences, but that these might be different for different people, so disputes need to be considered from other people's perspectives as well as their own;
- that while disagreements can cause strong emotional responses, they are best resolved calmly, where people control negative feelings and maintain respect for each other;
- to consider the motives that lie behind a person's actions – often a good intention can be frustrated by clumsy execution or thoughtlessness, rather than malice;

- to consider alternatives, options and choices carefully;
- to aim for a *win–win* resolution – or a compromise if this is not possible – where everybody feels positive about the outcome and the relationship can return to an even keel as soon as possible afterwards.

In the secure environment of the classroom, the children might use role-play to act out disagreements, perhaps exploring situations that have arisen during the week, either in real life or on television, as they learn the essential steps towards conflict-resolution.

Being assertive

Assertiveness is not the same as being pushy or aggressive. Rather, it is a kind of confidence or inner strength, based on sound moral judgement, which enables people to stand their ground when they are being pushed into something they think is wrong or something they don't think they should do – and even quiet people can acquire this invaluable quality.

The aim is for the children to be able to:

- decide what is right and what is wrong;
- positively promote what is right;
- resist peer pressure to do something that they know is wrong or unhelpful;
- refuse to support actions or ideas that may be damaging to individuals or communities;
- preserve their personal safety vis-à-vis adults and children who might wish them harm;
- resist media pressure and advertising.

For example, they might need to know how to say 'no' in such a way that the person receiving the message really believes that 'no' is the final and non-negotiable answer. Again, this can be practised in the safe environment of the classroom through role-play activities. The children also learn how and where to get any help or advice they might need when they have felt the need to be assertive in difficult circumstances.

Making good decisions in social situations

Although human beings are social animals, present-day communities are very sophisticated. The unwritten *rules* about how we interact with each other have developed over centuries and will doubtless continue to do so as society continues to evolve. And different cultures have different rules.

As adults, with all our experience, we still have to think about how we will act and react when faced with a new experience – how should I behave in a job interview, or when called for jury service, or at my first practice with an amateur dramatics group? Children are inexperienced in their social interactions and are faced with unfamiliar situations all the time. They may not know what to expect or what is expected of them. Consider their first visit to a swimming pool – some children adapt quickly (perhaps they have seen something similar before), some appear not to notice that a new set of behaviours is required and continue to behave as if they were playing in a paddling pool in their garden, and some watch carefully and copy those who they think might be doing the right thing.

Our aim is to ensure that the children:

- gain experience of a variety of social situations and are taught how to behave appropriately in each;
- learn a range of general strategies that can be adapted to new situations;
- develop the confidence and the willingness to draw on their experience, consider options, and make careful and wise decisions, based on a firm set of morals, fairness and consideration for others.

Health education and a healthy lifestyle

An introduction

In addition to the lessons about the personal, emotional and social aspects of life, PSHE education also covers a broad range of physical aspects:

- managing risk, danger and accidents;
- self-organization;
- how our bodies work and how they change as we grow older;
- illness, disease and keeping clean;
- the benefits of a healthy diet and exercise;
- the dangers of drugs, tobacco and alcohol.

The children learn that there are two main ingredients in keeping themselves safe and healthy – *maintaining good routines and practices*, and *responding to particular circumstances that might prove harmful*.

In each area, the children learn important facts and are helped to understand how those facts relate to them personally, and how to make sound, informed decisions. They also learn what sources of help are available to them and how to access that help when things do not go according to plan, as will inevitably happen at times.

Managing risk and danger

In real life, we can't avoid risks, even if we want to (and sometimes we actively court them for the thrill). As adults, we usually make a fairly good job of recognizing and assessing the dangers we face, basing our decisions on questions such as:

- How much do I want to do this?
- Have I done it before? How did it go? Are the circumstances the same this time?
- Have I seen other people do it successfully? How do I compare with those other people, physically and mentally?
- How bad would the consequences be if it all went wrong? What less serious outcomes are possible?
- Do the benefits outweigh the risks?
- How can I reduce the danger?
- Is it worth the risk?

Sometimes we continue with our plan, perhaps in a modified form. At other times, however, we simply will not even attempt to do something that we consider to be too dangerous.

Children, however, have a more limited experience of life than we do and are therefore less able to make informed decisions about this. For example, if they have never been to an ice rink before, they might not appreciate just how slippery – and how hard – ice can be. Of course, there will always be some accidents – it would be impossible to avoid these altogether. But we can help the children to prepare for many of the risks and situations they might face.

A good starting point is for the children to review what they already know about a situation and then perhaps to consider asking somebody with more or better experience about it. After this preliminary stage, they should consider each activity from the following three viewpoints.

Before the event:

- Make a plan that reduces the likelihood of accidents to oneself or others and reduces the impact if things go wrong.
- Consider whether they have the necessary skills to do it alone, or as part of a group.
- Consider clothing, equipment, special procedures.
- Know who should be informed.
- Devise a Plan B.

During the event:

- Be aware, remember the plan and then follow it, being careful.
- Avoid getting carried away.

- Resist peer pressure.
- Use Plan B if it all goes wrong.

If it goes wrong:

- Deal with the emergency.
- Decide whether to use first aid or just get help as quickly as possible.
- Use a mobile phone to dial 999 (no hoaxes!).
- Tell an adult and know what to say.

Using this model, the children learn about potential risks from:

– roads, railways	– waterways	– hot objects, fire
– sharp objects	– electricity	– germs, poisons
– the sun	– games, stunts	– peer pressure
– strangers	– bullying	– the Internet, phones

When children are young, we tend to give them instructions about safety that they should obey. Often these tell the children what they must *not* do, such as 'Don't touch the cooker'. The progression from this to allowing older children to make their own decisions is a long one and fraught with frustration as they get it wrong and bear the consequences – or, more worryingly, when they take unnecessary risks and *get away with it*, which merely fuels a belief that they know better than us! Ultimately, though, we want the children:

- to recognize the dangers they face;
- to understand the risks associated with those dangers;
- to have the knowledge, understanding, attitudes and skills to assess the risks, and to manage them sensibly.

By the time they are 11 years old, we would still expect the children to be checking with an adult in most situations, but they will soon progress to making those decisions by themselves, or with the aid of their friends when they are out and about. They need to have established good routines and a sound attitude before they reach this stage.

Looking after ourselves – self-organization

In the first ten or eleven years of their lives, the children acquire a vast amount of knowledge, understand a huge number of ideas and concepts, learn an enormous number of skills and, hopefully, develop admirable personal qualities and attitudes. Some of these will be learned at home, others at school, and others from sources such as television, the Internet and friends.

However, there are certain important skills that are rarely taught, but which we still expect the children to have picked up along the way. We need to check whether these really have been learned and to work with parents if it appears that they have not – skills such as:

- organizing their clothes and belongings, and knowing what clothes are appropriate for different occasions and different weather conditions;
- dressing tidily (including shoe laces), judging when clothes might need to be changed;
- grooming – looking after nails, hair, and so on;
- using a handkerchief or tissue;
- knowing their own personal information – full name, address, postcode, age, birthday, e-mail address, contact details for parents, parents' and grandparents' names, etc.;
- knowing their doctor's and dentist's name and address;
- knowing how to make a 999 call and when this might be necessary;
- finding their way around the locality, reading a bus timetable;
- knowing about agencies that can help families.

This might seem like a random list, but without knowledge and skills such as these, a child will be at a disadvantage both with friends and in life in general.

Our bodies – growth and development

A key feature of the programme is to value our body and look after it – after all, it's the only one we've got!

As they progress through the school, the children learn:

- to name the external parts of their body (for example, their facial features and various parts of their arms, legs, hands and feet), and describe the function of each;
- to name the various parts of their eyes, ears and teeth;
- about the human skeleton and muscles, and how these help us to stand, sit and move;
- the names of some internal organs – the heart, lungs, brain, liver, nerves, and so on – where they can be found and, in simple terms, what they actually do inside us.

The children learn how the human body grows and develops – from birth, through childhood, puberty, adolescence and adulthood to old age – together with the changing wants and needs that accompany each phase of life. Physical differences between males and females are discussed. It is made clear that, while we generally go through the same stages of development, we do so at slightly different rates and that variations from the norm are common.

The children are taught about some of the mental and emotional changes that accompany the physical changes that we see:

- the dependency of a baby;
- growing independence through childhood;
- the likelihood of mood swings as they approach puberty;
- the dangers of trying to conform to a *model* body image in the teenage years;
- the worry that comes from taking additional responsibility as a parent;
- the declining mental and physical powers and possible frustrations that accompany old age.

Discussion prepares the children for the next stages of their own development, while helping them to empathize with and understand other people.

Illness, disease and keeping clean

In the early years at school, the children are taught about basic personal hygiene, and lessons are reinforced by following regular routines, such as hand-washing, showering, covering their mouth when coughing or sneezing, using a tissue. Later, the children receive more formal lessons about caring for specific parts of the body, for example, the teeth, eyes, ears, feet, etc.

Older children learn that there are two types of *germs* – bacteria and viruses, both of which are too small to be seen with the naked eye. They also learn how diseases are spread (air-borne or by touch) and how this can be prevented or controlled by following good personal hygiene routines, and by processes such as refrigeration and keeping food covered.

Food and healthy eating

There is no avoiding it – food and drink are an integral and essential part of our everyday lives. In practice, each child's diet is determined by a combination of factors – what is provided by their parents, what their friends recommend, what they are persuaded to try, through advertising and publicity, what they believe is good for their health, and, for sure, what they like.

A school's *healthy eating* programme is normally delivered through a combination of PSHE lessons, science lessons and food technology lessons, as well as by the way the school deals with lunches, snacks, rewards and treats (National Governors' Association 2007: 1–55).

The basic message for the children is that they should enjoy their food, and that they should have a varied and balanced diet that includes more *healthy* foods than *unhealthy* ones. The aim is for the children to have reliable information about each of the foods and drinks that are available, and to understand how particular ingredients can affect their energy levels and their health in the short and longer term. We also want them to develop an attitude where they respect their bodies and build a determination to look after themselves and develop healthy practices where this is within their control.

The children learn that as all our energy comes from food and drink, we need to balance our nutrition and exercise, so that we have enough energy to do the things we want to do, but avoid putting on too much weight. In this respect, the *healthy eating* programme is very closely linked with the *exercise* programme.

Younger children learn to classify foods in various ways:

- meat, dairy, vegetables, fruit, nuts and seeds;
- natural, processed;
- healthy, unhealthy (the children also learn why particular foods are healthy or unhealthy, such as *a doughnut is unhealthy because it is high in saturated fat and refined sugar*).

Older children learn about the elements that foods and drinks contain – proteins, carbohydrates, fats, vitamins, water and minerals – and to give examples of foods that are rich in each of these.

They also learn that the key to a good, healthy diet is a well-balanced combination of food and drink. There are few foods that need to be excluded from the diet, but the balance should be suited to each child's age, size, weight, stage of development and exercise regime. Attention also needs to be given to any medical needs, illnesses and allergies. There might also be religious or cultural influences on diet that need to be respected.

The children are encouraged to try out foods that are unfamiliar to them and build a vocabulary of tastes and textures (sweet, sour, salty, soft, chewy, etc.). They are taught to read and interpret food labels, so that they know what ingredients have been used in processed food. They also learn how to plan and make simple snacks and meals, both hot ones and cold ones, sometimes using recipe books.

They are also taught a little about where our foods come from – how fruit and vegetables are grown (under the ground, above the ground, on trees), which meats come from which animals, which foods are imported (from where and why), and how far our food travels to reach us. In many schools, the children grow their own vegetables, which offers a good introduction to topics such as these.

Exercise

There has been growing concern that twenty-first-century children are too sedentary – they ride in cars more, they sit at computer games more, they play out less, and so on. So while in the past schools have used PE, games and swimming lessons to teach skills and tactics and to promote teamwork, they have now been given the additional role of encouraging the children to take more exercise overall. Again, the intention is that this will establish healthy patterns of behaviour while the children are still young, which they will take with them through their teenage years and into adulthood.

So, in PSHE education the children reinforce what they are learning in their PE lessons and find out about the physical benefits of exercise:

- how it builds fitness (strength, stamina, speed and suppleness), so that they can join-in more, and get more out of life;
- how it improves coordination and therefore makes other activities easier;
- how it builds heart and lung fitness, giving a foundation for good health later in life;
- how it releases endorphins, which make us feel more relaxed, which in turn improves mental health;
- how it can be fun, through making friends and joining in friendly cooperation and competition;
- how we can make measurable progress by setting ourselves targets and improving our performance to achieve them;
- how it helps us to take responsibility, both for ourselves and as part of a team, and make decisions.

The children also learn about the benefits of rest and getting enough sleep.

Drugs, tobacco and alcohol

These three substances are very confusing for children, and often cause unease. For sure, they are within their experience – they may have seen them at home, but will certainly have seen each of them being used and abused on television, often in dramatic ways. Yet they come in so many different forms and with so many different names – and what exactly are the effects? While the children may be aware that there are laws governing their use, they are often not sure what they are.

Our task is to help the children to recognize the risks associated with these substances and to manage them wisely, making informed and responsible choices about their health and their lives, and resisting peer pressure where this could lead them to harm themselves. The emphasis should always be on taking responsibility for oneself and one's safety. It can be useful to start with the question – 'What should I put into my body?'.

It is worth noting that, probably more than in any other area of the curriculum, the children's level of knowledge and understanding will vary a huge amount, depending on their home circumstances and whether they have older brothers and sisters. Indeed, some children may know more about this by the time they are just 10 or 11 years old than we do as adults.

Drugs

In this context, the word *drugs* has a broad definition, covering both *good drugs* and *bad drugs*:

- prescription medicines and tablets, and those bought over the counter;
- illegal drugs;
- unhealthy substances that people take into their body for pleasure, such as solvents, glue and so-called legal highs.

The children learn:

- how drugs are taken into the body – swallowed, inhaled, injected;
- that some people rely on medication to stabilize long-term medical conditions – for example, using an inhaler to counter asthma attacks;
- that it is common to use drugs to reduce the symptoms of familiar ailments, e.g. paracetamol;
- that all drugs, even the good ones, need to be treated with caution because exceeding the recommended or prescribed dose can be dangerous;
- about the importance of keeping the boxes and labels, so that dosages can be read and *use by* dates adhered to;
- that prescription drugs should be taken only by the person named;
- how and where to store medicines and tablets (as well as household cleaners and other poisons) so that younger brothers and sisters cannot access them by mistake.

The children also learn about the reasons why some people choose to take illegal and other harmful substances – for pleasure, or they are under peer pressure to appear *cool*, or because they are addicted.

This is swiftly followed by the case against taking these substances:

- they affect people's behaviour, often for the worse;
- they can be harmful to physical and mental health, and even life-threatening if an overdose is taken;
- the after-effects can make people feel ill, depressed or even suicidal;
- they are addictive, so they are very difficult to stop, and the user needs to take ever increasing amounts to achieve the same effect;
- they are usually expensive, so users cannot buy other things and do other things that they would like.

Finally, the children learn where to get help in an emergency, and where to get further advice, if it is needed.

Tobacco

Children learn about what forms tobacco can take, why people smoke it, the negative health effects of smoking and the legal position with regard to tobacco products. There is no doubt that society as a whole disapproves of smoking, although it does not go so far as to ban it outright. So this is another area where we want the children to recognize the risks and make informed and responsible choices.

Alcohol

Again, this area is covered by a lot of legislation, but the position is by no means clear-cut – certainly children are forbidden from buying alcoholic drinks, but the law about where and when children can drink alcohol with their parents is probably less well known. For adults, the official message is to *drink responsibly*.

The children learn the names of some alcoholic drinks, and discuss the relative strengths of these.

As with other recreational substances, there are positives:

- it can taste good;
- it can help people relax and make them feel good-humoured;
- red wine is thought to contain anti-oxidants, which are good for the heart;
- it makes some youngsters feel *cool*.

There are also negatives. If people drink too much (which is a different amount for different people):

- they can lose their judgement, physical coordination, inhibitions;
- they can become depressed, angry, violent;
- they are more likely to fall, or be injured, attacked or robbed;
- they may be drinking only because of peer pressure;
- they can't drive safely;
- they can become addicted, with the same harmful effects as illegal drugs;
- in the long term, it can lead to heart attacks, liver damage and early death.

Despite this, drinking is socially acceptable for adults of all ages, and among some teenagers, getting drunk is seen as a rite of passage.

As ever, we should also teach the children about dealing with emergencies and where to seek help if all else fails.

Sex and relationship education (SRE)

In their science lessons, the children learn about the physical aspects of reproduction in plants, animals and humans. Sex and relationship education (SRE) adds the personal, social and health aspects to this information.

The core of the programme is based on *friendship* as a special kind of relationship. As such, it draws on many of the other elements of PSHE education.

The aim of the programme is to help the children to move confidently from childhood through adolescence and into adulthood, by:

- establishing the principle that sexual activity should take place within a relationship which is stable and loving, between partners who are mature and equal in status;

- preparing children for the times when they might meet difficult situations, so that they can make informed decisions about safeguarding their physical and emotional well-being and health.

A suitable balance can be hard to achieve. On one hand, we would wish to help the children develop positive attitudes towards sex and sexuality in a suitable context as they mature; on the other hand, we should in no way encourage them, as children, to indulge in sexual activity themselves.

We teach SRE gradually, building knowledge, understanding, skills and attitudes, so that the content is, as far as possible, appropriate to the age and maturity of the pupils in the class, but is also responsive to the needs of individual children or groups within that class. However, this is difficult to gauge, because children mature physically, emotionally and socially at widely different rates:

- if the teaching is too early, some children may be unable to relate to what is being discussed;

- but if the teaching is too late, other children may not be prepared and protected in the way we intended.

Unfortunately, not all the information the children receive is as carefully planned as we or the parents would like. We need to be aware that much of children's SRE actually comes from television programmes, the Internet, older brothers and sisters, and friends. Information gained in this way is prone to exaggeration and sensationalism, and is unlikely to give a rounded and healthy picture. We need to work closely with parents to redress the balance.

Although additional support is made available to children who are thought to be particularly vulnerable, the general SRE programme includes a number of topics.

Attitudes and values – probably the most important part of the programme:

- self-respect, valuing our body;
- a willingness to talk about emotions, relationships and bodies;

- the value of mutual respect within relationships;
- the importance of taking responsibility for one's actions;
- a commitment to resist peer and cultural pressure;
- a guarded approach to the ways in which body image, relationships and sexuality are portrayed in the media;
- the principle that violence and coercion in relationships are never acceptable;
- the value of a stable, loving relationship as the ideal environment for a sexual relationship, and for bringing up children.

Knowledge and understanding

- the physical changes that occur in both males and females as they get older;
- the legal position concerning, for example, the age of consent;
- emotional changes and feelings they may encounter at puberty;
- sexual health – how to keep themselves fresh and clean, particularly as they approach and reach puberty;
- different types of loving relationships, which can bring great emotional benefits, or harm;
- the behaviours and actions that constitute sexual behaviour, and what is acceptable and unacceptable in terms of different sorts of touching, name-calling, etc.;
- not every sexual act necessarily leads to pregnancy, but it might;
- sexual relationships are a natural part of adulthood, but they are not a requirement;
- consent is critical;
- where and how to access help and advice.

Skills

- identifying and discussing feelings and emotions;
- managing and controlling emotions;
- managing friendships and personal relationships sensitively;
- managing the changes to the body that occur at puberty;
- managing disagreement and conflict in a civil, but assertive, way;
- recognizing possible risks and dangers, and using effective strategies to avoid them;
- recognizing and avoiding exploitation and abuse;
- making informed choices;
- resisting pressure to be sexually active;

- being able to say 'no' convincingly to suggestions that make them feel uncomfortable or they think are wrong;

- discussing values, concerns and actions in a mature way;

- asking for help and accessing advice and services.

A number of these topics might seem better suited to youngsters in their teenage years, but we need to recognize that some children become physically mature as early as 8 years old, even if they are less mature emotionally. These children need to understand what is happening to their bodies, and to understand what behaviour is acceptable and what is unacceptable, so that they can avoid being exploited.

Economic education and financial well-being

Financial capability – understanding and managing our personal finances

When young children *play shop*, does this truly reflect what happens when we, as adults, go to a supermarket? It is probably more likely that we walk into a large store, fill a trolley, scan our own goods, push a card into a slot, press a few buttons, bag up our groceries, and then walk out of the store, without ever speaking with a shopkeeper. If we do use a till, the checkout assistant will even give us cash back – so we take a trolley-full of groceries and we seem to be paid for doing so!

There is so much the children need to learn if they are to understand how to control their finances effectively and independently, both now and as they get older. They learn:

- where they can get money from;

- how to look after their money;

- how much things cost;

- how to make best use of money;

- what happens if they can't afford something they want.

Possibly the most important lesson the children learn is that we can spend our money only once. So we should consider very carefully what we really want from it – at a simple level, this means that if we buy an ice cream today, we probably can't have sweets tomorrow.

Where do we get money from?

The children discuss the main ways of acquiring money – younger children might receive pocket-money and presents, while older children and adults usually work. Many families also receive money from benefits of one kind or another.

The children learn about the variety of jobs that people do, and they will probably appreciate the suggestion that, if they are going to spend several hours each day at work, then they should get a job that suits them, and which they enjoy.

How should I look after my money?

The children are taught that they should not waste money – it should be used carefully, to buy things that they really want. They compare ways of keeping their money safe, including all sorts of money boxes and piggy banks.

Older children learn about banks and building societies, and how debit and credit cards are used:

- we use the banks as safe storage for our money;
- we have an *account*, so that the bank can keep track of our money;
- banks sometimes pay us a small amount of *interest* when we *deposit* our money with them (there might be lessons on percentages at this point);
- when we have deposited money at the bank, we can usually withdraw it at any time, or spend it by using a debit card (links with ICT here);
- banks do not just hold on to our money – they lend some of it to people who want to borrow for various reasons;
- banks make their money by charging more for their loans than the interest they give us;
- if we borrow money, it is called a *loan* – and we have to pay it back;
- using a credit card is actually borrowing money;
- banks will also swap our pounds for foreign currencies when we go abroad.

We also have to be very careful when giving payment details over the Internet.

How much do things cost?

In their maths lessons the children solve many *money problems*. The most valuable problems are those that relate to the children themselves and their lives, where prices are realistic and where the children understand the relative prices of items.

As the children mature, they move from knowing the cost of a packet of sweets to knowing the cost of a pair of trainers (tens of pounds), a computer (hundreds of pounds), or a particular model of car (thousands of pounds). But prices such as these are merely numbers without a sense of scale attached to them – the question of whether a £60 tennis racket is expensive depends on one's income. So the children also need to appreciate how much people earn.

The idea of *tax* is explained, together with a discussion of what taxes are spent on, including schools, colleges and education, roads, doctors and hospitals, and parliament and councils (links with citizenship).

The children learn that politicians make decisions about what will be provided and that while these services appear to be free, they are only free *at the point of use*, and they do still need to be paid for – through taxes.

They are also made aware of some of the costs associated with running a home, for example, rent/mortgage, light and heat, food, school lunches, holidays, etc., and the cost of using a mobile phone might receive special attention.

In this way, the older children get a real sense of the value of money, appreciating that it can be spent only once, and that much of it goes on *essentials* – so we need to be very careful about how we spend the rest, in order to get best value from it.

How can I make best use of my money?

The children will usually offer many personal examples of making choices about the way they spend their money. In lessons, the children practise weighing up options and making responsible financial decisions – ice cream or fruit? CD or tee-shirt? cinema or swimming? how to contact a friend – bus, bike, on foot, e-mail, landline, mobile or text? The children learn to estimate how far their money will go, using their calculation skills to total up their *wants*.

We want the children to become questioning and informed consumers, so they learn to evaluate products by reading labels carefully, comparing specifications and accessing reviews (both by word of mouth and on the Internet) before deciding what to buy. They are advised to treat advertising and special offers with a degree of scepticism, and to ask the question 'Does this product offer good value for money?'.

Looking beyond their own finances, the children learn that people's spending patterns depend on both their financial circumstances and their personal life choices:

- they are taught that people in different parts of the world have very different levels of income;
- they explore alternatives such as buying *quality* products that last a long time, as against buying cheaper *throw-away* items;
- they explore differing attitudes to money – some people want to be rich, while others wish only to earn enough to live comfortably and fund a hobby;
- they discuss the practice of giving money to charities (and doing sponsored events to support them);
- they consider broader ethical issues – is my spending having a good or bad effect on people locally and across the world, and on the environment?

What if I can't afford something I want?

The children are taught that we have *needs* and we have *wants*, and if our budget is limited, then our needs should be satisfied before our wants – for instance, buying our groceries should take priority and we may have to wait a while to buy treats.

And if the things we want are expensive, we might need to save up for them. However, some people are unwilling to save up. Instead, they borrow money from a bank (or building society), which needs to be repaid at a later date, together with some interest – there is nothing wrong with this course of action, just so long as it is planned carefully. The children learn that most people who buy their own home borrow money to do so, because flats and houses are so expensive.

Enterprise education

A good way to learn about handling money and making responsible financial decisions is to manage a budget. In the same way, probably the best way to learn about business is to run a business (in a safe, risk-free environment, of course). Enterprise education provides opportunities for both of these.

Typically, the children set up and run a manufacturing business, such as making and selling greetings cards, a school newspaper or home-baked cakes. Through this, they learn about:

- profit – the reason why most businesses exist;
- the relationship between cost, price and profit;
- the benefits of collaboration and team-work;
- showing initiative in a responsible, measured way;
- making best use of people's skills, through the careful allocation of tasks;
- the qualities needed to be entrepreneurial, such as self-belief, creative problem solving, attention to detail and perseverance.

They also learn about the process of getting a product from an *idea* to a *sale*:

- financing, costs and accounts;
- designing and trialling;
- sourcing raw materials;
- manufacturing;
- packaging and distribution;
- promotion, advertising and sales;
- banking and receipts.

The children are introduced to some of the risks of going into business: What if nobody wants to buy the things we have produced? What if we have to lower our price? We could end up with a loss, instead of a profit!

The children take a fresh look at shops and learn that they are enterprises, and that they exist to sell things so that the owner makes a profit and therefore makes a living. They might also see shop owners in a new light – as entrepreneurs who have a *can-do* attitude, show initiative to make their ideas a reality, take calculated risks and strive to provide what buyers want.

Careers education

At the primary level, careers education helps the children to:

- get a sense of the range of jobs that people do;
- find out about the satisfaction that people derive from doing their job;

- appreciate that, while all jobs have their own skills and demands, two of the most important skills are *the ability to get on with other people* and *the ability to communicate clearly*;

- find out what qualities people need to carry out particular jobs successfully — for example, a fireman needs to be physically fit, strong, brave, calm and caring — and how they can develop these qualities themselves;

- develop a sense of ambition and aspiration;

- be aware of qualifications;

- appreciate that education continues into adulthood alongside working in a job.

An important principle of careers education is that, whatever work we eventually do, as long as we do it well, we are making a contribution to our community, which brings us together and strengthens society.

Working with children on PSHE education topics

An introduction

PSHE education can be approached in so many different ways. A key requirement, however, is to match the topic to the age and maturity of the children.

Activities might include any of the approaches outlined in Chapter 2 (*With so many different types of learning, how do we go about teaching?*), but the following have proved particularly useful in PSHE education:

- discussing the qualities and actions of the characters in stories, television and video;

- discussion, role-play, simulations and games;

- discussion with visiting speakers, such as police, community health workers, bank workers, sports professionals — in fact, people who work in a variety of different industries;

- taking responsibility around school, for example, looking after the school environment, being play buddies or prefects for younger pupils on the playground, or looking after school pets;

- taking part in lunchtime and after-school activities, such as hobby clubs, sports teams, school council, residential visits, music and drama productions, etc.

An important skill for staff working in this area is that of *questioning* using open-ended questions, to find out exactly what the children know and don't know, what they understand and don't understand, and what their opinions and attitudes might be. Many of the issues being discussed have no *right/wrong* answers, and the children might have any number of misconceptions and misunderstandings that need to be cleared up before they can move on to the next level.

Some children will need help beyond the general class lessons, either from a member of staff at the school or from a specialist based elsewhere. In these cases, an individual programme might be drawn up, although its contents may not be generally available to all staff, because of the nature of the child's difficulties.

Many PSHE education activities will involve discussion, as the children explore themes and ideas. It can be very helpful to offer them prompts, such as:

- What is happening here?
- What do you think about this?
- What could happen?
- What could we do in this situation? What should we do?
- Who can help us with this?

It may be tempting simply to tell the children what is right or wrong, and what they should think or do – and there is a place for such a straightforward approach, especially when the children are very young. Eventually, however, we want the children to understand situations, and to decide for themselves what is right and proper and safe. We want them to be able to make sensible choices from the opportunities that will be made available to them and to cope with the difficult situations they may face.

In addition, every child is different in terms of their cultural and family background, their level of knowledge and understanding, their experience, their character, and so on. So the support they require will inevitably need to be individualized. This support is most effective when we have created a safe environment in which the children can share their feelings and opinions, and explore their values and attitudes, without attracting negative feedback.

Dealing with sensitive issues and difficult questions

Most people would agree that PSHE education is central to the primary curriculum and ranks alongside English and maths in importance. However, it is also a subject that has the potential to cause upset. Unlike other subjects, the children are not *outside, looking in on the content*, but rather, they are *living the content* – we are discussing *the children and their families as they live their lives*. While we have a responsibility to get our message across, we need to be careful to avoid alienating the children or their parents, who might have a cultural background very different from our own, as this might affect a child's willingness to accept a particular point of view that we are putting forward (QCA 2005: 11–12).

An essential first step is for all staff to be sure of the school's stance on particular issues. This area of the curriculum is usually well documented through policies and procedures, and these should be read thoroughly and followed carefully. This may include, among others:

– the school aims and ethos

– confidentiality

– behaviour/school rules

– anti-bullying

– healthy eating

– child protection

– sex and relationship education

– equal opportunities

– racist incidents

– physical activity

as well as any schemes of work used by the school, such as SEAL (The Social and Emotional Aspects of Learning) (DfES 2005).

The next step is to prepare thoroughly for the lesson, by grouping the children carefully, taking into account their maturity and their worldliness, as well as their level of understanding, and making sure that the children receive balanced information and a range of views. This also applies to contributions made by visitors to the classroom, of course. Another good idea is to pre-plan how we will respond to questions that may arise while discussing particular topics – for example, what questions might the boys or the girls ask as part of a sex and relationship education lesson?

Once the lesson has started, we need to be extra vigilant: Will we recognize a comment that amounts to a disclosure of abuse? How far can we let a discussion run before we intervene? Also, of course, we need to be sensitive to the feelings of individual children when we discuss issues that might be particularly difficult for them.

To protect everybody in this difficult area – both children and adults – it is a good idea to establish some ground rules, which are explained and understood (in child-speak, as necessary) beforehand. Rules such as:

■ respect what people say;

■ no one – neither child nor adult – will be obliged to answer a personal question;

■ no one will be compelled to take part in a discussion, although they should listen;

■ only correct names for parts of the body will be used;

■ meanings of words will be explained in a sensible and factual way;

■ if anybody wants to ask a question, but is embarrassed about asking it aloud, they may use a *question box*;

■ it is acceptable for teachers to avoid answering a question by saying that the parent is the appropriate person to answer that particular question, or that the question can be discussed individually after class, or that the question will be covered at a later stage in their PSHE lessons;

■ we have a set of values that we share absolutely – bullying, cruelty and racism are never acceptable in any form.

By adopting rules such as these, in most cases children can share their views without fear, and staff can be confident that the discussion will be meaningful and helpful to the children in terms of developing and maturing their views. Occasionally, however, a pupil will make a personal *disclosure*. In these circumstances we must be meticulous in following the school's policies, for example, those concerned with child protection and confidentiality.

17

Religious Education (RE)

Why are religions studied in schools?

Before we explore *religious education*, we probably need to clarify just what *religion* is, and why it has a place in the primary curriculum at all.

Let's start with what we know – religious groups have been with us since the Stone Age, and there are hundreds, if not thousands, of such groups across the world today. It seems that a large proportion of humankind has a need to believe in something beyond the here-and-now – something *spiritual*, something greater than humanity – that we can look up to. However, we can't necessarily agree on what that *something* is.

Some people believe in superior beings (often called gods) who possess exceptional or remarkable qualities. Others lead their lives according to the advice of a particular charismatic character in history who, they believe, possessed spiritual inspiration and wisdom. Others assign special powers to natural elements such as the wind, the earth or nature. And there is a widespread belief that humans have a spirit, or a soul, which is separate from the body it inhabits. Each of these would qualify as *religious*, or at least *spiritual*. But, of course, there is no proof that any of these forces actually exist. That is why religion is a matter of *faith*.

People embrace religion for a whole host of personal reasons, including:

■ satisfying a need for a spiritual dimension in their lives;

■ bringing meaning, perspective and structure to their lives;

■ offering answers to the big questions about creation, life and death;

■ providing opportunities to appreciate and enjoy beauty, joy, wonder and mystery in a serene and peaceful environment;

■ providing a set of moral and ethical values on which they can base their decision-making, as they decide what is right and wrong, and what is fair and unfair.

Together, these provide a compelling case for the children to learn about the principal religions and religious beliefs in our society.

What is religious education in schools really about?

First, let's be clear about what RE is *not* – it is *not* about nurturing, coaching or instructing children in a particular faith. Responsibility for that lies firmly with their family and community, if that is what they want. Nor is it the same as *collective worship*. In brief, RE is about helping the children to explore and understand the religious beliefs that people hold, and to consider these beliefs in the context of their own lives.

We do this by helping them to:

- gain a basic knowledge and understanding of religious beliefs and practices;
- consider religious ideas and reflect on how they compare with their own beliefs and values;
- develop a respectful and caring approach towards other people and their beliefs, to nature, and to all living things;
- cultivate and refine their own moral and ethical values and spiritual beliefs;
- develop an interest in spiritual questions and ideas.

To sum up, RE offers the children opportunities to learn about a range of religions, and to learn from them in ways that help them to grow as people.

(Ofsted 2010: paragraphs 12–18, 29–42, 86–91)

What is included in the RE programme?

The majority of primary schools in the UK are *maintained* schools, where a governing body manages a school in conjunction with a local authority. However, there are also a large number of *faith schools* and a growing number of *academies*. By law, all these schools have to provide religious education for their pupils. However, there is no national curriculum for RE – rather, programmes are drawn up to reflect local circumstances.

In maintained schools and academies, this means following a locally agreed syllabus, which has been drawn up by a committee that includes representatives of the various faith groups in the area. The content should be substantially Christian, but will also include some of the teaching and practices from the other principal religions represented in the UK (Buddhism, Hinduism, Islam, Judaism, Sikhism) (Leicestershire County Council 2009). Faith schools, on the other hand, can draw up their own programmes for RE, drawing on the traditions of their faith.

Interestingly, although schools are obliged to provide RE for all their pupils, parents may ask for their children to be withdrawn from the lessons if they so wish – they do not have to give a reason and the school must comply with their request.

The lessons

The children explore religion and belief by undertaking investigations. Of course, they will usually need something physical on which to base their investigation, perhaps:

- a story
- a statue or figure
- an article of clothing
- a celebration or festival
- a national charitable event

- a picture
- a building
- some food
- a journey
- an animal or bird

- a song
- an artefact
- a symbol
- a piece of sacred writing
- a child's new kitten

Discussion of the religious significance of the object should lead to an exploration of:

- a key religious concept, theme or question;
- what people believe; and
- the children's own ideas and consideration of where they stand on the issues raised.

It is likely that the children will return to particular starting points more than once during their school career. For instance, in the infant classes, they might listen to Hindu or Christian stories and be able to talk about them, describing who the main characters are, and what they like and dislike about them. By the junior classes, they are encouraged to suggest what believers might learn from a particular story and perhaps be able to identify which parts of the story support these lessons.

It is not just the objects that are repeated – the children return again and again to particular themes, as they study the messages given by the spiritual leaders from different religions, themes such as:

- belonging
- trust
- celebration
- rules for living
- myself
- responsibility

- belief
- communication
- good, evil
- love
- respect
- inspiration

- charity
- god
- creation, life, death
- wonder, appreciation

In their lessons, the children explore what different religions say about these themes, and how the actions of believers are based on religious teachings and beliefs. They are encouraged:

- to consider what they personally think about the opinions and teachings in relation to each theme;
- to compare their own views with those of believers;
- to consider whether they might wish to alter their opinion, on the basis of what they have learned.

Of course, it would be perfectly feasible to treat these themes as moral or social issues, without ever mentioning a religious perspective. For example, while discussing the work of charities, the children might explore issues such as fairness, kindness and equality of opportunity – after all, most charities are not affiliated to any religion. The difference is that, in RE, the children explore these themes through the eyes of believers. So, for instance, they might consider whether there is a difference in motivation between people who undertake religion-based charitable work and those who carry out non-religion-based charitable activities.

Other examples of themes that might straddle the religious/non-religious divide include:

- communities, belonging, tolerance (citizenship);
- Greek and Roman gods, why King Henry VIII established the Church of England (history);
- links between places, sustainability (geography);
- poverty, charity, equality, value, getting along together (PSHE education);
- inspiration, genres, styles, traditions (art and music);
- stories, poetry, drama (English).

Obviously, every child comes to the lesson with different background knowledge and a different level of understanding, so we need to set open-ended tasks and ask open-ended questions, to which the children can respond in a variety of ways – through discussion, writing, drawing, sculpture, drama, music, song and so on.

RE can be a most rewarding subject, both for staff and for pupils. It contains marvellous stories and beautiful art, and we meet fascinating characters. It stimulates our imagination and really gets children thinking. However, it can also be rather difficult for some children. For example, in science lessons, they learn facts about the life cycle of plants, animals and humans, and then, in RE, we introduce the possibilities of resurrection and reincarnation. Other children might have been told by their parents that the ideas we are discussing are nonsense.

We really do need to be aware of the sensitivity of some topics. So, as in PSHE education, we need a set of rules to govern religious discussion in the classroom. Perhaps the principle should be that, while everybody should be included in the discussion, nobody should be obliged to make a comment or be made to feel uncomfortable.

Learning about particular religions

Clearly, there is a huge amount of information that the children can learn about each religion – the people, artefacts, events, beliefs, teachings, values, forms of expression, the way of life that make each religion what it is, and so on (BBC Schools).

Spiritual leaders

The children learn about spiritual leaders and other significant people in each of the religions – their names, what they did, why they are important and how they act as role models for believers – people such as Buddha, Jesus, Muhammad and the Guru Nanak. They learn about the ideas and values advocated by these leaders, which shape the core beliefs in each religion.

The outward signs of religion

Religion is an abstract thing – the children can't see it, hear it, touch, smell or taste it. However, they can:

- read and hear stories from the sacred books associated with each religion, such as the Christian *Bible*, the Muslim *Qur'an*, the Sikh *Adi Granth*;
- see the artwork, artefacts, statues, buildings, signs and symbols;
- observe the rituals and practices;
- listen to the music, songs, hymns and chants;
- taste the special foods;
- smell the incense;
- touch the special clothes.

The sacred books in each religion are particularly important artefacts – they are not just records from the past, but speak to believers in the present and guide them in their own lives.

The children learn that, while the outward signs of religion might be colourful and appealing to all of us (for example, the architecture, the clothes and the music), for believers they are so much more than this – they provide a means of feeling closer to their god (or to their ideal state of mind). These artefacts are extremely important – they are used by believers to demonstrate their commitment to their religion.

So when the children hear a story with a religious heritage, or see a religious picture, sculpture, carving, sign, symbol or relic, they should be encouraged to consider:

- its religious significance;
- how it plays a part in the beliefs, principles and traditions of the religion;
- how it might affect believers in their day-to-day lives, both within their religious community and in the context of a broader society.

Stories

Each religion has its own set of stories. Some are central to the religion, such as the Christmas story and the Hindu story of Rama and Sita, while others deliver a lesson on how we should behave towards each other, for example Jesus's parables. Stories offer a wonderful introduction to religious ideas, as they allow the children to imagine themselves present at a particular event and to consider what they would have felt and done if they had been in the same situation. Stories also serve to introduce many of the key characters in each religion.

Festivals and celebrations

Festivals and celebrations are key elements in all the major religions – with their special clothes, food, dances, rituals, candles, pilgrimages, and so on – and yet each one is carried out and presented in its own special way.

The children learn about these by looking at pictures, listening to descriptions, watching videos, and so on, as well as by joining in events – for example, tasting hot cross buns just before Good Friday and discussing the significance of the cross in the Christian faith. When they watch or take part in a religious celebration, festival, tradition or ritual, the children should take note of:

- which religion it relates to;
- which element of religious belief is being highlighted;
- what believers think and feel when they are taking part;
- what believers get out of the experience;
- how it supports the teachings and values of the religion.

Prayer and worship

The notion of prayer and worship can be difficult for children, as the idea of speaking to an unknown being is far removed from the first-hand experiences normally associated with the early stages of learning. However, the children learn that, in religions where believers have faith in a god (Christianity, Hinduism, Islam, Judaism and Sikhism), prayer is a way for believers to show their devotion to their gods, to feel closer to them and to have a dialogue directly with them. Buddhists do not believe in a god, so they meditate rather than pray, focusing on awakening to *truth* and *enlightenment*, in the way that the Buddha did. The children also learn about the various rituals and practices associated with prayer in each of the major religions, and about their significance to believers.

How religious belief affects the way believers lead their lives

All religions offer a view on moral and ethical values – good and evil, honesty, respect, love, forgiveness, tolerance, justice, responsibility, human rights, etc. This leads naturally to a code of behaviour – a set of rules – that believers try to follow – for example, the Christian *Ten Commandments*, the Buddhist *Five Moral Precepts* and the Jewish *Torah*.

The children explore these values and behaviours and are taught that, for believers, they stem from religious belief rather than from human kindness alone. The children discuss these moral values in terms of their own lives:

- What does it mean to be *kind* or *charitable*?
- Just how do these values reveal themselves today rather than in the setting of a story?
- Is this how I mostly behave? Is this the best way to behave?
- What do I get out of it? What do other people get out of it?

A good way for the children to find out what it is like to commit to a religion and belong to a faith community is to talk with a member of that community, either by visiting one, or by inviting one into school. Of course, care needs to be taken to ensure that any information is given impartially, so that it remains in the realm of religious *education* and does not stray into religious *persuasion*. But what better way to find out the answers to such questions as: Are Jews allowed to work on Saturdays? Why do Sikhs wear turbans? Can they still ride a motorbike and become firemen? Do Muslims have to give to charity? What sort of charities?

Faith communities

The children learn that a group of people who share a belief is called a *faith community*. This may be local, national or international, and is usually led by an official, who brings the faith community together, gives spiritual guidance to the group and to individual members when there is a need, leads and performs ceremonies, and sets an example for the way the scriptures should be interpreted in the daily lives of believers in modern times.

In some countries, a particular faith community will comprise the majority of the population – for instance, we might say that India is a Hindu country, while Italy is largely Christian (Roman Catholic) and Pakistan is Muslim.

How similar are the major religions?

As the children learn more about the various religions, they come to appreciate that religions mostly encourage very similar values, and that these are very often incorporated into national laws, for example, those to do with lying, stealing and hurting others.

Religions also differ, however, both in their spiritual beliefs and particularly in their rituals. They all have their own words for their gods and the way they should be addressed. They all have their own practices, special days and traditions. And on a day-to-day level, they have different rules, such as whether believers should eat beef, pork, or any meat at all. The children learn about some of these differences, and are taught that they are matters of opinion, based on religious belief.

Older children are also taught that there are variations within each of the major religions – there are many different forms of Buddhism, Islam, Christianity and the rest. Sometimes, these variations have arisen because of geographical distance; in the past, followers in different countries would not have compared notes very often as to how the scriptures should be interpreted in everyday life. In other cases, a group of believers has disagreed with the establishment of the time and formed a break-away group, who hold enough of the same basic beliefs to regard themselves as belonging to the same religion, but think differently on enough issues to launch their religion under a different set of rules. The children might learn about some of the different beliefs held by Catholics, Anglicans, Methodists, Baptists and other groups who see themselves as *Christians*, for example, on the subjects of the acceptance of female preachers, ministers and bishops, and the way churches are decorated and services are carried out.

Developing enquiry skills through religious education

An important way for the children to learn about religions and religious ideas is through research and enquiry. There are a great variety of characters, objects, songs, events, etc. to be explored and investigated.

Research and enquiry skills enable the children to find out about specific religions and about the nature of religion itself: What is religion all about? What does it means to have a faith? What purpose does religion serve in people's lives? How do believers benefit from their beliefs?

Of course, the skills are similar to those used in other subjects:

- *Exploring and investigating* – being inquisitive; asking relevant questions about an aspect of religion or about the notion of religion itself; observing, in the wider sense of using all five senses – sight, hearing, taste, smell and touch; gathering facts, ideas and opinions from books, video, visits, interviews, ICT sources etc.; judging which pieces of information will allow them to answer their questions.

- *Communicating* – listening respectfully to opinions held by people with a faith; discussing questions and issues sensitively; understanding religious words and phrases and using them accurately; expressing religious ideas in a variety of ways through speech, writing, drawing, music and song, ICT etc.

■ *Interpreting* – understanding the meaning attached to artefacts, stories, works of art, symbols; suggesting a meaning or message contained in religious artefacts and texts.

■ *Analysing* – distinguishing between fact, opinion and belief; comparing elements of different religions.

■ *Evaluating* – weighing up evidence and making informed judgements about the religious ideas, beliefs and values that people suggest; identifying key religious values, and noting their importance to individuals, to religious communities and to society as a whole; connecting different aspects of religious teaching to create a coherent whole.

Alongside these enquiry skills, we also use RE lessons to help the children to develop skills in:

■ Using their imagination and reflecting (in the sense of *mulling over ideas*) – reflecting on religious beliefs and practices, and forming their own views on each of these; reflecting on the big questions in life, and reaching their own tentative conclusions and explanations; identifying and feeling positive emotions such as love, wonder, peace, delight.

■ Empathizing – seeing things from other people's point of view; considering the thoughts, feelings, attitudes, beliefs and values of others.

Encouraging the children's moral, ethical, personal and spiritual development

The aim of primary education is to help children to grow and develop in the broadest possible sense – not just academically, but also morally, ethically, personally and spiritually. In the best schools these elements filter through the entire life of the school – in lessons and assemblies, at breaks and lunchtimes and, importantly, in the way staff and children relate to each other. Undoubtedly, RE is particularly well placed to make a significant contribution.

Moral and ethical development

In the context of religious belief, the children consider *moral and ethical issues*, such as:

■ right and wrong, fairness;

■ the consequences of our actions;

■ our rights and responsibilities – and those of others.

When these issues are encountered through their study of religions, the children are encouraged also to reflect on them in the context of their own lives, clarifying their views and reaching individual conclusions about how they should behave.

Personal development

When taught well, RE offers opportunities for the children to develop a range of both personal qualities and positive attitudes. For example:

- self-awareness;
- curiosity, open-mindedness and a positive approach to life;
- tolerance, respect and concern for individuals and groups in society;
- respect for religious customs, artefacts, buildings and so on;
- calmness and politeness when discussing difficult issues.

Clearly, many of the personal qualities and attitudes listed above are not specifically related to RE. However, they do also provide a firm foundation for the children's spiritual development.

Spiritual development

At the children's level, *spiritual development* isn't easy to define but, by its very nature, it isn't concerned with *things* – it has much more to do with ideas such as feelings, insight, belief and faith.

We can say that children make progress in their spiritual development when they begin to:

- develop a set of values, principles and beliefs which guide their outlook on life and their behaviour;
- experience feelings such as joy, delight and calm;
- develop a sense of wonder, marvelling at the beauty and power of the natural world, and appreciating the less tangible aspects of life;
- appreciate the arts and personal achievements;
- feel inspired, and become creative and expressive in their own right;
- welcome *mystery* and *uncertainty* as an integral part of their life;
- accept that it is all right to ask questions, even when adults cannot agree on an answer;
- perhaps, relate to sacred things and to a *higher power* of some sort.

Certainly, progress in the area of spiritual development is a gradual process, but it will be evident in the way the children feel and the way they behave.

18

Science

What is science really about?

Scientists see their job as finding out about the universe and everything in it:

- Plants and animals, and their component parts – skin tissue, cells, seeds, etc.
- The materials and substances that things are made of – natural materials (e.g. rocks, oil, rubber, wool, water, cotton) and man-made ones (e.g. plastic, glass, silicon).
- Forces – both *natural forces*, such as the weather, gravity, electricity, light, heat and earthquakes; and *human-induced forces*, such as electricity, light, heat, lasers, nuclear power.
- Systems – the solar system, ecological systems.

Because science covers all aspects of the world, professional scientists tend to specialize in just one or two areas, perhaps:

– genetics	– ecology	– biochemistry	– meteorology
– astronomy	– mechanics	– forensics	– acoustics

But whatever their area of interest, they aim to *explore it, find out about it*, and *describe it*, with the ultimate goal of *understanding it*.

Using their five senses (sight, hearing, taste, smell and touch) together with a range of scientific instruments, their investigations begin with *what? where?* and *when?* questions, such as:

- What is this? What is it like? What properties does it have? What is it called?
- Where else have I seen something like this?
- When was it first noticed? Has it always been there or is it new?
- What happens if we try to change it in some way, perhaps by moving it, mixing it with something else, or changing environmental conditions?

They then move on to *how?* and *why?* questions, such as:

■ Why is it the way it is?
■ How does it *work?*

Of course, questions like these are not exclusive to *science* – they are the kind of questions that any inquisitive person might ask. But the way scientists go about answering them *is* scientific – they use what is called *the scientific method*. Essentially, this means that, whatever the object, substance, force or system might be, there can be no wild guesses. At an everyday level, anybody can be a scientist – it is just a matter of being inquisitive, asking questions in the right way, and answering those questions using this so-called *scientific method*.

In class, we encourage the children to ask questions which begin with 'I wonder why . . .' or 'I wonder whether. . .' or 'I wonder how. . .'. For example, 'I wonder whether it is true, as one of my gardening friends has told me, that copper wire will stop slugs from getting to my courgette plants', or 'I wonder how birds manage to keep their balance on a branch when it is windy'.

Scientists don't always *do* anything with the knowledge and understanding they gain – it is often left to other people, such as engineers, technologists, doctors and so on, to apply the knowledge. For instance, scientists discovered that sounds could be converted into pictures; but it was technologists who adapted this *sonar* technology so that fishermen are able to see shoals of fish beneath their boats and have a better idea of where to lower their nets.

Some discoveries, in astronomy for example, seem to have fewer practical applications, at least in the short term, but this does not discourage scientists, because sometimes research is carried out purely to gain knowledge and understanding (DES 1992c: paragraph A6).

Which areas of science do the children learn about?

We have five broad areas of learning in primary school Science.

Of course, the children still learn Biology, Chemistry and Physics, although these have been *re-branded* several times in various UK national guidelines over the past twenty years or so:

■ **Biology** is also called *Life Processes*, and *Life and Living Things*, and *Biological Systems*. The children learn about plants and animals.

■ **Chemistry** also goes under the names *Materials and Their Properties*, and *Material Behaviour*, and just plain *Materials*. As its name implies, the children learn about some of the hundreds of different substances in the world – gases, liquids and solids, both natural and man-made – exploring what they are made of, what properties, characteristics and qualities they have, and how they behave in different conditions.

■ **Physics** is variously known as *Physical Processes*, and *Energy, Movement and Forces*, and *Forces, Electricity and Waves*. In this area, the children learn something of the natural and man-made forces that operate around us – we can't see them, just feel their effects.

And they also learn about:

■ **Earth and the Solar System**, and
■ **Attitudes, values and interdependence** – the ways in which plants, animals, humans and the planet all depend on each other for their welfare.

Practical science, using the scientific method

The scientific method of enquiry has two elements – *transferable skills* and *scientific skills*.

Transferable qualities, attitudes and skills

Whatever topic scientists are working on, *doing science* is very much a hands-on activity, carried out by active people with enquiring minds. The qualities and attitudes that allow children to do *good science* are also invaluable in other areas of learning and investigation, whatever the subject:

■ curiosity;
■ a willingness to work steadily and methodically, perseverance;
■ creativity – how is the best way to go about investigating something? what will the process be?;
■ showing respect for evidence;
■ flexibility of thought – the gradual refinement of what we believe when new evidence comes to light;
■ acceptance that not everything is clear-cut, and recognizing that more evidence might be needed before a conclusion can be reached;
■ cooperating with others;
■ sensitivity to living things and the environment.

Without these qualities, skills and attitudes, any enquiry would be considered clumsy, flawed and unscientific, so we need to help the children to develop these approaches over time.

Scientific skills

As the children move on from the 'I wonder . . .' stage and start to think as a scientist, they learn to work through three distinct phases:

- planning an investigation (*before* the experiment);
- obtaining evidence and presenting it clearly (*during* the experiment);
- considering the evidence and reaching a conclusion (*after* the experiment).

Planning an investigation (before the experiment)

This phase has several steps:

- Turning a general query into an *investigation* – changing the 'I wonder . . .' into a specific, answerable question, such as 'What happens if I do this, or this, in this way?'.
- Researching what other people have already found out about the topic – the children can use this to plan their study or to check their results afterwards.
- Making a *hypothesis* about what they might find out – that is, using what other people have found out, using their own experience and, importantly, using their imagination, to suggest a tentative prediction about what might happen – 'I think it might be that . . .'.
- Deciding what information and evidence to collect.
- Deciding how to go about it – choosing what apparatus, equipment and methods to use in the investigation in order to get this information.
- Planning a *fair test* – keeping everything the same, apart from the one *variable* being investigated, so that they know that any effects could not have been caused by anything else.

Obtaining evidence and presenting it clearly (during the experiment)

- Observing (where it is safe to do so) and describing what they see/hear/ smell/taste/feel – both carefully and accurately.
- Enhancing observations by measuring carefully and accurately, using various pieces of equipment and apparatus to collect further *data* in the form of numbers and measurements. In different topics, this will include counting objects and measuring time, length, distance, weight, capacity, brightness, loudness, strength, speed, angles, temperature, perhaps using ICT in the form of electronic sensors as appropriate.
- Managing risks – science is a practical subject, with a potential risk of burns, cuts, electric shocks, collisions, etc., and the children increasingly learn to assess hazards, minimize the likelihood of accidents and even abandon an activity if the risks appear too great.
- Collecting up the results carefully and accurately, in a systematic way, through writing, drawing, recording, etc.

Considering the evidence, and reaching a conclusion (after the experiment)

- Deciding which results are relevant to the investigation.

- Sorting, grouping and classifying the information gained.

- Bringing various pieces of *evidence* together (both observations and data), and looking for patterns by linking them together in their mind and on graphs and charts, again using ICT where this is useful.

- Believing the evidence – when children have had the imagination and courage to make a hypothesis, there is always a temptation to *fix* the results, but this is just not the scientific way.

- Talking and writing about their observations and data.

- Drawing conclusions – it is important that the children limit their conclusions to the results obtained. Let's imagine that, when we carried out the *slug and courgette* investigation, we found that *the courgettes were not nibbled when surrounded by the copper wire*. In gardening terms, this is a good result, but what could a scientist conclude from this? That all slugs will be kept out by copper wire? *(but this would need another experiment, introducing black, brown and orange slugs to the garden)* or that copper is the only metal that will deter slugs? *(a new experiment would be needed here too, using different metals)*. Or can we even conclude that it was the copper wire that kept them out? Were there other reasons why the slugs left the courgettes alone? For instance, did the next-door neighbours have some luscious lettuces in their garden, which the slugs found more attractive? (in which case, the experiment was flawed because it was not a *fair test*). Unfortunately, the most that a scientist can conclude with any confidence is that, *on the basis of this investigation, no slugs crossed the copper wire. More investigation will be needed.*

- Deciding how accurate their original hypothesis was.

- Explaining their conclusions – and how the evidence persuaded them – by communicating them to other people through speech, writing, tables and diagrams, models, video, etc.

(The Scottish Government 2004: 255)

The scientific method vs. knowledge and understanding

Clearly, this *scientific method* needs to be taught, used and practised in the classroom. But what about *scientific knowledge and understanding* – is that to be regarded as less important? Well, of course not – without the *content*, there would be no science. So, in practice, the children should learn the facts (*knowledge*) and concepts (*understanding*) as they carry out practical work using the *skills* and *attitudes* of the scientific method.

Biology (Life processes; Life and living things; Biological systems)

An overview

Using the *scientific method* as far as possible, the children are introduced to the living world, learning mainly about plants, animals and humans (but also a little about bacteria and viruses), finding out what they are like, how they *work*, how they are alike and how they vary, and how they thrive in different environments.

The children learn that, while we differ in so many ways, plants, animals and humans each:

- have a finite life-cycle;
- go through similar stages – birth, growth, reproduction, ageing and death;
- have the same sorts of needs – nutrition, light, warmth, and so on.

This can lead the children to a better appreciation of how they can look after themselves, their pets and their gardens, keeping each as healthy as possible.

Plants

Because most of the plants the children come across are green plants (garden plants, wild flowers, grasses, weeds, trees) rather than ferns and fungi, the children concentrate on these, learning about:

- The parts of the plant – leaves, roots, flowers, stems, seeds – the range of shapes, sizes, colours, types in each of these, and what each of these parts *do* for the plant, and how they do it.
- Their growth and nutrition – the importance of light, water, warmth, food; the roles played by leaves and roots; how water and food are transported through the plant; caring for plants.
- Their life cycle – annuals, biennials, perennials.
- Reproduction – germination, flowering, pollination, fruit, seed production and seed dispersal.

Of course, plants vary a great deal, ranging from small plants such as cress to 400-year-old oak trees. However, the children learn that they all have similar parts, needs and life cycles.

Animals – with an emphasis on humans

It is important that the children appreciate that humans are animals, and share many functions with them. With this in mind, they learn about:

- *Parts of the body* – external parts, their names and functions; major internal organs, their names and functions, how exercise affects the heart, lungs and sweat glands.

- *Nutrition* – proteins, carbohydrates, fats, vitamins and their roles; how diet can have positive or negative effects on particular parts of the body.

- *Circulation* – the heart as a pump; the role of arteries and veins.

- *Movement* – how the skeleton and muscles support the body and enable movement.

- *Growth and reproduction* – the need for warmth, water, food, shelter; the *mechanics* of conception, birth, growth, ageing and death.

- *Health* – good and bad drugs; the positive effects of exercise – for circulation, movement, growth, digestion.

(DfEE and QCA 1999: 79, 85)

Certain topics in science (for example, cleanliness, vegetarianism, smoking, reproduction, death) can stir up strong opinions and emotions, depending on the children's personal and family circumstances. We need to be clear that, in science lessons, we explore and explain scientific processes in a factual way. Discussion about morals and ethics are included in PSHE education lessons.

Classifying the vast array of plants and animals

Victorian biologists worked hard to observe, draw, photograph and catalogue as many plants and animals as they could find. These are fundamental scientific skills, which are as important nowadays as they were over a hundred years ago. In encouraging the children to find out about the *variation* in life forms, we should prompt them to ask questions such as:

For plants:

- Where does it live (geographically)?
- What is its normal habitat? How is it suited to this habitat?
- What do the stems, leaves, flowers, fruit, seeds, roots look like (shapes, sizes, colours)?
- How long does it live?
- How does it change as it grows?
- How are the seeds spread?
- Is it the favourite food of any animal? Where does it enter the *food chain*?

For animals:

- Where does it live (geographically)?
- What sort of habitat does it prefer? How is it suited to this habitat?
- Where and how does it make its home?
- How big does it grow and how heavy?
- What colours and patterns does it have (males and females are often different)?
- What is the texture of its coat/skin?
- How does it change as it grows?
- What does it eat and drink?
- How is the body adapted to collect and eat this food?
- How long does it live?
- What predators does it have?
- How does it defend itself?
- Is it susceptible to any particular diseases?
- What sort of family or society does it live in?
- How does it move around?
- What other animals is it related to? How so?
- Are any body parts (or personality traits) particularly important to its lifestyle?

The next step for scientists (and therefore for the children) is to group and classify the plants or animals, using the information they have gained about them. To do this, they identify both similarities and differences, and then decide which of these are *significant*. A picture of *families* and *family ties* can then be constructed – for instance, we know that horses and dogs are both *mammals* (because they both give birth to live babies, which are suckled by their mothers) – but what makes a dog a dog and not a cat? What exactly is an amphibian – is it a *genetic* thing or a *lifestyle* thing? There are so many interesting questions to be asked and answered, which children often find fascinating.

Classifications that the children learn about include:

- Plants:
  - green plants, shrubs, trees
  - mosses, fungi, grasses, algae
  - shapes, colours, textures of stems, leaves, flowers, seeds, fruits
  - roots, bulbs, tubers
  - evergreen, deciduous
  - annuals, biennials, perennials
  - edible, poisonous.

■ Animals:
  – mammals, birds, fish, reptiles, amphibians, crustaceans
  – insects, spiders and other *minibeasts*
  – vertebrates (with a backbone), invertebrates (without a backbone)
  – herbivores, carnivores, omnivores (diet).

The children learn to use a *key* as an aid to identifying individual plants and animals. The children ask themselves a series of questions, with each answer narrowing their search and bringing them closer to identifying, for example, a particular plant: Has it got broad leaves? What colour are the flowers? What shape are the roots? The answers are matched up with information in a reference book or database. *Branching databases* are designed for this very purpose.

Plants and animals thrive in different environments

We encourage the children to explore a range of habitats – gardens, hedges, woodland, parks, beaches, rock pools, etc. They observe and note the range of plants and animals that live there or visit, and make hypotheses about why they might be able to thrive in these particular places, habitats and ecosystems – for example, because their bodies are well suited to the conditions, or because there are few predators, or because there is plenty of food about.

They might then compare these local environments with places further afield – warmer countries, Arctic wastes, deserts, mountain tops, and so on. The children learn about how many different sorts of habitats there are in the world – variously on land, under water, in trees and under the ground – and about the range of plants and animals that exist even within a small habitat. They learn about some of the physical features that allow certain plants and animals to thrive in particular environments, for example, waterproof feathers help a duck to shrug off pond-water, while cliff-top plants such as *thrift* are short, with tough leaves, which helps it to resist the wind and salt-spray. They learn a little about how plants and animals respond to changes throughout a day or a year – being awake or asleep, breeding seasons, hibernation, migration, etc. They also learn about the importance of food chains in the animal world – carnivores, herbivores, omnivores, predators and prey. If we follow the food-chain down, green plants are almost always at the bottom of the chain.

Children also learn a little about micro-organisms – bacteria, viruses, yeasts and moulds – and where they live. They may be so small that they are impossible to see with the naked eye, but they are alive and can have a dramatic effect on our lives. Among other things, we rely on them to keep our digestive system working, to make bread and yogurt, and to neutralize our sewage. On the other hand, they can also cause illness and death.

The children are encouraged to develop particular *attitudes* when working with plants and animals, showing respect for all life-forms and washing their hands carefully when coming into contact with live (or dead) specimens.

Chemistry (Materials and their properties; Material behaviour; Materials)

What materials are we talking about?

In primary schools, we talk about things being made from *materials* or *substances*. These include:

- solids, liquids and gases;
- naturally occurring materials (such as leaves, rocks, soils, clay, oil, water, wool);
- naturally occurring materials which have been *refined* (such as sugar, milk, leather, salt, metals);
- man-made mixtures (such as fabrics, plastics, soap, paper, inks, cola).

What sorts of properties do these materials possess?

Given a material to study (for example, a piece of cooking foil or a wooden stirring spoon from the home technology room), the children are encouraged to use the *scientific method* to find out as much as they can about its *physical properties*, noting how it is similar to some materials and different from others. They ask questions such as:

- Is it shiny/transparent/coloured?
- How hard/strong/flexible is it?
- Is it waterproof?
- Does it boil/melt/freeze?
- Does it conduct heat/electricity?
- What does it feel like?
- What does it smell like?
- Does it float?
- Is it magnetic?
- Is it an acid, alkali or is it neutral?

By grouping objects and materials with common qualities and characteristics, children also learn how we make use of these properties in real life – for example, *transparency* in windows, bottles and spectacles.

As information is collected, in a systematic way, the children compare materials so that they can be *classified* according to their qualities and properties – which ones are pliable, which are good for heat insulation, etc.

Changing, mixing and separating materials

So far in this section, the emphasis has been on *gaining knowledge about different materials*. Now we move into the realm of *understanding how materials work*. This is investigated either by experimenting with the material by itself, or by mixing two or more materials together.

In each case, scientists make a hypothesis about what might happen when they cause a change to the materials. Then they carry out their investigation – monitoring carefully what happens – exploring this and other possibilities. Any changes to the material are described as *reversible* or *irreversible*, depending on whether the change can be *undone*.

For example, when the children heat or cool materials, depending on the temperatures used, they might observe a *change of state* (*when a material changes between its solid, liquid and gas forms*):

- *melting* – a solid turning to liquid (e.g. warming ice cream);
- *evaporation* – a liquid turning into a gas (e.g. water to water vapour);
- *solidification* – a liquid turning to a solid (e.g. glass moulding);
- *condensation* – a gas turning into a liquid (e.g. water vapour to water).

Obviously, these changes are all reversible. The understanding gained here will help the children understand the *water cycle*, in geography, as we depend on evaporation and condensation for our rain. On the other hand, if we burn a piece of wood (and it becomes smoke and ash) or if we boil an egg, the changes cannot be reversed.

Scientists also like to see what happens when they mix materials and then try to separate them out again afterwards. Sometimes, the materials remain separate, such as flour and sand, or flour and water. In such cases, the mixing is *reversible*, because the materials can be separated, by *sieving* or *filtering* the mixture, or by using a magnet if the mixture contains iron filings. Sometimes one of the materials dissolves in the other, such as sugar in water, but this is still reversible, because the water can be evaporated off (and collected through condensation) and the sugar will be left behind.

Other mixtures, however – for example, a mixture of vinegar with baking soda – are *irreversible*. In effect, a new material is formed – there is a *chemical change*, which cannot be *undone* back to the original materials. By hypothesizing and then checking, scientists try to understand what is going on during a chemical reaction like this, what happens to the original materials and what new materials are created. The children might use examples from cooking for their experiments.

Identifying substances

A task undertaken by the older children is to *identify an unknown substance*. A substance is brought into class and, through experimentation and checking it against information about different substances, they seek to identify it, often by a process of elimination. For example, a saucerful of a white substance is brought in:

- by observation, it is made up of white, shiny crystals;
- at room temperature, it feels cold to the touch;

- it melts at room temperature and the crystals change to a transparent liquid;
- this liquid has no distinctive taste or smell;
- when the liquid is warmed, it evaporates and boils at around 100°C.

This data would lead them to conclude that this white substance is, in fact, *snow*.

Some questions can be answered with a yes/no answer, while others need some sort of measurement. These measurements are carried out very carefully, sometimes using specialist equipment, following *the scientific method*.

Physics (Physical processes; Energy, movement and forces; Forces, electricity and waves)

Forces

Physics is about the *forces* (both natural ones and those produced artificially by scientists) and the *energy* all around us. These come in many forms, including:

- light	- heat	- sound
- movement	- electricity	- stretch (springs or elastic)
- gravity	- magnetism	- wind power
- nuclear power	- solar power	- fossil and other fuels
- wave power	- tidal power	- human and animal energy
- microwaves	- lasers	- TV waves
- X-rays	- air pressure	- water pressure
- air resistance	- friction	- earthquakes

Although the children need to learn some facts about these forces and their names, much of this section is about *understanding*. This can prove difficult, because we cannot actually see forces or energy – we can only observe their effects, and, in some cases, these are too powerful or dangerous to demonstrate without specialist equipment. For this reason, only a few of these forces are taught in primary schools, some even being left until university.

With regard to these forces and sources of energy, scientists are particularly interested in questions such as:

- Where do they come from? What causes them?
- What do they do?
- How do they do it?
- How can we control them for our own benefit?
- What happens when two forces are working in the same place at the same time?

One of the principles the children learn is that energy can sometimes be converted from one form to another, for example:

- wind power into electricity;
- friction into heat (by rubbing their hands together);
- stretch into movement (e.g. elastic bands);
- light into heat (using a magnifying glass);
- human energy into movement into light (using a *wind-up* torch) – an example of a two-step conversion.

In primary schools, the children learn about a number of different forces and, using the scientific method, study some of these in more detail, as outlined below.

Some forces can make things move

The children learn that *a force being applied to an object* is described as either a *push* or a *pull*. This is likely to result in the object moving in a particular direction, at a particular speed.

In real life, the dominant force is:

- *Gravity* – the *pull* towards the centre of the Earth, which keeps us on the ground, and makes things fall downwards, rather than float in the air.

There are also:

- *Magnets and magnetic materials*, where the children learn what materials are attracted to them, how they work, attraction and repulsion, why we talk about *north* and *south*, and how electromagnets work.
- *Stretch* – springs and elastic exert a force on things that are attached to them.
- *Water pressure* – floating happens when water's upward *push* on an object is at least equal to gravity's downward *pull*.
- *Friction* – when objects scrub together as they move, and slow down – without friction, our shoes would slip on the ground, as if on ice; we can use shiny surfaces or oil to reduce friction.

The children also learn about what happens when two forces are applied at the same time:

- When two forces act in the same direction, an object's movement will accelerate.
- When two unequal forces act in opposite directions, the stronger will win out, but more slowly than would otherwise be the case.
- When two forces are equal in strength and operate in opposite directions, the object will remain still.

The children look at some examples taken from everyday life – for example, when we walk uphill, our human energy has to overcome gravity, air resistance, and the friction between our shoes and the path – that's why it's so difficult. When we go swimming, our human energy propels us forwards, while friction against the water slows us down and the up-thrust of the water is struggling to stop gravity from drowning us!

Electricity

Electricity is important mainly in terms of how it can be converted and used – for example, to create light and heat, and to make buzzers and motors work.

The children learn about:

- appliances that use electricity;
- how electricity can be *made* (that is, converted from another form of energy);
- storing electricity (in batteries);
- batteries and mains power (noting the dangers);
- simple electrical circuits and circuit diagrams (using conventional symbols to record this);
- how switches work, different types of switches;
- static electricity (using a balloon).

Light

Children learn:

- about the sources of light, including the sun, fire, electrical devices;
- that darkness does not exist of itself – rather, it is the absence of light;
- about materials that are transparent, translucent or opaque;
- about shadows – how they are formed, their shapes and uses;
- about reflection, from mirrors and shiny surfaces;
- how eyes works and how to care for them;
- that we see things only when light bounces off them and then reflects into our eyes;
- that light travels in straight lines, unless we change its direction with a mirror, a lens or a prism;
- about the light spectrum, as seen in the colours of the rainbow.

There is also some discussion about other sorts of rays within their direct experience, such as X-rays and lasers.

Sound

Children learn:

- that there are lots of different sounds in the world – natural sounds, mechanical sounds, and animal and human noises, including speech;
- that sounds are caused by vibration;
- that sounds made by acoustic musical instruments are produced by shaking, plucking, hitting or blowing, each one causing a vibration that we can feel as well as hear;
- that, in order to be heard, vibration must travel to the ear through the air, water or a solid (the vibration being passed on rather like dominos falling in a line);
- about our ears – how they work and how to care for them;
- about echoes;
- about the speed at which sound travels (more slowly than light, hence lightning before thunder);
- how to measure sound in terms of loudness (in decibels) and pitch;
- that a shorter string or a shorter pipe will produce a higher pitched sound than a longer one;
- what happens when two sounds happen at the same time – *harmony* and *dissonance*.

There are lots of opportunities to link science with music in this topic.

Heat

Children learn:

- that when something is hot, it contains *heat energy*, but cold things don't have *cold energy*, they just don't have much *heat energy*;
- how to measure heat, using thermometers (below zero, as well as above);
- which materials conduct heat well and which are good insulators;
- that heat might change a solid to a liquid, or a liquid to a gas.

It is perhaps worth repeating here that the children should gain knowledge and understanding in all these areas by taking an active part in practical work, using the *scientific method*.

Earth and the solar system

In this area, the children are taught that planet Earth is just a small part of a larger order. They learn:

- that a solar system is the space around a star, in which planets and any other objects are subject to its gravitational pull as they orbit around it;
- that the star that we call *the Sun* is the star at the centre of our own solar system;
- about the planets and moons within our solar system;
- why the Sun appears to move throughout the day, and how day and night come about;
- how to tell the time from the position of the Sun;
- about the relationship between the Sun, Earth and Moon;
- the Moon's phases and how these come about;
- how months, seasons and years come about.

Attitudes, values and interdependence

An introduction

So far, this chapter has focused on the scientific *knowledge*, *skills* and *concepts* learned by the children at primary school. The final piece of the jigsaw is to explore *attitudes* and *moral values* in the context of science.

The children learn that we are all part of the world community, and that we rely on each other to keep ourselves safe and well. Everything we do can have an effect on others (that is, other people, plants and animals, environments or the whole planet), and equally, things that happen elsewhere can affect us, too.

We need to apply these principles to each of the scientific topics as we teach them, so that the children explore ways in which humans, plants and animals rely on each other to survive and thrive; ways in which advances in science and technology affect us – both the intended, beneficial effects and the unplanned, harmful ones; and ways in which we can live our lives in a sustainable way, avoiding the waste of natural resources and long-term damage to the planet.

Plants and animals

The children learn that interdependence between plants and animals is a two-way process.

Animals rely on plants because the diet of all animals can be linked back to plants through *food chains*, even when they are carnivorous themselves. Also, the food given to farm animals is mostly manufactured from plants and their seeds. Animals that eat plants often have physical features which help them collect particular foods, for example, sparrows' beaks are short and strong – ideal for cracking open seeds and nuts.

Plants rely on animals particularly in terms of their reproduction – insects transfer pollen from plant to plant as they search for food; larger animals trample plants, which throws seeds up into the air and allows the wind to distribute them over a large area; and seeds can also be spread as they pass through the body of birds and animals that have eaten them (not only that, but these seeds are surrounded by fertilizer, giving them every chance of a vigorous, healthy start).

The effects of science and technology

Science and technology are very closely linked – while science increases our knowledge and understanding, technology uses that new knowledge and understanding to change the way we live and, hopefully, to improve the quality of our lives. However, some good ideas can have unfortunate negative effects, too.

All our actions have an effect on somebody or something else, so each topic we teach should include a discussion about:

- who is affected – children, adults, plants, animals – locally, worldwide;
- which industries are affected – e.g. medicine, agriculture, travel, communication;
- where the anticipated benefits lie;
- what the accidental harmful effects might be – e.g. an increased risk of danger, poor health, change to an ecosystem, pollution, global climate change;
- how long it is likely to be before the effects have their full impact – immediately, a few months, a few years, a generation, or more.

For example, when the children learn about micro-organisms, they discuss how some bacteria help our digestive system, while others cause illness; when they study electricity and electrical circuits, older children learn about the pros and cons of gas/coal-fired, nuclear, wind and wave generation, and discuss sustainability; and when studying air resistance, the children learn that when cars are *streamlined* they are more efficient and therefore need less petrol, and that this has a beneficial effect on the world's natural resources.

The children return to issues like these again and again during their school career, each time with greater knowledge and understanding of the science, and each time with greater experience of considering the ethical and environmental issues.

References and Further Reading

BBC Schools. Available at: www.bbc.co.uk/schools/religion/ (accessed 10 January 2012).

Becta (2009) *AUPs in Context: Establishing safe and responsible online behaviours*, Coventry:Becta. Online. Available at: www.teachtoday.eu/sitecore/shell/Applications/~/media/Files/United %20Kingdom/Becta/Becta%20AUPs%20in%20context%20-%20downloaded%20on%2025 %20January%202011.ashx?db=master&la=en&vs=1&ts=20110704T1820334896 (accessed 6 January 2012).

CILT (The National Centre for Languages (2009)) Available at: http://upskilling.primary languages.org.uk/?q=content/frenchmodules (accessed 10 January 2012).

DCSF (2009) *Special Educational Needs (SEN) – A guide for parents and carers (revised)*, London: DCSF. Available at: www.education.gov.uk/publications/eOrderingDownload/00639-2008.pdf (accessed 12 January 2012).

DCSF (2010) *A Guide to the Law for School Governors*, London: DCSF. Available at: http:// media.education.gov.uk/assets/files/guide%20to%20the%20law%20for%20school%20 governors.pdf (accessed 12 January 2012).

Department for Children, Education, Lifelong Learning and Skills, Welsh Assembly Government (2008) *Foundation Phase Framework for Children's Learning for 3 to 7-year-olds in Wales*, Cardiff: Department for Children, Education, Lifelong Learning and Skills, Welsh Assembly Government.

Department of Education Northern Ireland, Online. Available at: www.nicurriculum.org.uk/ microsite/the_arts/music/keystage_2/singing_and_performing.asp (accessed 11 January 2012).

DES (1989a) *English in the National Curriculum (England)*, London: HMSO.

DES (1989b) *History in the National Curriculum (England)*, London: HMSO.

DES (1992a) *Art in the National Curriculum (England)*, London: HMSO.

DES (1992b) *Music in the National Curriculum (England)*, London: HMSO.

DES (1992c) *Science in the National Curriculum (England) Non-Statutory Guidance*, London: HMSO.

DES (2004), *Every Child Matters: Change for Children*, London: DES.

DfE (2011) Citizenship General Article. Available at: www.education.gov.uk/schools/teachingand learning/curriculum/primary/b00198824/citizenship/ks1; www.education.gov.uk/schools/ teachingandlearning/curriculum/primary/b00198824/citizenship/ks2 (accessed 7 January 2012).

DfEE (1999) *The National Numeracy Strategy*, London: DfEE.

DfEE and QCA (1999) *The National Curriculum Handbook for Primary Teachers in England*, London: DfEE and QCA.

DfES (2002) *Languages for All: Languages for Life*, London: DfES.

DfES (2005) *Excellence and Enjoyment: Social and emotional aspects of learning: Guidance*, London: DfES.

Dutton, D. (1990) The Difference Between Art and Craft. Available at: www.denisdutton.com/rnz_craft.htm (accessed 12 January 2012).

English Outdoor Council, Values and Benefits of Outdoor Education, Training and Recreation. Available at: www.englishoutdoorcouncil.org/Values_and_benefits.htm (accessed 13 January 2012).

Leicestershire County Council (2009) *Agreed Syllabus for Religious Education*. Available at: www.leics.gov.uk/religiouseducation_agreed_syllabus.pdf (accessed 11 January 2012).

Macdonald, A. (2009) *Independent Review of the Proposal to make Personal, Social, Health and Economic (PSHE) Education Statutory*, London: DCSF.

Members of Primary Curriculum Support Programme (Ireland) (2008) Warm-up and cool-down activities. Available at: www.irishprimarype.com/tips/WarmUp_CoolDown.pdf (accessed 10 January 2012).

National Governors' Association (2007) *Food Policy in Schools: A strategic policy framework for governing bodies (revised)*, London: National Governors' Association. Available at: www.food.gov.uk/multimedia/pdfs/foodpolicygovernor2.pdf (accessed 12 January 2012).

Ofsted (2009) *Mathematics: understanding the score*, London: Ofsted.

Ofsted (2010) *Transforming Religious Education*, London: Ofsted.

Ofsted (2011) *Modern Languages Achievement and Challenge 2007–11*, London: Ofsted.

QCA (1998a) Scheme of Work, Geography Unit 4 Going to the seaside. Online. Available at: webarchive.nationalarchives.gov.uk/20100612050234/http://www.standards.dfes.gov.uk/pdf/primaryschemes/geo4.pdf (accessed 12 January 2012).

QCA (1998b) Scheme of Work, History Unit 6C: Why have people invaded and settled in the past? A Viking case study. Available at: http://webarchive.nationalarchives.gov.uk/2010 0612050234/http://www.standards.dfes/gov.uk/pdf/primaryschemes/his6c.pdf (accessed 12 January 2012).

QCA (2000) Scheme of Work, Art and Design, Unit 1C: What is sculpture? Available at: http://webarchive.nationalarchives.gov.uk/20090608182316/http://standards.dfes.gov.uk/pdf/primaryschemes/art1c.pdf (accessed 12 January 2012).

QCA (2003) *Information and Communication Technology (ICT) Teacher's Guide (revised and updated)*, London: QCA. Available at: www.traffordelarning.org/trafford/sections/public_html/teaching/curriculum/ict/documents/6119_teachers_guide_ict_schemes_of_work_pdf (accessed 13 January 2012).

QCA (2004) *Design and Technology: The National Curriculum for England (revised)*, London: QCA.

QCA (2005) *Sex and Relationship Education, Healthy Lifestyles and Financial Capability: Teacher's handbook for the units of work*, London: QCA.

QCA (2008) *Early Years Foundation Stage Profile Handbook*, London: QCA.

QCDA (2010) *The National Curriculum Primary Handbook*, London: QCA.

Rose, J. (2009) *Identifying and Teaching Children and Young People with Dyslexia and Literacy Difficulties*, London: DCSF.

Snowling, M.J. (2008) *Dyslexia*, London: Government Office for Science. Available at: www.bis. gov.uk/assets/bispartners/foresight/docs/mental-capital/sr-d2_mc2_v2.pdf (accessed 12 January 2012).

The Scottish Government (2004) *A Curriculum for Excellence*, Edinburgh: The Scottish Government.

Tickell, C. (2011) *The Early Years: Foundations for life, health and learning – An Independent Report on the Early Years Foundation Stage to Her Majesty's Government*, London: DfE.

Glossary

Becta★   British Educational Communications and Technology Agency
CILT   The National Centre for Languages
DCSF★   Department for Children, Schools and Families
DfE   Department for Education
DES★   Department of Education and Science
DfEE★   Department for Education and Employment
DfES★   Department for Education and Skills
HMSO   Her Majesty's Stationery Office
Ofsted★   The Office for Standards in Education (to 2006)
Ofsted   The Office for Standards in Education, Children's Services and Skills (from 2006)
QCA★   Qualifications and Curriculum Authority
QCDA★   Qualifications and Curriculum Development Agency

★Agency discontinued.

Index

Taylor & Francis

eBooks

FOR LIBRARIES

ORDER YOUR FREE 30 DAY INSTITUTIONAL TRIAL TODAY!

Over 23,000 eBook titles in the Humanities, Social Sciences, STM and Law from some of the world's leading imprints.

Choose from a range of subject packages or create your own!

Benefits for you

▶ Free MARC records
▶ COUNTER-compliant usage statistics
▶ Flexible purchase and pricing options

Benefits for your user

▶ Off-site, anytime access via Athens or referring URL
▶ Print or copy pages or chapters
▶ Full content search
▶ Bookmark, highlight and annotate text
▶ Access to thousands of pages of quality research at the click of a button

For more information, pricing enquiries or to order a free trial, contact your local online sales team.

UK and Rest of World: **online.sales@tandf.co.uk**

US, Canada and Latin America:
e-reference@taylorandfrancis.com

www.ebooksubscriptions.com

ALPSP Award for BEST eBOOK PUBLISHER 2009 Finalist
sponsored by

Taylor & Francis eBooks
Taylor & Francis Group

A flexible and dynamic resource for teaching, learning and research.